1 MONTH OF
FREE
READING

at

www.ForgottenBooks.com

By purchasing this book you are eligible for one month membership to ForgottenBooks.com, giving you unlimited access to our entire collection of over 1,000,000 titles via our web site and mobile apps.

To claim your free month visit:

www.forgottenbooks.com/free859087

ISBN 978-0-365-20221-9
PIBN 10859087

For support please visit www.forgottenbooks.com

THE GOLDEN HIND SERIES
Edited by Milton Waldman

MAGELLAN

·THE GOLDEN HIND SERIES

*Volumes published and
in preparation*

DRAKE

JOHN SMITH

HUDSON

RALEIGH

FROBISHER

DAMPIER

MAGELLAN

SCOTT

HAWKINS

GRENVILLE

FERDINANDVS MAGELLANVS FRETI PERVVIANI TERRÆQVE AVSTRALIS INVENTOR

MONVMENTA QVÆRIT

Ferdinand Magellan

By
E. F. BENSON

NEW YORK

HARPER & BROTHERS PUBLISHERS

MCMXXX

PREFACE

ERDINAND MAGELLAN is one of those who, as Robert Browning says, are "named and known by that moment's feat," and though that feat took three years in the doing, he is still a man of one achievement. Unlike some great general who has half a dozen victorious campaigns to justify his title to immortality, unlike some great painter who has a score of deathless canvases to his credit, unlike Newton who accomplished years of epoch-making work before he made his great discovery, unlike (in his own line) the English admiral, Francis Drake, who not only circumnavigated the world, but defeated the Spanish Armada, and carried through a dozen amazing adventures to the sore undoing of Spain, Magellan's claim to immortality is based on one feat alone, but that was of a unique splendour, and carried out in the face of stupendous difficulties. Had it not been for that one voyage, we should never have heard of him. His very name would have been unknown except possibly to the industrious historian who, studying the campaigns of Almeida and Albuquerque in India, might conceivably have made mention in a footnote to one of his innumerable pages that one Ferdinand Magellan, seaman and subsequently captain

in the Portuguese navy four hundred and more years ago, behaved on two occasions with considerable gallantry.

But an idea occurred to Magellan, and since, on his return from India, King Manuel of Portugal had no further use for his services, even as his predecessor, King John II, had no use for a certain Italian called Columbus, Magellan, like Columbus, took himself and his idea to Spain. And this idea was so prodigious, and the accomplishment of it so unparalleled in the history of exploration, that by virtue of it his deeds and his days generally seemed worth a little ferreting out and a trifle of study, in order to see whether this man, who is known to most people as a name, Spanish or Portuguese, rather than a human being, after whom, vaguely, an obsolete strait in the most remote part of South America was called, could not be shaped into a living personality. History, as a mere series of events, as a collected chronicle, is as dead as the bones in the vision-valley of Ezekiel (and, behold, they were very dry !) unless it is animated by some human interest attaching to those who made it. But if it can be breathed upon by the spirit of the living folk who caused these things to happen so, it becomes winged with the romance that belongs to the great deeds of men.

Magellan's feat, in itself, was a supreme achievement: he was the first person in the world who demonstrated not by theory, but in terms of ships actually sailing on the sea, that this world is round (or thereabouts), and that by sailing out beyond the known ultimate of the West, a voyager will arrive at the known ultimate of the East.

To us that is a commonplace, but it must be remembered
that when Magellan was born no ship of the two great
maritime Powers, Spain and Portugal, had ever sailed
beyond the Atlantic. The Atlantic washed the shores
of the known world, and not yet had Columbus found
its further coast, nor had Bartholomew Diaz rounded
the Cape of Good Hope, and though it was certain that
there were lands and seas to the East of Africa, and islands
fragrant with the spices brought to Europe by Moorish
traders, no European eye had ever beheld them. For
hundreds of years no substantial additions had been made
to men's knowledge of the surface of the world : it was
indeed probably larger in the days of Alexander the
Great than in A.D. 1480. Then suddenly, in the space
of thirty-five years, the world was unrolled like some
wondrous manuscript, and (out of the three explorers
who spread it out) the last and longest section, stretching
from the coasts of Brazil westwards to the Spice Islands
of the East, was smoothed straight and pinned down by
Magellan. Not for sixty years, so sown with peril and
difficulty was the route, did any ship pass through his
Strait again and traverse the Pacific.

Singularly little is known of Magellan's life until
within a year or two of his leaving Seville on the voyage
from which he never returned. We hear of his performing two meritorious pieces of service in the East, but
his earlier years are not so much mysterious as merely
undistinguished : we do not yet feel that here is a great
personality of whom we unfortunately know little. Then
King Manuel, on his return, told him that he had no
further employment for him, and immediately he becomes

significant. But as soon as he became significant, he became mysterious also : we know that there was a great force moving about, a will that drove its way through mutiny and a myriad obstacles towards the accomplishment of its aim, but we rarely get any information that puts us into touch with him personally. Yet from such hints as may be legitimately linked together, we find enough to enable us to realize a human image of the man, and by combination and inference arrive at a figure of great psychological interest, one who was lonely and formidable and self-sufficient, and at the end blazes out into a religious fanatic. If the attempt here made to do this attains any measure of success, it may help those who thought of the first circumnavigation of the world, and the discovery of the Strait of Magellan, to perceive that one definite human personality, of rather terrible steel, inspired that amazing achievement.

I have found no new material to work upon : the Spanish historians, and the journals of those who accompanied Magellan on his voyage, or supplied information on their return to Spain, have been my sources. I have constantly consulted Mr. F. H. H. Guillemard's *Life of Magellan*, who has brought together all the historical books that bear on the subject, though sometimes I have disagreed with his conclusions : I have also freely quoted from Lord Stanley of Alderley's admirable translation of the diaries of Pigafetta and others contained in his *First Voyage by Magellan* (Hakluyt Society, 1874). But it soon became clear that if I gave references to these historians and diarists every time I used the information they supplied, these pages would largely consist of footnotes.   In order therefore to avoid distracting the reader with a criss-cross of such (for a single sentence, in the narration of the mutiny, may contain facts derived from three or four of them), I have omitted footnotes altogether, except when these authorities, as sometimes happens, contradict each other, or are otherwise irreconcilable. In such cases, I have given a reference or a footnote to indicate the reason for the choice I have made.

Finally, with regard to the spelling of certain names, Portuguese or Spanish, I have adopted the modern equivalent wherever possible.   It seemed, for instance, too rich a sacrifice on the altar of pedantic accuracy to speak of my hero at one time as " Fernão de Magalhães," and at another as " Hernando de Magallanes."

E. F. BENSON.

CONTENTS

		PAGE
PREFACE	. . . .	v

CHAP.

I. GEOGRAPHICAL	I
II. MAGELLAN SEES THE EAST	18
III. KING MANUEL HAS NO USE FOR MAGELLAN .	35
IV. MAGELLAN APPLIES TO SPAIN	55
V. KING CHARLES APPROVES	74
VI. THE GREAT VOYAGE BEGINS	97
VII. MAGELLAN ARRIVES AT PORT ST. JULIAN .	III
VIII. THE MUTINY	125
IX. THE FINDING OF THE STRAIT	140
X. THE TRAVERSE OF THE STRAIT	152
XI. THE PHILIPPINES	170
XII. THE DEATH OF MAGELLAN	199
XIII. THE SPICE ISLANDS	216
XIV. THE CAPTAIN-GENERAL	239
APPENDIX	249
INDEX	255

ILLUSTRATIONS

FERDINAND MAGELLAN . . . . . . *Frontispie*
    From the engraving by Crispin Van de Passe.

MAP OF THE WORLD SHOWING THE VOYAGE OF THE
"VICTORIA" . . . . *Facing page* 6

MAP OF MAGELLAN STRAIT (CANAL DE TODOS LOS
SANTOS) . . . . ,, ,, 15
    From the Admiralty Chart.

FERDINAND MAGELLAN

CHAPTER I

GEOGRAPHICAL

T is a legitimate and indeed a laudable curiosity that desires to know what signs and foreshadowings of genius glimmered like distant signals out of the dim and early years of those who have developed into the architects of the world's history and the pioneers of its progress, and to trace in what can be learned about the environment of their boyhood the influences which determined their careers. But though this latter quest often brings interesting details to light, though we can often find in the circumstances that surround the boyhood of great men causes that strongly make for such predispositions, it is very easy to press too hard on this chase, and overlook the fact that of all qualities genius is the least liable to influence and that it makes but little response to encouragements from without, just as it is little deterred by external hindrances. It proceeds along the uncharted track of its destiny in a manner singularly independent of wayside beckonings.

Such certainly was the case with Ferdinand Magellan, for that noble and solitary sea-bird, whose flight was over the great waters, and who found a path where footsteps were not known, lived, till he reached the age of thirteen or thereabouts, in the stony uplands of the only province of Portugal which has no sea-board, and from which no possible glimpse can be obtained of the element

of which he was truly native.   These earlier years of
boyhood are, according to modern psychology, the most
formative, but in his case, as far as the sea furnished
suggestions in his development, we must write them
down as wholly barren.   Those therefore who confid-
ently discover in the environment of his childhood the
predisposing influences which drove him on, in the face
of greater difficulties, dangers and discouragements than
ever fought against human enterprise, to wing his way
round the world, must fall back on the reflection that the
people of this mountainous province, far inland, were a
grim and hardy race, whose life was a perpetual struggle
with the inclemencies of nature.   For the climate of
Traz-os-Montes has been tersely summed up as consisting of nine months of winter and three of the fires of
hell.   What more apt nursery (these psychologists beg
us to tell them) could be found for one whom adventure
led through tropic seas and Antarctic winters ?   Very
likely that is so, but in turn we may remind them that
this nursery would suit their theories more aptly if some
sight of the sea could have been visible from its windows.
Again, we do not find in the very sparse records of
Magellan's early years any hint that he had drunk of
that seething ferment of exploration and discovery with
which all Portugal was tipsy, till when, at the age of
twenty-five, which was decidedly mature for the appren-
tice-adventurers of that day, he started on his first
voyage as a volunteer seaman in Almeida's expedition
to India.   No call from the sea, imperative and irresis-
tible, haunted his boyhood, or, if it did, he closed his ears
to it ; while as for those who would seek to find in
anecdotes of his youth the foreshadowings of his genius
they must resign themselves to the entire absence of
such, for we have no knowledge whatever of what
manner of youngster he was.   No doubt the boy was
father to the man, but he was a silent father, and kept

his aspirations to himself.   At any rate not a shred of them has come down to us.

So much as is certain about his cradle and his race must be briefly recorded by way of introduction, though there emerges therefrom nothing vivid or personal : it serves but as a background to the figure we hope to portray.   The year of his birth, though nowhere specifically stated, was probably 1480, and he was of noble birth, as is attested not only by two Portuguese genealogists, and by the Will which Magellan himself executed before leaving Lisbon on his first voyage to India, but by the fact that at the age of thirteen, or thereabouts, he left his highland home to be educated at the Royal Court, first as page to Queen Leonora, wife of King John II of Portugal, and on the accession of King Manuel in 1495 to serve in some similar capacity to him.   These royal pages were, at this time, always the heirs of some noble family, and thus they received the liberal upbringing and education that should fit them for their future.   Both these genealogists are agreed that his mother's name was Alda de Mesquita Pimenta, but they differ as to his father's name, the one calling him Gil, the other Ruy.   We need not weigh the reliability of these authorities, for they both seem to have been in error, since there exists an acknowledgment of the payment of his salary at Court, dated 1512, and signed by Magellan himself, in which he describes himself as the son of Pedro.   We must conclude that probably Magellan knew best.   Though the elder of Pedro's two sons, he had three sisters all of whom were senior to him.   The eldest of these, Teresa, married John da Silva Telles, and Magellan in his first Will, dated 1504, and dealing with his inherited Portuguese property, names them jointly as his heirs with succession to their son Luiz.   He enjoins also that his brother-in-law shall quarter with his own arms those of Magellan, which, he says, belong to " one of the most distinguished, best and oldest families in the kingdom." At the date of this Will, Magellan, aged twenty-four, was unmarried, and he adds the proviso that, if he himself should subsequently beget legitimate offspring, his property, " the little property I have," should pass to them. When he made his second Will, which he did on the eve of his departure for his last voyage in 1519, from which he never returned, he had married, had a son Rodrigo, and was expecting another child, but he had ceased to be a Portuguese subject, and had been naturalized as a Spaniard. To Rodrigo therefore, Spanish born, he bequeathed such property in Spain as might accrue to him as the results of his voyage, but he did not disturb the succession to his Portuguese property. Should Rodrigo die without legitimate issue, and should his own direct line fail, he named his younger brother, Diego de Sousa, as his heir as regards his Spanish property, subject to the proviso that he should live in Spain, and marry a Spaniard ; failing him his sister, Isabella, was to succeed, subject to the same conditions. The significance of this separate disposal of his Spanish and Portuguese property will appear later.

From these two Wills then, with the help of the Portuguese genealogists, we can construct all we know, directly and inferentially, about the Magellans as they lived at Sabrosa in the inland province of Traz-os-Montes before Ferdinand went as a boy of thirteen to be educated at the Court at Lisbon. The eldest child of Pedro Magellan was Teresa ; the second Ginebra, of whom, apart from her husband's name, we know nothing ; the third was Isabella, who was still unmarried at the date of her brother's second Will in 1519. Then in order of birth came Ferdinand Magellan himself, and his younger brother, Diego.

Except for Teresa and her line, which eventually suc-

ceeded to the Portuguese property, and emerges somewhat tragically out of the dimness, all is shadowy ; a
matter of Wills and nomenclature.   They lived, we must
suppose, the life of countryfolk of gentle breeding,
owning land, but no great estate, with its stock of horses
and cattle and its exiguous harvest of grapes and corn.
Pedro Magellan, the father of these five children, certainly died while Ferdinand was still young, for in 1504,
when he was twenty-four years old and made his first
Will, he had come into his estate, since he had the disposal of it.   But of him personally, and of his earlier
boyhood, we know nothing whatever.   Pictures have
been made of this boy of strong character and country
breeding, who pined for the mountains and the rain-
storms, the snows and the grilling heats of Sabrosa, for
the austere stone-built house with the arms of his ancestors
on the gateway, when translated into the softer airs of
the sea-coast, and for the quiet of that sequestered life
when thrust into the gorgeous hive of the Court at
Lisbon, buzzing eternally with news of fresh discoveries
and unconjectured continents ; but such depiction is
purely imaginative and highly improbable.   From all
we subsequently learn of that silent and adventurous
soul, whose wings were never furled while there was a
glimpse of the unknown within the straining compass of
his vision, we should more reasonably figure him as a
boy enraptured with the wider living and the tidings
brought in by those who had pushed back the limits of
oceans and lands as at present explored.   There lay the
sea to which his life was to be dedicate, and the sunsets
that brought dawn to horizons yet unvisited.

The discovery of new lands, and of the seas that were
the highway that led to them, was at the time when
Magellan came to Lisbon as page to Queen Leonora
a passion that gripped the whole nation with the magic
of its allurement : Portugal was the first maritime Power

in the world, and her ships were continually beating up and advancing into the confines of the unknown. This fever for adventure has often been compared with the voyages of the great English sea-captains in the reign of Elizabeth, but there is a very radical difference between the two which must not be overlooked. Drake and Hawkins and the rest were not pioneers in geographical discovery to anything like the extent that the Portuguese were ; their main objective was to wrest sea-power from Spain, and, going where she had gone, to capture from her, by exploits frankly piratical according to our modern codes, the freights of her golden argosies from the New World. But Portugal, though in rivalry with Spain, was not fighting her nor robbing her ; her penetration into unknown seas and lands, though in the service of imperial interests, was peaceful as far as other civilized nations were concerned ; she wanted to discover and to trade, and, when her expansion threatened to come into collision with the expansion of her neighbour, Papal arbitration was sought for. In 1490 there was room for them both ; east and west lay abundance of undiscovered lands rich in gold and spices, and Portugal was discovering (certainly to her great advantage) rather than appropriating in the later Elizabethan manner.

The wizard who had set this spell at work in the minds of his countrymen was Prince Henry of Portugal, the Navigator, who, though not a practical seaman, must be held to be the greatest of pioneers in cosmography. He was the younger son of King John I and was born in 1394. After distinguished services against the Moors, he left his father's Court, and devoted himself to geographical study, and to the sending out of maritime adventurers to explore the vastnesses of the unknown world. He established himself on the south-western coast of Portugal at Cape Sagres, a few miles to the east of Cape St. Vincent, and built there what was known as

the " Infante's Town " with palace, church and obser-
vatory, and at the base of the promontory founded a
naval arsenal. There he lived, recluse from the world,
but intensely occupied with the visits of the sea-captains
of Portugal who brought him the news of their further
nosings into ultimate seas, and of the lands that fringed
them. There in his remote quarters, with the highway
of the Atlantic washing the base of his promontory, and
the setting sun striking an avenue of gold out into the
west, he collected and collated and charted these glean-
ings of knowledge so perilously won, and sent forth a
succession of other labourers into the harvest-fields of the
sea. Henry VI of England asked him to take command
of his armies, and in 1443 made him a Knight of the
Garter, but neither honours nor advancements lured him
from his chosen work, and he remained at Sagres busy
with his charts and maps till his death in 1460. He
was the founder and preceptor of this school of Portuguese adventurers.

No huge discovery rewarded him in his lifetime :
Portuguese ships had not yet passed the Equator at the
time of his death, but he had mapped out the road for
maritime expansion down the West Coast of Africa, and
realized in theory its further projection. Some day, if
his sea-captains pressed on, winning their way down that
interminable continent, the land would come to an end,
and there would be a sea-way open eastwards to the
fabulous wealth of India and of the remoter Spice Islands,
and of the furthest markets of Cathay. Hitherto these
products of the Orient had reached Europe by way of
the Mediterranean, and of some yet unexplored route by
land from the seas beyond. This trade was in the hands
of the Moors ; cinnamon and pepper, silks and porcelain and jewels, all were brought west by the circumcised
race which had once been lords of Portugal. But
Prince Henry was convinced that there was a sea-route

open along which his Captains might sail their ships from
the Moluccas into the Tagus, and discharge there the
spices and the treasures they had embarked at Oriental
ports.   But dearer to his heart than the riches of the
unloading ships was the knowledge of the route that they
should traverse, which presently became manifest, even
as he had foreseen it, for Africa was found to be but finite,
and from beyond its southernmost cape there lay the way
to India.

After Prince Henry's death the Infante's Town
became more generally known as Sagres Castle, and in
1587 Sir Francis Drake, spying round the coast for a
base for his ships that waylaid the treasure-bearing fleets
of Spain that came from Nombre de Dios and Panama
laden with gold for King Philip in his wars with England,
seized the little bay at the foot of the promontory and
stormed the castle on its summit.   It was too strongly
built to be taken by assault, and he piled firewood against
its walls and burned the defenders out and razed the
fortifications ; for he could not suffer a fort to command
his anchorage.   But many years before that Prince
Henry's charts and chronicles of exploration had been
removed to the Royal Library at Lisbon, and even if
they had been there they would have been already obsolete.   In Drake's day they would be curiosities merely,
like out-moded maps, for since then regular traffic had
been established eastwards with the fabled Spice Islands,
Columbus had found the New World, two navigators,
Magellan and Drake himself, had noosed the globe in
the wake of their ships, and a third, Cavendish, was on
his way.   Swiftly indeed had advanced the knowledge
which the Prince-Navigator had devoted his life to gain,
and it was from him and his researches, in the main, that
the impetus had come.

In 1481 there succeeded to the throne of Portugal
King John II, who carried on the Navigator's tradition.

Cape by cape Portuguese ships pushed their way down the West Coast of Africa, following out Prince Henry's scheme of penetrating southwards and further south till there lay to the east the open sea, while in the first year of his reign the new King had despatched two travellers, Pedro de Covilhão and Alfonso de Payva, to ferret out a land-route towards India and the mythical kingdom of the Christian King, Presbyter John. As early as the eleventh century the legend of this monarch, king and priest like Melchizedek, was widely credited in Europe ; but, by the fifteenth century, it was believed that his kingdom was situated somewhere in Abyssinia, and while the sea-route round Africa was being explored these travellers set forth to strike the trade-route of the Moors from the East, for it was known that the spices and silks and produce of the Orient came into Europe along the East Coast of Africa. They got to Abyssinia, and Covilhão seems to have reached Calicut by way of the Arab sea-route from Zanzibar. On his way home he was imprisoned in Abyssinia, but sent information to Portugal about his journey, saying that beyond the southern Cape of Africa was open sea. But that was already known, for in 1487 Bartholomew Diaz rounded the Cape of Good Hope, and thus credited to Portugal the first of the three great discoveries which were to revolutionize geography.

The second of these great discoveries (as indeed also the third) would assuredly have been scored up to Portugal as well, had not in each case a piece of unwisdom and unkingliness caused them to be won under the flag of Spain. There had come to Portugal a Genoese sea-captain called Columbus : he was a skilled navigator, he was for ever studying charts, and he married a Portuguese, Felipa Perestello, daughter of one of Prince Henry's Captains. He had heard the story of how Martin Vincente had picked up at sea, four hundred leagues west of Cape St. Vincent, a piece of strange wood, unknown to the forests of Europe, and this was to Columbus what the falling apple was to Newton. The ordinary man would have thought it curious, and the matter would have rested there, but the constructive mind, with the insight of genius, found in these two trivialities the keys to the discovery, in one case, of a continent and, the other, of a great natural law. Columbus did not himself realize what he had found, nor till the day of his death did the entire truth dawn on him, but now, on the accession of King John II, he entered the Portuguese maritime service, and put before the King his aim of reaching Asia, not by sailing eastwards but by sailing westwards. King John consulted his Council, who turned the scheme down as being chimerical, but he was not wholly satisfied with their rejection of it, and by a very shabby piece of work privately sent out ships to test Columbus's proposition. They returned without having accomplished anything, and Columbus, rightly disgusted at this underhand manœuvre, betook himself and his idea to Spain in 1484, much as Magellan did thirty-three years later. Both took with them the project which their genius had built on hints and obscure indications, and for which Portugal had no use. But Spain was of truer intuition and of wider enterprise, and in 1492 Columbus set out to discover the new world. Too late Portugal suspected what she had missed, and sent out ships to intercept him, just as she did when she tried to stop Magellan sailing westwards to the Spice Islands in 1519. So, about the year that Queen Leonora's young page arrived, a country boy from Sabrosa, at the Court at Lisbon, Columbus returned to Barcelona with the news that he had discovered the western route to India. Thirty-six days of sailing westwards from the Canaries brought him within sight of those shores which he believed to be the Eastern Coast of Asia. The vast sea beyond them had never yet been beheld by European eyes, nor was it seen by them till in 1513 Balboa stood on the peak in Darien.

This discovery of America caused a fresh distribution of the kingdoms of the world to be proclaimed by Pope Alexander VI in the Bull promulgated on May 4th, 1493. Spain and Portugal were the favourite spiritual children of the Holy Father, who was himself a Spaniard by birth, and, now that both were pushing out east and west into the unknown with this amazing vigour, there was considerable danger (the world being round) that their claims would seriously come in conflict. The Holy Father therefore, appealed to by both parties, made a very honest attempt, considering that he was a Spaniard, to give an equitable decision. Spain had been exploring westwards, Columbus had discovered America for her ; Portugal had been exploring eastwards and Diaz had rounded the Cape of Good Hope. Therefore Holy Father very sensibly decided that the entire Western Hemisphere and all that was therein, known now or subsequently discovered, should belong to Spain, and all the Eastern Hemisphere to Portugal. Had King John not behaved in so shabby a manner to Columbus, and had Columbus discovered America under the Portuguese flag, Holy Father would have been 'n a very difficult position, for Spain would certainly not have liked both hemispheres assigned to her neighbour. But, happily, such a situation did not arise ; and, once granting that the Pope had the right (concerning which neither he nor his spiritual children had any doubt whatever) to apportion the world as he pleased, his arrangement seemed very tactful and suitable.

The next point to settle was where, on the surface of the globe, East was to become West, and where, somewhere on the far side of it, West was to become East again. Through what seas or islands or conti-

nents the more remote semicircle of that line of demarcation would lie, nobody could possibly tell, because
nobody had yet been there. But as regards the nearer
semicircle of that line on this side of the world, Pope
Alexander decided that it should lie due north and south
of some spot ·in mid-Atlantic situated one hundred
leagues west of the Azores and (not or) the Cape Verde
Islands. Islands so remote as these, thought this somewhat inaccurate Pontiff, might be regarded as one point
for the purposes of measurement, and probably on the
maps that he consulted they appeared to lie in the same
longitude, which is very far from being the case. But
King John of Portugal was very ill-satisfied with this
disposition : a line drawn so near to Europe would
almost certainly give Spain the whole of the newly discovered continent, which, had he not treated Columbus
with so gross a shabbiness, would all have been Portuguese. So he begged that this line of demarcation
should be shifted three hundred leagues further to the
west, which would give Portugal a better chance of securing any parts of the new continent which should lie eastwards of the longitude of Columbus's discovery. There
was some bargaining over this, and next year, in 1494,
the position of this line of demarcation between east and
west, which constituted the boundaries between the
kingdoms of Spain and Portugal, was, by the Tortesillas
Capitulations, shifted two hundred and seventy leagues
further west of Holy Father's original assignment.

Both beneficiaries set out with renewed vigour to
explore the moieties of the world's surface which had thus
been bequeathed to them *in sæcula sæculorum.* The seas
of the entire world, broad and narrow alike, were subsequently granted to the same fortunate nations for their
joint possession, and the unconscious humour of this
enviable bequest remained undetected till Elizabeth's
sea-captains, notably Hawkins and Drake, took it upon

themselves to point it out. At present this amended division of the world by the dividing line which no one was capable of drawing with the smallest approach to accuracy, or had the slightest idea where its remote bisection lay, gave satisfaction till the discovery of Brazil and subsequently the objective of Magellan's voyage of circumnavigation, caused some highly disquieting complications to arise. Brazil, according to this amended demarcation, lay within the Portuguese hemisphere, and, so far as that went, that was highly satisfactory to Portugal. But she now became afraid that, by having caused the Spanish hemisphere to have been screwed round westwards, in order that she might secure just such eastern lands of America, she had also caused the Spice Islands, on the other side of the world, to come into the Spanish half-world. These complications, and the adjustments thereof, scarcely belong to our story : it may, however, be mentioned that as a matter of fact the Spice Islands still remained in the Portuguese half-world. But the dividing line was difficult to fix, and King Charles continued to consider that they were his. Eventually, in 1529, Portugal paid Spain 350,000 ducats for their indisputed possession.

King John II died in 1495 ; he had carried on with ability and success the traditions of the Prince-Navigator, and though he had made a very disastrous and costly mistake with regard to Columbus, which had lost Portugal the New World, his policy of expansion and discovery had been conceived on broad and progressive lines. He was succeeded by King Manuêl ; and, under him, not discovery alone but conquest and consolidation went forward with redoubled vigour. The new King was a true Empire-builder : he grabbed whatever portions of the earth's surface he could possibly lay hands on, and held them tight, not only by erecting forts for military occupation but by establishing others to guard the routes to his new acquisitions so that they remained, though remote, in some sort of touch with Portugal. Like Queen Elizabeth of England, he was served by men of conspicuous ability ; like her, he was cursed with a native strain of incredible parsimony. Under him Portugal penetrated into the fairy-land of the Orient towards which she had been feeling her way so long. In 1497 Vasco da Gama repeated Diaz's voyage round the Cape of Good Hope, but, instead of then turning back, he went on up the hitherto unexplored East African Coast. On Christmas Day of that year he landed on those unknown shores, and in commemoration of the Birthday christened the territory by the name it still bears, Natal. Then coasting to Melinda, a little north of Mombasa, he found himself at the African end of the Arab trade-route to India, already traversed by Covilhão, and leaving the coast Gama struck eastwards across the Indian Ocean. He dropped anchor in the harbour of Calicut, and the jewel of India gleamed in the crown of Portugal. Within the space of eleven years, Diaz had rounded the Cape of Good Hope, Columbus had discovered America (though he thought he had found the East Coast of Asia), and Gama had landed in India. Magellan was seven years old and still in remote Sabrosa when Diaz made his voyage, but he must have gone to Lisbon just about the time when Columbus found a New World, and he was eighteen when Gama landed in India. We may safely assume that these events, which had intoxicated all Portugal with the noble wine of adventure, had set him bubbling with the heady ferment.

Smaller confluents, some of which flowed from remote and significant table-lands, kept pouring into this widening river of geographical knowledge ; they joined it chiefly from its western bank. South America was found to trend far eastwards from the point originally discovered by Columbus, and Pinzon, one of his captains, coasting southwards along Brazil, in 1500, arrived clearly within the hemisphere assigned to Portugal, for the eastern portion of Brazil and Pernambuco, which was the southern limit of his voyage, lay easily to the east of the line of demarcation as amended on the petition of King John II. That same year Cabral, a Portuguese Captain with a fleet *en route* for India, sailing wide of the West African Coast in order to take advantage of the trade-winds, was driven far out of his course by gales from the east and came within sight of the same coast. In 1501 and 1503 Gonzalo Coelho and Christopher Jacques pushed exploration further southward along the coast of Patagonia (then unnamed) and penetrated, as we shall find strong reason for believing, to the neighbourhood and probably the entrance of the Strait of Magellan itself. Columbus in a subsequent expedition had learned from natives that a vast sea lay beyond the narrow lands of Central America ; and, though till the day of his death he personally believed that he had discovered the eastern confines of Asia, it is clear that, even before Balboa saw the Pacific, it was generally believed that Columbus had found a continent hitherto unknown and separated by a thousand leagues of sea from the coast of Asia. North America was still unexplored ; it was believed to consist of a chain of islands, and how vague and erroneous generally was the imagined configuration of America can be gathered from the map made in 1515 by Leonardo da Vinci, who charts it as a long island stretching not north and south but east and west. To the north of it Leonardo delineates widely sundered islands, the chief of which is Florida ; its western cape lies in the same longitude as China, while its eastern portion, on which appears Cape St. Augustine and Brazil, approaches Africa. It is interesting, however, to observe that Leonardo did not share the view that South America joined the Terra Australis Incognita of other cosmographers, but draws it as separated from that conjectured continent by a wide stretch of ocean. This was suspected, as we shall see, by Magellan, but not verified till Francis Drake in his Circumnavigation of the World, in 1578, was driven southwards after passing into the Pacific through the Strait of Magellan, and saw the Atlantic and Pacific meeting " in a wide scope."

But Eastern exploration during these years was the main objective of Portuguese seamanship, for Portugal, as was natural, was pushing on into the Eastern Hemisphere assigned her by Pope Alexander. Cabral, it is true, had found Brazil, but his discovery was accidental ; he had been driven by easterly winds on a more westerly course than he had intended, and the object of his voyage was to pass round the Cape of Good Hope, and in these early years of the sixteenth century the maritime vigour and enterprise of Portugal were like the growth of springtime in her search for the lands of the further Orient. Vasco da Gama, now the heroic subject of odes and rhapsodies innumerable for his first exploit, left Lisbon again for India in 1502, and made himself execrable for the abominable cruelties and massacres he ordered at Calicut. Next year another fleet under Alfonso d'Albuquerque followed his tracks up the East Coast of Africa, and then north to the entrance of the Red Sea and the Persian Gulf, thus traversing another section of the Arab trade-route to Europe, and in 1504 three more Portuguese fleets rounded the Cape. But the actual annexation of India and the Spice Islands beyond was not attempted at present : India would not run away, and none but the ships and soldiers of Portugal had Holy Father's privilege and protection in those waters. Unfortunately they teemed with Moorish ships whose Captains cared not a rap for the Vatican, and were glad to earn merit by disembowelling, in the name of Allah the all-merciful, every Christian they could lay hands on : it was therefore a preliminary task in the conquest of the East to get an effective grip on the route that led there. No conquest of Indian soil was worth anything if the invaders were isolated in the network of Moorish trade-routes : they would be no more than a fly entangled in the encompassing web. But by the autumn of 1504 King Manuel deemed that the time was ripe for an expedition of conquest, and Francisco d'Almeida was appointed Viceroy of India with orders to proceed there and hold it in the name of the King. His fleet was gathered in the Tagus, and among the volunteers who flocked to his flag was Ferdinand Magellan. He did not resign his appointment at Court, but obtained leave to enlist as a seaman.

CHAPTER II

MAGELLAN SEES THE EAST

AGELLAN had been enrolled as a seaman in the autumn of 1504, and he made his Will in anticipation of a long and perilous service. It is dated December 17, 1504, at Belem, the fort on the Tagus where, no doubt, having left the Court, he was then undergoing his training as a sailor. His father, as we have already noticed, must have died previously, for it was in his power to bequeath the family estates at Sabrosa to his sister, Teresa, wife of John da Silva Telles, and her heirs. He himself was unmarried at the time, but he provided that, if before his death he married and had legitimate offspring, these estates should pass to his son or daughter. In this Will we get for the first time into some sort of touch, light though that is, with the man himself. He alludes, with the pride of birth, to his family as being one of the oldest and most distinguished lines in the kingdom, but side by side with that we find a certain significant simplicity in his direction that, should he die during his service abroad, his funeral should be that of a common seaman. Equally characteristic of him we shall find to be his desire that the chaplain of his ship, to whom he bequeaths his clothes and his arms, shall say three requiem Masses for the peace of his soul ; characteristic, too, is the provision that twelve Masses shall be said yearly *in perpetuo* in the church of San Salvador at Sabrosa. We get just

this authentic glimpse of a young man proud of his distinguished lineage and with a sense of simplicity, of duty and of religion, and our view of him shuts down again. But that crossing of the bar of the Tagus was the marriage of Magellan to the sea, and faithful he was to his mistress. Not for seven years was he to behold the coasts of Portugal again, and he never returned, as far as we know, to the stone-built house among the hills at Sabrosa, with his arms carved on the gateway of his inheritance. It passed to the heirs of his sister, Teresa, but the arms, by order of the King, were defaced.

By the spring of 1505 the fleet was ready to sail ; the number of its ships was probably twenty, but they carried on board the finished timbers, ready to be put together, for several such vessels as Drake in his raids on the Spanish Main sixty years later called his " dainty pinnaces." These were not ocean-going vessels, but were set up when the passage of the high seas was accomplished, and used for coasting-purposes, for attacks, and for general off-shore businesses. Fifteen hundred soldiers composed the fighting force, and among them were many young men of high birth who, like Magellan among the seamen, had enlisted for the sake of brave adventure ; the equipment of arms and ammunition, and the details of gunners and smiths and carpenters, were of the most comprehensive kind. Never yet in all the expeditions that had swarmed out of the hive of the Tagus had there been so important an occasion. Hitherto the ships had gone out in mufti for these preliminary scoutings : now, as was fit on this more official departure, a state-ceremony speeded them, for Portugal by virtue of her privilege was to take formal possession of her new dominions, and King Manuel to substantiate, in the person of Almeida, his title of King of Portugal and India which he had used since Vasco da Gama had returned from his first expedition there. The latter was

now appointed Admiral of India, and Almeida, as accredited Viceroy, was to unfurl the Royal banner of
Portugal on the walls of Cochim.

So before sailing a solemn service of dedication was
held in the Cathedral, attended by all who were going
forth on the King's service ; all made their confession
and partook of the Mass and took their vows of loyalty
to the King. From his hands Almeida recei.ed the
newly consecrated banner, and the Royal heralds proclaimed him Viceroy of India. That night the fleet
anchored opposite the fort of Belem on the estuary of
the Tagus, and next morning, March 25, 1505, King
Manuel paid a state visit to his fleet and bade it God-
speed. Then upon the high-tide and under sail and
oar the ships slid over the bar, and stood out to sea.

Interesting and picturesque, full of surprising adventure and monstrous with massacre, is the history of
Almeida's campaigns in India and of his Viceroyalty
there, but any detailed account of it would be quite out
of place in a Life of Magellan, for during the next four
years he was merely a common seaman, and played no
more part in these events than any other nameless man
aboard. Indeed the sum of our information about him
is that in 1506 he was on the ship commanded by Nuño
Vaz Pereira which was sent back to the East Coast of
Africa to establish forts there for the protection of the
route to India, and that he was wounded in the naval
battles of Cananor and of Diu. But, though any narrative of Almeida's administration is alien to our purpose,
it is necessary briefly to sketch the lines of Portuguese
policy in the East, for it bears directly and crucially on
the international situation which arose when, fourteen
years later, Magellan, no longer an unknown seaman in
the service of Portugal, but Commander-General of a
Spanish fleet, set out on the voyage which resulted in the
first circumnavigation of the world, and enthroned him

in the hierarchy of explorers. Until-then the only known route to the Orient, via the Cape of Good Hope, lay in the hemisphere assigned by Pope Alexander to Portugal : no Spanish ship could pass along it, for purposes of trade or conquest, without committing international trespass, and India and the Spice Islands were entirely inaccessible to Spain. The Spanish sphere lay west of Europe, its eastern limit being in mid-Atlantic, and from that Portugal was similarly excluded. But little did Almeida or King Manuel suspect that, among the indistinguishable seamen of the fleet, was a dark and silent little fellow, now on leave from his duties at the Court of Lisbon, where his absence was as inconspicuous as was his presence on Pereira's ship, whose destiny it was to arrive at the furthest East by sailing west. The most far-seeing cosmographer had not yet reckoned that as being among the practical possibilities of navigation, and thus there was no thought at present of Portuguese interests in the Orient ever coming into conflict with Spain at all. There were two races only there who would resist the establishment of Portuguese power in India, namely the native Indian states and the Moors ; the former because their territories and independence were thereby threatened, the latter because the trade with Europe which had hitherto been exclusively in their hands would thus be diverted into these European ships which passed round the lately discovered route by the Cape of Good Hope.

Almeida's programme then was to get a grip on India, and, by breaking the hold of the Moors over the trade-routes, to establish safe and regular communication by sea between Portugal and the East. The naval engagements at Cananoi and Diu, followed in each case by the bloodiest of massacres, were the decisive actions in the period of Almeida's Viceroyalty up to 1509.

These two victories had completely broken the Moorish

hold over the trade-routes and given Portugal a firm grip
on India, and it was time to push further eastwards
towards the limits of the hemisphere which Pope Alexander had assigned to Portugal.   The next step during
the consolidation of the new Indian kingdom, now free
from any serious Moorish menace, was to get possession
of the Strait of Malacca, through which passed the
wealth of the islands beyond, cinnamon and cloves and
pepper, worth their weight and more in silver, and all
the merchandise from China, silks fine as mist, and
sumptuous porcelain.   Noble as was that fever for discovery which had raged in Portugal since the days of the
Prince-Navigator, there always burned in it the lust for
domination and for riches, and that, in the main, inspired
this Easterly advance.   The treasures of India itself, its
Golcondas and Mysores conjectured but as yet unknown,
would wait, and there was no fear of their being filched
as long as the Portuguese maintained their grip on the
coast.   Not yet were they equipped for penetration
inland : it was all they could do to maintain a firm seat
on the route of communication with Europe.   And
India was only a wayside station, a point that must be
held in order to pass on to these fabulous Spice Islands,
the exact position of which, with regard to the Spanish
and Portuguese spheres, was still undetermined.   Spain
had her eye on them ; it was doubtful (especially since
nobody knew exactly where they were) whether that
shifting of the line of demarcation, made at the instance
of King John of Portugal, might not possibly have
brought them within the Spanish sphere.   It was of the
highest importance, then, that Portugal should establish
herself there, before any serious argument arose as to
their position.

Communication with Lisbon was now a regular service ; every autumn the laden ships from the Orient
started on the wings of the north-easterly monsoon for

the long passage from India round the Cape, which was
now a familiar piece of navigation to Portuguese pilots :
every spring there came out of Lisbon more ships and
men for the conquest and the holding of the East.   Up
till 1509 Almeida, though already officially superseded
as Viceroy by Albuquerque, had refused to give up the
reins of government to his successor, and when in this
year there came from Portugal a small squadron of three
ships under a new commander, Diego Lopes de Sequeira,
with orders to proceed to Malacca in order to secure
command of the Strait, Almeida, judging that this squadron was not of sufficient strength to adventure itself in
seas hitherto unknown, added to it a ship from the India
fleet in command of Garcia de Susa ; and in it sailed
Magellan   and   one   Francisco   Serrano.   From   this
moment, Magellan, of whom hitherto we have only
caught the most fleeting glimpses, begins to emerge,
and it is in connection with Serrano, who soon became
the most intimate if not the only friend whom Magellan
ever had, that we first see him detaching himself from
the background.

Except for the bare fact that Sequeira's squadron did
get to Malacca, and that there the Portuguese first
beheld the gate through which all the trade and merchandise from further East passed from the Pacific into the
Indian Ocean, the expedition was a disastrous fiasco.
Though the Italian, Luigi Vartema, had already been
there, he had certainly gone there in Moorish guise, and
the Sultan of Malacca had never consciously set eyes on
Europeans before.   But he had doubtless heard of their
victories over the Moorish traders on the Indian coast,
and of their capture of Moorish trade, and since all ships
that passed through the Strait paid toll to his sovereignty,
he had no wish to see Malacca pass into the control of
the Portuguese.   So, while he laid his private plans,
which were not of the friendliest, he gave them the

warmest welcome ; the Portuguese sailors were bidden to make themselves at home on shore, and Captain Sequeira, unwilling to be behindhand in the cultivation of cordial relations, allowed the Malayans free access to his ships. A day or two passed thus, with sailors constantly in the bazaars, and the natives visiting the noble ships of King Manuel, and Sequeira sublimely ignorant that the Sultan had aught but the most amicable intentions towards him. Presently the plans of this most perfidious monarch were ripe, and when Sequeira, whose orders were that he should return after this friendly penetration into the gate of the Pacific, told him that it was time to be off, the Sultan said that the bales of pepper and spices which the Portuguese had traded in were all ready for them, and suggested that Sequeira should send his boats ashore with the crews to load up and transfer the precious stuff to the ships. The guileless Sequeira gave the order ; Francesco Serrano was put in charge of the shore-going boats, and off they went, leaving the ships nearly empty of sailors, but swarming with genial Malayans. This done, Sequeira sat down to play chess in his cabin, with eight natives admiring him.

This fatuous confidence was luckily not shared by Captain de Susa, on whose ship Magellan was a seaman. He guessed that there was another game going on beside Sequeira's chess, and with a sudden inspiration he drove the grinning crowd of natives from his ship and despatched Seaman Magellan to the flagship to tell the chess-player that there was surely treachery afoot. Presently, so he believed, and so ran his message by Magellan to Sequeira, some signal would be given by that pleasant Sultan, on which the party ashore would be attacked and surrounded by hordes of natives, while the Malayans, in swarms aboard the denuded ships, would easily overpower the few Portuguese who remained.

Sequeira scarcely looked up from his game when

Magellan delivered the message ; maybe he thought light of it and cared more for his ivory men and their manœuvres, but it is more likely that he realized that coolness alone could save a desperate situation, for eight Malayans were closely surrounding him. Pondering his move, he told Magellan to order a man aloft to see if all was well with the party ashore, and then to row back to his ship. The man climbed up to the crow's-nest, and on the instant he saw a streamer of smoke ascending from the Sultan's palace, and, simultaneously, Serrano and his party dashing back to the boats moored by the quay, pursued by a horde of Malayans. Captain de Susa had seen that too, and now into Magellan's boat, as soon as he was alongside, there leaped Castelbranco, one of the officers, and the two rowed at top speed for the quay to the rescue of Serrano and his party, whose boat was already in the hands of the Malayans. They drove them off, and Serrano and his men tumbled in and escaped to their ship. The other parties ashore never reached the quay, but were all captured, and it was only through Magellan and Castelbranco, and their promptitude in making a dash for the shore, that his friend Serrano and those with him were saved. The rest were prisoners and were put to death. Sequeira's expedition had ended in disaster : he had lost sixty men killed, and certainly one ship which had gone ashore, and was a-swarm with natives. He tried to arrange a ransom for the Portuguese who were in the enemy's hands, but failed to effect anything, and set sail again for India with no spices aboard and short of men.

Though the evidence is only inferential, it seems fairly certain that Magellan was at once promoted to the rank of an officer for his promptitude in averting what might have been a capital disaster. On the voyage back to Cochim, Sequeira's squadron was attacked by armed Chinese junks and the assailants managed to board one

of the Portuguese ships.   Again Castelbranco and
Magellan went to their assistance from Susa's ship,
and the phrase that they " had only four sailors with
them " seemed rather to imply that the other two were
officers.   But this conjecture (for it is no more than
that) receives solid support from the next mention we
get of this elusive man, of whose life we have hitherto
got only glimpses.   On the arrival of Sequeira's ships
at Cochim, Albuquerque sent back to Portugal three
ships with cargo of the Orient, following the first annual
autumn detachment which had already sailed, and in
one of these three ships was Magellan.   His ship and
another out of the three ran ashore at night on the Padua
Bank of the Laccadive Islands, while the third, unaware
that any accident had happened to them, continued her
course to Portugal.   These three ships, in fact, though
forming a squadron, were in no sort of touch with each
other, and this incident, as we shall see, struck root in
Magellan's mind.   There was no use, thought he, in
sending three ships together unless they stood by each
other and afforded mutual support and succour in time
of need, and he remembered that when he started on his
last voyage, in which he circumnavigated the world.

Now, when this grounding of two ships on the Padua
Bank took place, it is quite clear that Magellan was a
seaman no longer.   They had run hard aground, and
all efforts to float them again proved fruitless.   Luckily
there was a calm sea (for otherwise they must have been
bumped and battered to bits), and the crews and the
cargo were safely transferred in small boats to one of
the islands.   A council of officers was held next morning, and it was decided to despatch the ships' boats, with
as many men as they would hold, back to Cochim :
should they succeed in reaching it, they would bring
back sea-going vessels to rescue the remainder.   While
they were gone there was no fear of starvation for the

temporary castaways, for the ships had been provisioned for the voyage to Lisbon, and there was abundance of food. . . . And here we get a sudden glimpse, unexpected and strangely illuminating, as to the workings of navies of that day. The boats would just hold the Captains and officers of these two ships but no more, and these prepared to go off themselves, leaving all the crew behind. To us now such a procedure is unthinkable : officers and men would be treated as units of equal worth, and lots would be drawn as to who should go, while the two Captains of the ships would most undoubtedly stop with their men. But in King Manuel's day an officer was considered of higher individual value, when danger or death was in the hazard, than a seaman, and so the officers prepared to set out in the ships' boats. Then something like a mutiny occurred : the men refused to let the boats start unless a due proportion of them were given places therein. And now it becomes clear that Magellan had become an officer, for he volunteered to stop behind with the seamen. Instantly the mutinous symptoms subsided : if Magellan stopped, the men were perfectly willing to let all the rest go, and we may certainly infer from this episode that he was not only an officer, but one whom the seamen trusted. As the rest of the officers now crowded into the boats, Magellan was busy there helping to stow provisions for their voyage, and one of the seamen, thinking that he repented of his offer, said to him, " Sir, did you not promise to remain with us ? " But he need have had no qualm : Magellan had no thought of leaving them.

Here then on this Padua Bank, throwing in his lot with the seamen, just as in his Will made before he started for Lisbon he had enjoined that if he died on the voyage he should have the burial of one, we begin to get a more intimate sight of Magellan than his previous history has given us. And most interesting of all, for

us who want to realize him as a human figure, is the
reason given by one of the Portuguese historians for his
thus volunteering : he had a friend, we are told, among
those who were to be left behind, and that was Francesco
Serrano, whose life Magellan had already saved at
Malacca. While Serrano, a seaman, had to stay,
Magellan would not leave him. Off went the boats,
under promise that if they arrived safely at Cochim they
would send a ship of rescue. This was done : a caravel
instantly set out for the Padua Bank and picked up
Magellan and the marooned crew. But the two ships
which had run ashore were now wrecks, and instead of
returning to Lisbon, Magellan went back to the Indian
coast.

During the spring of 1510 Albuquerque had taken
Goa, but he had been unable to hold it, and in the ensuing
autumn prepared for another attack on it. Previous to
this expedition, he held a Council of all the Captains of
the Portuguese ships, and we find that Magellan took
part in it. It looks therefore as if his conduct on the
Padua Bank had earned him further promotion, and
indeed we find it spoken of in tones of the highest com-
mendation even by those Portuguese historians who are
most bitter against him for his subsequent naturalization
as a Spaniard. The point on which Albuquerque desired
to know the opinion of his Captains was whether he
should take with him to Goa, to help in the blockade of
the place, the ships which were now due to start with
cargoes of the East for Portugal. Magellan was against
Albuquerque's stopping the immediate despatch of this
convoy, and spoke in that sense : if the start was delayed
they would miss the north-easterly monsoon. The
merchant-captains supported this view, and Albuquerque
against his personal inclination decided that no ship outside the regular fighting fleet need accompany him to
Goa, unless its Captain wished to do so. It was settled

thus, and without the merchant-ships he set out for Goa, which he took in the month of November. The incident in itself was trivial, but it holds a certain significance, for it shows that Magellan had now won a certain standing in the Portuguese Navy, and that he did not hesitate to express a view which he knew would be unpopular with his Admiral.

With the taking of Goa a period of relative tranquillity settled down on the Indian coast. But there was still Sequeira's dismal failure to capture Malacca to be retrieved, and that was an affair of the first importance, for until the town and the strait which it commanded were in Portuguese possession no further progress could be made towards securing the trade from the Spice Islands and the Coasts of Cathay. That gate still stood firmly locked, and beyond it, not to be reached till it was flung open, lay those thrice precious treasuries. Desirable they had always been, but since the Portuguese had occupied this Indian coast the fame of these Spice Islands, the value of their produce, of their groves of incense-bearing trees, had become more fabulous yet, and with their spices was mingled some unique fragrance of romance that made of them a faery-land beyond the perilous seas. The Moorish ships that came through from beyond, the Chinese junks that strolled into the ports now held by Portugal, reeked of precious and tropical nards ; and that El Dorado lay somewhere beyond the gate that had been slammed in Sequeira's face. Of that sea practically nothing was known, except that it washed the shores of China, and that the Spice Islands basked in it : it was just the Great South Sea, conjectured (but no more) to extend to the coasts of the new continent which Columbus had discovered.

But this time there was to be no bungling ; and, in the summer of 1511, Albuquerque, himself in command, set out with a fleet of nineteen ships again to attack the

town that was the key to the further and richer Orient.
It lay ranged for miles along the shore of that narrow
strait, and every furlong of it was contested, for it was
strongly garrisoned, it had abundance of artillery, and,
as its Sultan knew, it was the last line of defence of the
riches within : when once the Portuguese wolf had
broken through, the flock of islands was at his mercy.
For six weeks the struggle for it went on, but at the end
it was in the hands of the western invaders, and the long
eastward passage from Lisbon to the islands of the
Pacific (not yet known as such) was open.   Since Diaz,
twenty-four years earlier, had rounded the Cape of Good
Hope and thrown open a maritime route to India, no
more important achievement had crowned Portuguese
enterprise than this forcing of the final gate.   They had
broken their way into the richest treasury of the inheritance devised to Portugal by Pope Alexander VI : the
Malay Archipelago, Java, the Moluccas, the Celebes,
and the Philippine Islands were now unbarriered and
the coasts of China.   Whether the Moluccas lay so far
east that they fell within the western or Spanish hemisphere or not, the only gate through which they could be
reached was in possession of Portugal, and the control
was hers.   Spain might not trespass along that Eastern
highway of the seas, but the insignificant Captain of one
of these Portuguese ships was he who would show Spain
another route into the Pacific through Spanish waters.
He had already shown Albuquerque that he could form
opinions of his own ; it was not many years before King
Manuel would be using the utmost resources of his
Royalty in fruitless opposition to that indomitable will.

The effect of the fall of Malacca was no less prodigious in the new world which Albuquerque had opened
to Portugal than it was in the old world when the tidings
of his exploit reached the Court at Lisbon.   His prestige
flamed high through the unbarriered East, Sultans and

Kings of the islands beyond whose troops had fought to oppose him now hurried to make friends with a power they could not resist. With Malacca in his possession, Albuquerque lost no time in pushing forward again and securing the islands on which the soul of Portugal was set. He showed a wise statesmanship in the instructions he gave to the Captains of the three ships which he instantly despatched eastwards into the Pacific, bidding them adopt the most friendly and conciliatory attitude in all parts into which they penetrated. They took with them native pilots and interpreters, and their immediate mission was to establish peaceful trading, load up with spices and return.

Antonio d'Abreu was appointed Admiral of these three ships which now went eastwards from Malacca : he sailed in the flagship, of which the name is unknown. Francisco Serrano, Magellan's friend, and now a seaman no longer, was Captain of the second, and one historian, Argensola, specifically states that Magellan was Captain of the third. No other historian mentions him as having gone on this expedition ; and, though their silence does not, of course, prove that Argensola had made a mistake, the argument that Magellan did not, on this occasion, sail into the Pacific is based on premises which cannot be disputed. For this expedition started from Malacca in December, 1511, and we find that in the following June Magellan was indubitably back in Lisbon. We do not know exactly when this squadron, now sailing east-wards into the Pacific, returned from its exploration, and brought back to India the reports of those who had actually seen the fabled isles ; but it seems quite im-possible, considering that the prevailing winds in spring in the Indian Ocean are westerly (thus speeding the fleets that Portugal now annually sent out at that season), that Magellan should have sailed east from Malacca in mid-December, have made an extensive voyage in the

Pacific, and yet have been back in Lisbon during June. The importance of this as regards what we call " records" is considerable, for in his circumnavigation of the world Magellan met his death, sailing westwards, in the Philippines. If then, as seems certain, he did not command a ship in this expedition, he missed the complete circumnavigation by (roughly) some fifteen hundred miles. It need, perhaps, hardly be stated that this makes not the smallest difference to the splendour of the achievement which must always give him rank as the greatest navigator known, but technically he failed in person to accomplish the entire circuit.

But, though Magellan cannot have sailed from Malacca with Antonio d'Abreu, the history of that exploration which revealed to Portugal her enchanted goal must be briefly touched on, for the destiny of his friend, Francisco Serrano, who certainly was in command of one of these three ships, had a vital bearing on his own. This squadron, now ploughing new seas with every favouring breeze, coasted along the northern shores of Sumatra and Java, and from there struck across the Banda Sea, making land again at Amboina, one of the southernmost of the Moluccas group. From there Abreu sailed to Banda, and found so great a store of spices that he gave up all idea of visiting the more northerly islands and turned homewards again. He had accomplished the object for which he had been sent, Amboina and Banda had received him in the friendliest manner, and his ships were laden with peppers and cloves and cinnamons to their full capacity. Some hundred and forty miles west from Banda on this return voyage Serrano's vessel ran ashore, and lost touch of the others. But the magic of the East and this fragrant faery-land of the Spice Islands had taken hold on him ; and, when his ship was repaired again and floated, he set her course not for Malacca, but back to Amboina. The natives there had already experienced the friendliness and fair dealing of the Portuguese, and they welcomed Serrano's return. There was at that time a quarrel going on between the Kings of Ternate and Tidore, two of the most northerly islands of the group, and Serrano, seeing the possibility of an undreamed-of career opening before him, sailed from Amboina to Ternate, and offered his support and services to the King. He was most cordially received, for his service was a pledge of Portuguese support when next their ships came through the gate of the Pacific, and he became, like Joseph in Egypt, the Grand Vizier to the King of Ternate. By rights, of course, in performance of his duty as Captain of one of King Manuel's ships, he should have followed Abreu back to India. Perhaps he thought that he would do the King more signal service by remaining here and making a Portuguese focus in the islands of his desire, or was it that the magic of the East was too strong for him and he could no longer tolerate the thought of life anywhere but in these isles of the Pacific ? Henceforth, at any rate, till the day of his death Ternate was his home, and from here he sent many letters to his friend, Magellan, saying that he had found a new world richer than India and that here he would live out his days. Without being unduly fanciful, we may guess that the thought of Serrano out there in Ternate, high in the favour of the King, became a magnet to Magellan and strengthened his resolve to make the Spice Islands the goal of his own ambitions. That stuck in his mind, it simmered and fermented there, and when a few years later Magellan had that interview with King Manuel which determined his destiny he wrote off at once to Serrano, as we shall see, to say that he would be with him soon, " if not by way of Portugal then by way of Spain."

Rejecting then, for stern reasons of chronology, the idea that Magellan took part in this first European voyage in the Pacific, we must figure him as saying fare-well to Serrano at Malacca, and going back in December, 1511, with Albuquerque's fleet to India.   He must then have been ordered to return with some home-going squadron to Portugal and have arrived in Lisbon not later than the following June, for on the 12th of that month he signed in Lisbon a receipt for the monthly salary, paid partly in cash, partly in kind, of his post at Court.   He had not, as already noticed, resigned this appointment, and though he had been absent for seven years, in the King's service in the East, he now took it up again.

CHAPTER III

KING MANUEL HAS NO USE FOR MAGELLAN

AGELLAN had left Lisbon as a sea-
man, and he returned as Captain in
the King's navy. He had been
wounded at least twice, and he had
two very meritorious pieces of service
to his credit : the one when by his
quickness he had succeeded in rescu-
ing Serrano's party which had been
attacked by the natives on the quay at Malacca on the
occasion of Sequeira's abortive expedition there ; the
other when, by volunteering to remain with the wrecked
seamen on the Padua Bank, he had averted a mutinous
outbreak. It was no doubt in recognition of these, and
of his long service, that his rank at Court was raised,
together with the salary attached to it, and when next
month, in July, he again gave a receipt (still extant) for
his salary, he signed it with his new title of " fidalgo
escudeiro " : in English parlance we should say that he
had been given an " order." All officials attached to
the Court at Lisbon appear to have had some such order
(much as is the case in the entourage of Royalty to-day),
and to each grade there was attached a certain fixed
salary. Accordingly we find that in this July receipt
Magellan (escudeiro) signs for a salary of 1850 reis
instead of 1000. This actual enrichment was on no
very opulent scale, for 1000 reis were equivalent to five

shillings (though their purchasing power in the sixteenth
century was from eight to ten times that of modern
money), but his salary was thus nearly doubled. Insignificant and unworthy of record as these details may
seem, this question of Magellan's pay at Court very
soon crops up again laden with weighty issues ; for,
with the implications involved in it, it directly contributed to the fact that the great exploit and adventure of
his life was undertaken not by a Portuguese but by a
Spaniard.

He had been away then for seven years, and had taken
a modest though highly creditable part under Almeida
and Albuquerque in their magnificent intrusions into
the unknown world of the Orient.   He had been present
when the gate into the Pacific had been thrown open, he
had seen Serrano's ship slide away into the great South
Sea, which he himself before long was to christen Mare
Pacifico, and now on his return from these years of conquest and discovery in the East, he found that the West
too had been yielding up fresh secrets of the round world
to the explorers in the Spanish hemisphere.   Columbus,
before his death, had made four voyages to Central
America, and there was not now much doubt that
beyond it lay the great South Sea : such, at any rate, was
the belief of those who had studied his charts and log-
books.   It was also certain that southwards from the
new regions of his voyage there stretched the shores of
a gigantic continent : south and yet south it extended,
and that could hardly be Asia.   Christopher Jacques
had returned from his voyage of 1503 with some sort of
chart of the Brazilian coasts, and of the shores of Patagonia (not yet known as such) which lay beyond.   There
was also talk, fireside talk, tavern talk among sailors,
about the existence of some strait far away to the south
which might prove to be the western, American gate
into the Pacific, much as Malacca was the eastern,

Asiatic gate into the same sea. There were even said to exist maps made by one of those explorers which showed it. All was vague, but there seemed to be some foundation for such a conjecture. In any case this huge continent must surely come to an end some time, if an explorer pushed far enough south, even as Diaz had found that the corresponding continent of Africa, which had barred all voyaging to the East, terminated in the Cape round which now every year the navies of Portugal went forth and back between Lisbon and India. Others said that America stretched south till it joined the polar ice, or the conjectured Terra Australis ; but, since nobody had been there to see, nobody could yet pronounce on that subject. America might come to an end, and there would be open sea beyond, which was one with the Pacific ; or there might be that strait they talked of, and the navigator sailing into the ultimate west would find himself in the ultimate east. . . . Such talk was in the air, the uncondensed vapour of conjecture and argument, and it persistently hovered over Magellan's mind when now, after seven years of Oriental adventure, he lived the tamed life again in the routine of the Court with its tediums and etiquettes and trivial ceremonies. And these uncondensed vapours began to liquefy and fall like dew on the cold steel of his mind. Surely there must be some passage for the navigator there ; and, if he went westwards still and ever westwards, he would on some remote evening see the sun setting behind those Spice Islands, which to the eyes of his friend, Francisco Serrano, had risen from the sea with the flames not of sunset but of sunrise behind them. It is difficult for us, to whom the globe is now a map for all to read, to put ourselves back to the times when far the greater part of it was undiscovered, but we must do that in order to understand that raging geographical fever that then heated men's blood into so noble a delirium.

For the space of a year, until the summer of 1513, Magellan remained at the Court of Lisbon, always seeking out pilots and captains of ships who had returned from remote voyages, and diligently studying the theories of navigation. But this summer there was trouble in Morocco with Portugal's hereditary enemies, the Moors. Azamor, a port of considerable size on the coast, refused to pay the tribute to which it was bound under its treaty with Lisbon. This was equivalent to revolt, and King Manuel, fearing that it might spread to other cities, resolved to deal out stern stuff to the Moors. He instantly commissioned a fleet and an army wholly disproportionate to the mere business of reducing one coast-town, and a vast navy, ten times more numerous in ships than that with which Almeida had been sent to conquer India, with eighteen thousand soldiers on board, was despatched to reduce a town that did not contain as many inhabitants. Any resistance on the part of Azamor was, of course, quite out of the question; the town surrendered, and the Duke of Braganza, who was in command of this immense armada, returned to Portugal in triumph. As far as the ostensible object of the expedition was concerned, it was attained by this demonstration in force.

But now the real purpose of King Manuel emerged, for General de Meneses, who took over the command, began overrunning the country, burning crops, raiding villages and capturing cattle. This might be supposed to serve as a deterrent to other Moorish tribes and cities who were disposed to follow the foolish example of Azamor, but no doubt King Manuel's real object was to provoke the resistance of the more powerful Moorish chieftains, and with his large force to crush it, and thus have no more bother with the Moors of Morocco. Such indeed was the result of these harrying raids, in one of which Magellan's name is first mentioned. He is not recorded in the lists of naval officers, but now he appears as serving among the troops.   In some skirmish he was wounded in the knee, and from that time forth to the end of his life he was lame of a leg.   In consequence of this wound he took no further part in active service on this campaign, but, with another officer, was put in charge of a camp at the base into which were herded the droves of cattle captured from the Moors.   Meantime in the spring of 1514 news came to the Portuguese, who still occupied Azamor, that the Moors in large force were advancing on the town under the command of the King of Fez.   They were heavily defeated in two actions by General de Meneses, and the campaign was over.   King Manuel, according to plan, had provoked a general rising and crushed it.   The Portuguese troops began to be drafted home.

Magellan, lame from his wound, was still in charge of the stock of captured cattle and horses, and an accusation was now brought against him that he had been selling these to the Moors.   He was neither arrested nor, it seems, formally charged ; but, instead of asking that the matter should be cleared up, he embarked among the returning troops without leave from his superior officer.   The explanation of this amazing conduct, that he wished to prove his innocence to King Manuel, will not hold water, for on arrival at Lisbon he did nothing of the kind, but, seeking an audience with the King, he merely asked for an increase of salary, on account, we must suppose, of this crippling wound.   In the meantime the King had received despatches from the officer in command at Azamor, stating that he had not given Magellan leave to return home, and, further, that there was this charge against him of selling captured cattle. King Manuel therefore, with justice that, if anything, inclined to leniency, ordered Magellan to return to Azamor and stand his trial on this double charge.   He refused to listen, as was perfectly proper, to anything that Magellan had to say. . . . So far the story seems scarcely credible : we should feel inclined to class it with those of that crop of defamations which sprang up about Magellan when, a few years later, he evoked the execration of all Portugal. The sequel, however, of the general accuracy of which there can be no doubt, possibly supplies the key.

Now if Magellan had left Azamor, while discharging military duties there, without leave, he was guilty of the gravest sort of insubordination, and would have been lucky on his return there to have been dismissed the King's service altogether and not have paid for it with his life ; if he had been proved guilty of selling captured cattle for his own profit, the consequences would have been hardly less serious. But on his presenting himself to Pedro de Susa, who had succeeded General de Meneses, neither of these charges was proceeded with, and instead he was given some official certificate which exculpated him from both, and granted him permission to return to Lisbon again. It looks, then, as if in his absence this charge of having stolen captured booty and disposed of it to his own enrichment (which may have been no more than malicious gossip) had been investigated and proved to be without foundation. Otherwise it is impossible to see why he did not now have to answer it. But it is harder to explain why he was not court-martialled for leaving Azamor without leave ; for, if he had really done so, he could not possibly have escaped it. It is certain, however, that no proceedings of the sort were taken, and we are driven to suppose, not for the sake of excusing him, but of finding some sense in the whole story, that General de Meneses must have given orders that a certain draft should go home, forgetting that Magellan was in it, or that some similar misunderstanding, for which Magellan was not to blame, had occurred.   The sequel, in fact, supplies a credible foundation for the whole story.   With this second return of Magellan from Africa, he leaps into the foreground of our picture.

He went back at once to Lisbon, now bringing with him the proofs of the correctness of his conduct as certified by his commanding officer ; and, with that quiet implacable determination which henceforth we see to be the very hall-mark of the man, asked for another audience with the King in order to prefer precisely the same request as before, namely an increase in his salary, all discussion with regard to which the King had broken off before, refusing to listen to one who was accused of theft and of desertion.   The audience was granted him, and at the appointed hour Ferdinand Magellan, aged thirty-four, short of stature, burned brown from his long service in India, and going clumsily by reason of his crippled knee, limped up the hall where the King sat to hear petitioners.   Manuel looked wryly on him, he always disliked him, and Magellan, making obeisance, presented the signed papers that exonerated him. King Manuel glanced at them and gave them back to him ; perhaps he said he was glad that this had been satisfactorily explained, but he u..derstood that Captain Magellan had some request to make of him in seeking audience.   So Magellan made his request, and it was that his salary at Court should be raised to the extent of one shilling a month.   King Manuel gave an imme-diate refusal : he did not like Magellan and he disliked much more to be asked for money.   And then Magellan asked if the King would let him go from Court and give him employment in his navy, and again the King re-fused.   And then finally Magellan asked for the King's leave " to live with someone who would show him favour, where he might obtain more good fortune than with the King."   Manuel had a ready assent to this, for thus he could show contempt of his petitioner, and he told him he might do just as he pleased about that. Then Magellan bent to kiss his hand, and King Manuel withdrew it, so that he did not get this privilege. . . . So the audience was over and he limped away clumsily from the Presence, foot behind foot, not turning his back. And a snigger ran round the circle of the lords in waiting and the equerries and the ushers, for someone whispered that the lameness of the tawny little fellow was feigned in order to move the King's compassion. Magellan heard that whisper and he flushed beneath his tan, for it stung him more shrewdly than the King's curt monosyllables.

So he went out from the Presence, leaving the Court sycophantically amused and gratified at the snub administered to him. Nothing could have been more contemptuous than the King's manner to him : he had refused with one point-blank word the first two requests he had made, but even more wounding than that was Manuel's willing assent that he might offer his service to whomsoever he pleased. And then he had refused to allow him to kiss his hand, as if, owing to this request which he had granted with such ready scorn, Magellan was no longer in his service. But the interview, brief, and to Magellan incredibly bitter, contains, like the first act of some subtly devised play, the whole foundation of the amazing drama that followed ; each word spoken dripped with destiny, and neither King nor petitioner can ever have forgotten those few minutes in the hall of audience. They need comment, out of all proportion, as it would at first seem, to their apparent significance.

Now at first sight Magellan's request that the King should raise his salary to the figure of an extra shilling a month strikes us as purely ludicrous, and not less ludicrous was the King's refusal to do so. But if we look

away from the face-value of this most exiguous boon,
and regard instead what was the implication contained
in it, the ridiculous side of it fades out altogether. The
King (as well as his petitioner) knew that this was a
serious and solid request, which had a real meaning
behind it, and he subsequently gave as a justification for
his refusal the reason that if he had granted this boon
" he feared an entrance should be opened to ambitious
persons." The ambitions of such were not really concerned with an additional shilling a month of pocket-
money, nor were Magellan's, and the King knew that
as well as anybody. For fifty years ago, officials of the
Court at Lisbon received their salary entirely in kind,
board and lodging of various grades of dignity was
given them, but when in the reign of King John II the
personnel of the Court grew more numerous this payment in kind was commuted into a monetary salary (just
as the butt of sherry which had previously been the re-
muneration of the English Laureate was commuted in
the poetic reign of Pye into an annual payment of £23)
and the standing and dignity of the officials of the Court
was estimated on the basis of their incomes. Magellan's
request therefore was not just for a nonsensical shilling
a month, but that which the shilling symbolized, and
Bishop Osorius, who can find no words strong enough
to express his condemnation of Magellan's subsequent
naturalization as a Spaniard, admits that there was here
" a slight offence " on the part of the King, in refusing
Magellan's request. He had served in the African
campaign and had been wounded there, and for this he
deserved recognition. Osorius goes on to make the
whole matter quite plain : " And as the Portuguese "
(he says) " think that the thing most to be desired is to
be enrolled amongst the King's household, so they consider the greatest honour to consist in an increase of
this stipend. For, as there are various ranks of King's

servants, so the sum of money is assigned to each servant according to the dignity of his rank.   The highest class is that of noblemen, but as there are distinctions of nobility, so an equal salary is not given to all.   Thus it happens that the nobility of each is estimated according to the importance of this stipend, *and each one is held to be more noble in proportion to the more ample stipend which he receives.*"

Now this very explicit passage causes the farcical aspect of this Royal audience in which a noble of Portugal asked his King for a rise of a shilling a month in his salary, and was told by the King he could not have it, to vanish altogether.   What Magellan was asking for was a recognition, in a rise in rank, of his services to the King.   Looked at in this light, his second request, when the first was refused, to be given further employment in the King's navy, follows reasonably and logically. It amounted to this : " If your Majesty will not recognize my previous service, give me, at any rate, the opportunity to serve you further," and this was a very proper expression of his loyalty and devotion.   Indeed Magellan had very good cause to seek such an assurance, for Vasco da Gama, who had discovered India, had for years been put on the shelf by King Manuel, who was always jealous of those who had done their country most signal service, and Gama's title of Admiral of India had been a sheer emptiness, fine-sounding but signifying nothing.   Almeida, too, had suffered from this engrained ingratitude, for after five years of incessant struggle in India and the most creditable administration of the Viceroyalty he had been superseded by Albuquerque.   But the King would give no such promise ; Magellan might look forward to dangling about the Court till the sap and dazzle of adventure had died out of his veins.

We may picture him pausing when the King thus

denied him not only promotion but any further chance
of earning it.   And then came his third request, also
a logical inquiry resulting from the answer he had just
received.   As the King had no further use for his
services, might he offer them elsewhere ?   To that
came an affirmative more stingingly contemptuous than
either of the refusals had been : he was perfectly at
liberty to do so.   It is most improbable that at this
moment King Manuel definitely understood Magellan
to mean that he asked leave to be done with Portugal
altogether, and seek employment from the King of
Spain, because when Magellan did so, and the nature
of that employment was known, it was a most unpleasant
surprise to King Manuel, and he did his best to get
Magellan back, and, failing that, to prevent him making
the great voyage.   He disliked the man ; he would not
recognize his previous services, or give him the opportunity to serve him further, and as a final and complete
snub, to show his total indifference as to what he did,
or where he betook himself, he gave his Royal permission
to him to do exactly what he liked.   His final gesture,
in withdrawing his hand from the obeisance of one who
had served him, man and boy, for over twenty years,
was a calculated and unkingly insult.   Thereafter King
Manuel was to get in a state of high agitation for his
lamentable manners, and, even more, for his entire lack
of judgment in appreciating Magellan's qualities.   That
he was socially unpopular there is no doubt ; a charge
of stealing from the stores of an army, resting on no real
foundation, is not brought against a popular officer,
nor are innuendoes made that his honourable lameness
is feigned *per misericordiam*.   And the King disliked
him too, and was pleased to show that he did not want
to have anything more to do with him.

It was not then, as Bishop Osorius states, King
Manuel's refusal to grant Magellan this rise of salary,

with its corresponding rise of rank, that led to his de-
naturalizing himself, but the King's contemptuous
refusal to hold out any hopes of a future career in his
service, and his permission to let him do what he liked
with himself : he had given Magellan his *congé*, and he
might kiss somebody else's hand, but not King Manuel's.
Whether, as has been suggested, he had ever told the
King of the project that was now taking shape in his
mind, which he had hoped to attempt under the flag of
Portugal, even as Columbus had hoped to find the New
World in the same service, is quite unknown. There
is, in any case, no record of his having stated that the
project was to seek the Spice Islands by a westerly route,
and subsequent developments seem to point to the fact
that he had not. We must not therefore suppose that
King Manuel pooh-poohed Magellan's scheme ; indeed
that would have been uncharacteristic of one who throughout his reign always encouraged any scheme which he
thought could advance discovery. King Manuel merely
thought that Magellan was of no use, and signified that
in the most unmistakable manner.

Fresh from this public and deliberate humiliation,
Magellan bethought him of his friend, Francisco
Serrano, who four years ago had vanished into the dawn
eastwards from Malacca, and who continued to write
to him of the wonders of those islands which Magellan
had never seen, and of the King of Ternate whose minister
he was ; Portuguese ships came there regularly now, by
way of India. And now Magellan wrote back to
Serrano, bidding him wait for him, for he would be with
him soon " if not by way of Portugal, then by way of
Spain." This phrase, simple as it sounds, is ambiguous,
and capable of two interpretations. The most obvious
is that he intended, as he was soon to do, to denaturalize
himself and offer his services to Spain. Possibly that
is the signification of it, but there is another which more

commends itself, namely that " by way of Spain " meant
by way of America, which in Pope Alexander's disposition was Spanish.   That certainly was also Magellan's
intention, and for the remainder of his days in Portugal
he set himself, now free from any duties to his sovereign,
to work out that scheme in order to present it, no tentative sketch nor vague adumbration of an idea, but a
design, feasible and finished, with himself ready to
expound it, for the consideration of his new master.
This motive seems to account for what is otherwise
rather puzzling, namely that he did not, on his demission
by King Manuel, at once leave Portugal for Castile.
But here he was working among the pilots and ship-
masters whom he knew, and from whom he could glean
information about the Brazilian coast and something
about the land that lay south of it.   Here too, in Lisbon,
there was undoubtedly something known about a strait
that lay further south yet, the entry of which at most
had been seen, but nothing more.   By now the existence of the Pacific, the great South Sea, was no longer
a matter of mere probability, for in 1513 the Spanish
Captain Vasco Nuñez de Balboa had climbed the peak
in Darien (an exploit poetically attributed by Keats to
stout Cortez) and not only had seen it, but had crossed
the Isthmus of Panama and gone down to the shore
where, sword in hand and fully accoutred, he had waded
into it and, in the best Hohenzollern style, had claimed
it and all that therein was, and all the islands that swam
in it, for his master the King of Spain.   That strait then,
thought Magellan to himself, opens into the Great
South Sea, and in that sea there swim the Spice Islands.
It seems now to have occurred to him that perhaps after
all, though Portugal had claimed them, and the only
access to them at present was through Portuguese waters,
they lay not in the Portuguese sphere of dominion,
as devised to her by Pope Alexander, but in the sphere

of Spain, and that access to them could be found through
Spanish waters. Hence his letter to Serrano. But the
strait, if it existed, was the key that opened the door into
the Pacific, and it seems clear that there was now something known, or rumoured, about it, and the source
from which that rumour sprang was Lisbon.

For in the year 1515, very shortly after King Manuel
found that he had no use for Magellan, Johann Schöner
of Nuremberg manufactured a globe on which the strait
subsequently known as the Strait of Magellan was
definitely marked. It was not correctly placed ; it was
not correctly drawn (for no one had been through it),
but it was there, a corridor from the far-South Atlantic
into the Pacific.[1] The information which he thus embodied on his globe was derived from a German pamphlet
which had been translated from the Portuguese. This
document described the discoveries made on the east
coast of South America by a Portuguese expedition
which was privately financed by Christopher de Haro
and others. This expedition must have been that of
Coelho, which went out in 1501, or that of Christopher
Jacques in 1503, for, as far as is known, no other Portuguese expedition explored the coasts of Brazil and
southwards, and we may therefore assume that the
Portuguese document on which (translated into German)
Schöner founded the globe which marks the strait was
an account of one of these voyages. Since the days of
Prince Henry the Navigator, maps and narratives of
such voyages were preserved in the library at Lisbon,
and it is at least highly probable that the narratives of
Coelho and Jacques were preserved there. It is suggested therefore that what kept Magellan in Lisbon
after his dismissal by the King was to get all possible
information about the strait before taking his scheme to

[1] For a full account of Schöner's globes see *Life of Magellan*,
Guillemard, p. 192, etc.

the King of Spain.   The material on which he worked was here, and we cannot doubt that, if King Manuel had given him promise of employment or had taken the least interest in him, the project that was soon to be offered to Charles of Spain would have been submitted to him.   Brazil, according to the ecclesiastical allotment of the world, was in King Manuel's parish ; a Portuguese expedition sailing to Brazil would not have trespassed outside it, and thereafter its course, though lying in Spanish waters, was where no sail, Portuguese or Spanish, had ever come.   Without doubt King Manuel could have been patron of Magellan's voyage (even as King John II, his predecessor, could have sent forth Columbus, and by right of discovery have claimed dominion over the New World), had he not come to the unfortunate conclusion that Magellan was of no use to anybody.

Here for the present then in Lisbon, ill-looked on by reason of the King's disfavour, Magellan remained, for he was darkly busy with learning what could not be learned elsewhere, before he took himself and his knowledge to one who might be less contemptuous of him. He had no position now at Court, for the King had dispensed with his services, and he could spend his time with mariners and geographers, and delve into such observations of noon and night and the wheeling stars as bore on practical seamanship.   Associated with him now, and soon to be more closely knit in the study of such things as applied to the voyage which he contemplated, was a strange and rather sinister figure, one typical of the age.   This was Ruy Faleiro, a scholar and a student, highly skilled in the theory of navigation though no practical sailor, and a notable astronomer.   It was whispered that he was a dealer in black arts and was tutored by a demon who both taught and obeyed him, and told him secrets about the stars which invariably proved to be true, so that, if Faleiro said that at midnight on such a day a great planet would rise over Africa, such information might be considered trustworthy.   In those days astronomers were astrologists as well ; the man who could point to the heavens, and show Jupiter to be dominant there and notably shining in a favourable quarter, would affirm that the celestial signs looked kindly on some contemplated adventure, and prophesy a fortunate issue for the consultant.   Such divination was not held to be Satanic in origin ; kings and captains consulted the stars through the medium of those learned in them, for they held that these celestial signs were set in the heavens by Divine ordinance for the guidance of mankind, and Magellan himself shared that view, for he took with him on his voyage an astrologist skilled in the interpretation of the stars.   Faleiro's profession, in short, was perfectly respectable, and his reputation as being leagued with the powers of darkness was not due to that, but probably to his black and venomous temper, bordering on the insane, which in a few years was to develop into madness.

But though Magellan, like everyone else of his day, believed that the stars were, if not the arbiters of a man's destiny, the signs, for those who could read their language, of the fate that was appointed for him, it was not Faleiro's knowledge of the baleful or beneficent regard of the planets towards adventurers on the earth that he desired, but the astronomer's skill in using these celestial lamps to guide the path of those who sought to traverse the unknown seas, and by their aid determine into what longitude the uncharted tides and winds had borne him. They might also have their bearing on destiny ; an astrologer could divine the future from their contemplation, but Magellan's business with Faleiro was in his capacity of astronomer rather than astrologer. Faleiro had made a terrestrial globe with lines of longi-

tude from pole to pole, and it was mounted on fine points
and turned easily on those pivots, slowly circling. Lisbon
was zero, and on the surface were sketched the shapes of
continents and islands as at present verified by exploration, and further afield, east and west, were fainter out-
lines as conjectured. In the Royal library at Lisbon
before he had fallen from favour, Magellan had seen a
chart that marked a long coast-line south of Brazil,
and the entry of a strait, and perhaps Faleiro recorded
these in tentative dotted lines. Again, Magellan had
letters from his friend Serrano in the Spice Islands ; he
knew how long it had taken him to sail there from
Malacca ; a rough calculation might be made as to how
far eastwards of the gate of the great South Sea Ternate
lay, and the general position of the Spice Islands could
be indicated. Then Faleiro lit the lantern hanging
from the ceiling in his cabinet of astronomical apparatus,
and set the globe so that this lantern which signified the
sun was poised above Lisbon, and so it was noon in
Lisbon. When the globe was adjusted like that, India
was somewhere on the vague edge of the circle of shadow,
and America, more conjecturally, situated on the edge
of the shadow opposite. " It is evening in India," said
Faleiro, " and noon in Lisbon and dawn in America.
Then I turn the globe and night falls in India, and
America comes out into full day. And now the shadow
of evening is falling over Lisbon and noon is blazing
over America and in India it is midnight. Then India
revolves through the night and the ray of dawn falls on
it again, but it has long been day in your Spice Islands.
. . ." And then Magellan put out his brown, lean
finger and stopped that smooth revolution of Faleiro's
globe. " Turn it back again," he cried, " and let it
be full noon over the line that Holy Father drew across
the Atlantic, to make the boundaries of Portugal and
Spain. Now look into the shadow and see on which

side of midnight the Spice Islands are lying. . . . It is
as I thought ! It is after midnight with them : they lie
in the Spanish half of the world. . . ." Again and again
they went into this, and more and more Magellan became
convinced that Serrano was waiting for him not in the
Spice Islands of Portugal but in the Spice Islands of Spain.

Faleiro cared as much for the pure science of the stars as
for any application of it to a useful end ; their actual
movements were as fascinating to him as their bearing
on human destiny and their aid to navigators. But it
was the applied science which concerned Magellan,
and, skilled navigator as he already was, this queer friend
of his, who had never steered a ship in his life nor furled
a sail, gave him data for the taking of many observations
which were at present matters of approximate guess-work
rather than exact calculation. But as their joint studies
progressed, and their acquaintanceship ripened into
scientific intimacy rather than human friendship, Faleiro
began to take a keener interest in the practical side of
this abstract knowledge of his, and it was not long before
Magellan told him the whole of that project which possessed his brain, and which should place him for ever
at the head of the world's great explorers. Faleiro had
long been employed on a treatise on methods of ascertain-
ing longitude by the sun and the stars, and now he
devoted his vast erudition to the working out of this
project of a passage to the Spice Islands by sailing west ;
the two became partners in it. Faleiro was a cross-
grained fellow, jealous and suspicious of others ; and
this suited Magellan very well, for he did not want his
scheme spoken of, and he was grim and taciturn himself.
The passionate search for knowledge on the one side, and
on the other the passionate desire for adventure that
would put it to the proof, was a link between them ; then,
too, they were both ill-looked on in Lisbon. But King
Manuel, for them both, was creeping into the shadow

much as India did when Faleiro set his globe slowly revolving eastwards.

Underneath their study there grew the thought of what they would do with their scheme when study had ripened it to full fruit.   There was as little chance for Faleiro to become Astronomer Royal to His Majesty of Portugal as for Magellan to be entrusted with a new command now that the King had bid him take himself and his service where he pleased, and as the project approached completion they talked over the idea of bettering themselves under the rays of a less malignant star.   Already Magellan had long contemplated such a step, and now it was settled between them, in the autumn of 1517, that Magellan should at once leave Portugal and cross the frontier into Spain, carrying the full statement of the joint scheme with him.   From Seville he wrote to Faleiro the news of his friendly and encouraging reception, and a few weeks later Faleiro followed him.   In Lisbon nobody cared, probably nobody knew, for the two were lonely men and they had kept the scope and purpose of their work to themselves :   the flitting of a shady and morose astrologer and of a naval officer for whose services the King had no further use was a matter of total unconcern to any but themselves.   It was not until news trickled through to Lisbon that the King of Spain had a mind to employ this man of whom his Brother of Portugal thought so contemptuously that the name of Magellan was mentioned again at Court.   And, when it was known what the work was, the wind began to whistle and soon there burst forth a tempest of malediction that is without parallel in the pages of history.   But not until Portugal was afraid that she had lost the services and the genius of a man who was, after all, a capable fellow (or so King Charles of Spain accounted him) did King Manuel care a jot whether he acted on the permission given him

with such sincere scorn, and naturalized himself a
Spaniard.   Thereafter the King must have considered
his conduct of that interview again, and presently he
began to wonder whether he had not made the mistake
of his life.   It would have been cheaper to have given
him an extra shilling a month than, possibly, to forfeit
the revenues from the Spice Islands.

CHAPTER IV

MAGELLAN APPLIES TO SPAIN

O in October, 1517, there came to Seville this swarthy little fellow, thirty-seven years old, and lame of the right leg, and he had in his pocket the plan of a voyage through an untraversed, if not wholly undiscovered, strait, which he believed would lead into an untraversed sea of unknown dimensions, at the far end of which was a group of islands from which to-day Portugal derived a prodigious revenue. But when this small lame man arrived there by way of Spain, he would take his observations and see whether he was not in Spain still. From there he would return to the country of his adoption by way of the Indian Seas and the Cape of Diaz, and so he would have circumnavigated the round world. Of all the projects of Portuguese or Spanish adventurers, from the days when Prince Henry the Navigator sat in his castle at Sagres and foresaw that some day his Captains would find open sea beyond the South Cape of Africa, this was the hugest conception that ever man had attempted to realize : no greater indeed could be imagined, for the longest road in all the world was that which encircled it. All had been thought out now, and the scheme was ready to be put before anyone who would finance and further it.

At present no definite exposition of the voyage was to be laid even before the King of Spain, for Magellan had a partner who was still in Portugal, and the partners were pledged to a mutual secrecy : they must consult together before the entire scheme was divulged, and jointly arrange what share (equal as between themselves) in the profits of the voyage was to be assigned to them. Magellan, as a practical navigator, had gone on ahead of his partner to establish relations in Seville with those interested in maritime adventure, and generally to prepare the ground. The record of a man who had been round the Cape of Good Hope with Almeida twelve years before, who had fought at Calicut and Goa, who had been in charge of a wrecked crew on the Laccadives, who had twice sailed to the eastern gate of the Pacific at Malacca, and who in these honourable services had thrice been wounded, was an introduction likely to command the attention of the maritime committees at Seville, even though King Manuel had said that the bearer of it was not worth his salt. Indeed, that might be taken as something of a recommendation, for had not His late Majesty of Portugal and his advisers said the same about the great Columbus ? It was rather promising, in fact, that King Manuel thought so little of him. Besides his chart and detailed plan of the route, which he was pledged not to disclose in its entirety till Faleiro's arrival, Magellan had with him, by way of establishing the genuineness of his record, the letters that Francisco Serrano had written to him from Ternate, and a black slave, Enrique, whom he had brought back to Portugal with him from Malacca, and who had become a Christian. Unlikely though this picturesque Enrique would seem to be, he was nevertheless quite authentic, for by his Will, executed before Magellan set forth on the great voyage, he bequeathed Enrique his manumission on the grounds of his having become a Christian, and a sum of money for his support. And he had a globe, perhaps that which had spun slowly in

Faleiro's cabinet of astronomy, and on it, very enticingly, were marked the Spice Islands within the hemisphere of Spanish dominion. . . .

Among these seamen and naval experts of Seville were many men of Portuguese birth who, like Magellan, had left their native land to seek in Spain the opportunities which they could not find in Lisbon ; we learn, indeed, that there came with him from Portugal many such sailors and sea-captains. But the implication that it was he who had induced them to come with hopes of partaking in some great adventure is extremely improbable, for secrecy had been of the essence of his business, and till he got to Spain the very last thing that he would have done would have been to hint at it in the hearing of Portuguese ears. Immediately on his arrival at Seville he attracted the attention of a compatriot, Diego Barbosa, who had come to Spain for precisely the same reasons as he, namely that he could not get employment at Lisbon, and had now for fourteen years filled an important post as Superintendent of the Arsenal. Barbosa had seen service under King Manuel before his naturalization as a Spaniard, and his son, Duarte, had made several voyages in the Indian Seas, and had written a description of his adventures, which he had lately completed. It is probable that the Barbosas were related to Magellan, though the degree of kinship is uncertain, but that some near tie of blood existed is likely on credible grounds, and explains why, immediately on Magellan's arrival at Seville, Diego Barbosa welcomed him as a permanent inmate of his house.

The key to the whole of the scheme was, of course, the traverse of the strait which Magellan believed to provide the gate into the Pacific from the Atlantic, and this was the secret which Magellan had promised not to disclose till he had consulted with Faleiro. But he had gone to Seville in order to get support for the voyage ;

and, as soon as he arrived and was welcomed by Barbosa, he told him enough to arouse his keen interest, and to procure for Magellan an audience with the Board of the India House at Seville in order to lay his project before them. India House (so named not from Eastern and Portuguese India, but from the West Indies) was a bureau of information with regard to commerce and navigation, and its activities were mainly concerned with America, for Spain was concentrating all her maritime energies on her dominions in the New World. Magellan laid his proposition before the Board ; in it he offered to demonstrate the shortest route to the Spice Islands, and prove by the calculations he had made with Faleiro that they lay in the Spanish sphere. But, as covenanted with his partner, he gave them no precise information as to what was the key of the route. India House was glad to collect information as well as to furnish it to mariners ; it was part of its business to finance schemes of exploration which seemed to promise fresh revenue for Spain from her new dominions ; and we may safely say that there had never been submitted to the consideration of its very capable Board so startling a dossier. For the very cream and crown of the contents of the Portuguese Hemisphere, as at present accepted, was exactly that group of remote islands, dripping with fragrant wealth, which everyone knew must lie somewhere very close to the slicing stroke of the Pontifical knife that had cut in two the orange of the world, of which one half belonged to Spain and the other to her neighbour. And now this rather grave young man, lately arrived from Portugal, short of stature and limping, but with something certainly striking and compelling about him, told them that he could find a Spanish route to this El Dorado, and prove it to be Spanish territory. He had a very good record of naval service, he had gone far East, and produced for their inspection some very interesting letters from a friend of his who had resided in the Spice Islands for seven years, and a black slave whom he had brought from Malacca. These all looked genuine ; moreover, Superintendent Diego Barbosa, a most respected official of the Arsenal, recommended this cousin of his to their notice, and that was in his favour.   But when it came to a disclosure of his route he would not tell them how he proposed to reach the great South Sea from the Atlantic, and they could not judge of the feasibility of the scheme without knowing that.   There were three of them on the Board, and they talked the matter over, and came to the conclusion that they would not touch it.   They had many wild and hare-brained schemes laid before them, all seeking to be financed, and this seemed one of them.   They were busy, too, with providing ships and guns and money for missions the success of which was already assured, for nothing could be more satisfactorily real than the gold of America, and convoys must be arranged for its conveyance to the Spanish exchequer.   Perhaps, too, as has been most acutely suggested, they were shy of a scheme which, if it had anything solid in it, would most certainly embroil the Spanish Government with Portugal, for Portugal had assumed that the Spice Islands were hers, with no protest from Spain, and would not lightly see her rights questioned.   In other words, if Magellan's scheme was fantastic it stood self-condemned ; while if it was sound it was perilous.   But apart from that, his refusal to disclose where this new route lay must have irritated a Board whose speciality was geography.

But there was one member of this Board who, though he acquiesced in its decision, which was based in the main on incredulity, was far more impressed than the others by the applicant : the parallel of Hans Sachs among the Mastersingers of Nuremberg, when they had blackballed Walther, suggests itself.   Hans Sachs,

it will be remembered, had heard in the song of the rejected candidate for the Guild something new, something
that revolutionized the accepted school of harmony, and
as he mused on it he knew that a master of music had
arisen.   Just so did Juan d'Aranda ponder over what
this Portuguese sea-captain had told them, as being
something far ahead of all that the pundits of India
House knew about geography.   All they knew was
that the Spice Islands lay remotely east from Malacca,
and that to Malacca there was no route but round the
Cape of Good Hope, which was now the highway for
Portuguese ships.   But Magellan did not mean that :
his route lay through Spanish waters.   It could only
be round the southern point of America, or through
some passage there. . . .

Magellan had gone back from the interview with the
Board at India House to Barbosa, reporting failure.
They had been civil, but otherwise he had prospered no
more than he had done at his audience with King Manuel,
which had driven him to Spain.   Spain had no more
use for him than Portugal, though he had held out for
them such a lure as was not meet to show Manuel.   But
now he was back where he was before ; this great
chance had come to nothing, he was unbelieved in,
unwanted, and undaunted.   And then there came a
messenger from Señor Juan d'Aranda to say that he
would like to see Captain Magellan.

At this interview Aranda hinted, and made broad his
hint, that he guessed where or whereabouts Magellan's
projected route lay.   Otherwise Magellan, who had
just refused to divulge the secret to the Board whom
it was vital for him to interest in it, would not have
divulged it, as he now did, to one of the men who had
turned down his scheme.   Aranda had thought it over
and had guessed ; and, thus confronted with the secret
which he had withheld from the Board, Magellan acknow-

ledged it. He also said that he had refused to answer the direct question put to him at India House because he was pledged to secrecy with his partner, Faleiro, whom he presently expected to join him from Lisbon. It is difficult to know what else he could have done : it was no use denying the truth of Aranda's conjecture, for then Aranda would have been possessed of an idea of his own, which he could use as he pleased. Magellan would then, too, have repudiated the project on which, with Faleiro, he had spent years of work. His only chance of keeping his ownership of it was to admit Aranda into the secret, and this he did. "Very proper," said Aranda, "you did quite right, and your secret is safe with me."

Safe indeed it was, for Aranda had seen that here was something that might prove as colossally remunerative as the voyage of Columbus, and he had not the smallest intention of disseminating it. But with equal propriety, Aranda wrote to friends of his at Lisbon, making general inquiries about Magellan and his partner. Magellan had represented himself as being a master-navigator in practice, and claimed for his partner a knowledge of cosmography, of methods of taking solar and stellar observations, of the courses of the stars, which was unequalled by any man alive.

At this critical juncture of cross-currents Faleiro arrived from Lisbon, and found that his partner's application to India House had been unsuccessful. Magellan said nothing to him about Aranda's having guessed the secret, and he did not know that inquiries were being made about them both in Lisbon. But Faleiro found that his partner had been more fortunate in the pursuit of romance than of finding backers. Magellan was already affianced to Beatriz Barbosa, daughter of his host, and the marriage took place before the year was out : that Barbosa, a man of standing, should consent to

the marriage of his daughter with a penniless cousin was
not, as we shall see, so surprising as it at first appears.
But Faleiro, crusty and bachelor of habit, must have
wondered whether those years of work were to be
rewarded by his being asked to stand godfather.

Aranda's friends were prompt in answering his
private inquiries, and their replies were satisfactory :
Magellan's record, as represented by him, was quite
correct ; he had seen long and honourable service in the
East, and had a thorough practical knowledge of navigation ; Faleiro was a student of high reputation for his
learning.   Not a word was said of the iniquity and base-
ness of those men in leaving their country and seeking
employment in Spain, for, as has been already stated,
not a soul in Portugal from King Manuel downwards
cared a penny piece what they did with themselves :
it was only when it became likely that Magellan's
abilities had been worth retaining that he became a
master of villainy in leaving a country where he had been
explicitly informed that he was not wanted.   So, on the
receipt of these testimonials, Aranda, highly excited,
went to the partners and promised to do all he could to
obtain the favour and support of the King of Spain
himself for their voyage.   Aranda, in fact, became their
impressario, and they could not have had a better.

It was now for the first time that Faleiro learned that
Magellan, though sworn to secrecy, had told Aranda
(or that Aranda had guessed) that the route by which
they intended to reach the Spice Islands was westwards
through the untraversed strait which they both believed
to exist.   He now gave a touch of his quality, and flew
into a violent passion, accusing his partner of having
violated his promise.   It did not matter to him that the
effect of this breach of faith had been to secure exactly
what they both wanted, namely a powerful friend who
would open an approach for them to the King, and he gave

Magellan the rough side of a lunatic's tongue. That Magellan had broken faith with him, though with so admirable a result, is indisputable, and it is impossible not to have some sympathy with Faleiro, especially since Magellan had not told him, on his arrival at Seville, what he had done.

The quarrels between the partners were no concern of Aranda's, and he at once wrote to Sauvage, Chancellor of Castile, asking him if he might bring Magellan, late of the Portuguese Navy, to see him with regard to an expedition which might prove of high profit to the King. Even before the answer arrived they all set off for Valladolid, where was King Charles, lately come from the Netherlands ; but Faleiro, still sulky and resentful, would not travel with Aranda, who went on ahead. He seems, however, to have acquiesced in Aranda's paying all expenses.

To what extent Aranda had disclosed the project to Chancellor Sauvage is nowhere recorded, but we may be quite certain that he withheld the information that His Majesty's India House would not touch it. He had, however, said enough to interest that extremely astute and powerful person, whose reply, when it came, was favourable : he would like to know more about it. An enormous step was gained, the Chancellor was willing to listen to the scheme of these unknown refugees from Portugal, and this was entirely the work of Aranda. He therefore began to consider where he was to come in. After Magellan's rebuff at India House, he and Faleiro had no more chance unaided of securing official recommendation to the King, or of obtaining an influential audience for their scheme, than of reaching the moon : the moon was not less accessible than the Spice Islands. It was only reasonable that if, through Aranda's agency, the scheme was taken up, and the partners and originators of it, as was the custom of the day, received a share in the eventual profits of the voyage, he should get a slice of it. He was spending time, money and trouble on a speculative venture ; should he fail in getting it through, or should it prove unremunerative, his pains would be thrown away, and it was only just that if owing to his services it materialized he should have a share in the profits of the partners, Magellan and Faleiro. These, it is hardly necessary to state, might possibly be colossal. For if the voyage was successful, and Magellan penetrated into the Pacific, all new islands he discovered there would be fresh jewels in the Crown of Spain, and would pay revenues to the King. Magellan & Co. would doubtless receive some percentage on such revenues should the King finance the scheme, and it was that on which Aranda staked. As a business man, he thought that this had better be settled now.

So Aranda waited for the arrival of Magellan and Magellan's wife and Faleiro at an inn within a day's ride of Valladolid, and after dinner intimated that nothing had yet been settled about what he should receive (should there be any receipts) for his services. He proposed as a basis for discussion that if the Spanish Government financed the scheme, and paid Magellan & Co. a percentage on the profits of the voyage, he should receive one-fifth of that percentage. If, however, Magellan & Co., with merely the sanction of the Government, raised the money by private subscription from merchants or bankers, Aranda asked for nothing ; but in this case he intended to subscribe to the syndicate himself. Faleiro thereupon showed the consistency of his character by again flying into a violent passion, and swore that he would not agree to Aranda's receiving anything whatever : apparently it was to be considered sufficient reward for him to have had the privilege of helping Faleiro. Aranda's estimate of the value of his services seems rather excessive : probably, according to

Spanish custom, he expected to be bargained with, and Magellan, totally disregarding Faleiro's ridiculous out_ burst, duly proposed that Aranda should receive one_ tenth instead of one-fifth of their profits. So there were the two limits defined within which bargaining would take place. That was enough for the present ; and Aranda, following correct etiquette in these matters, said that if Magellan & Co. did not wish to give him anything he would still do his utmost to advance their cause, since he was thus serving the interests of the King. No one, of course, took that seriously : it only meant that Aranda wanted more than one-tenth. Accordingly he left the partners to talk it over, and rode on to Valladolid alone. Magellan & Co. joined him next day, and offered him one-eighth of their profits : he instantly accepted this (it was about half-way between the two limits) and drew up a formal agreement to confirm it. After this piece of refreshing comedy they all shook hands and got to business, Aranda continuing to pay expenses

Aranda had therefore become a subsidiary partner in the firm, and it was his business, serving his interests and theirs, to get hold of high and influential personages to whom the scheme was to be submitted, in order that they in turn might obtain the support of the boy-King Charles, who after a youth passed in his Netherland dominions was now newly come to his Spanish realm. The first of these, from whom Aranda had already received an encouraging answer, was the Lord Chancellor of the Kingdom. The second, who might, if favourably impressed, be expected to exercise a private and domestic influence on the King, was Guillaume de Croy, His Majesty's late tutor, to whose advice the King was accustomed to listen with docility. Both of these were from the Netherlands, and it was important to impress on them, a thing which one of the members of the Board of India House was well qualified to do, the vast enrichments that would accrue to His Majesty's Spanish realm should undiscovered islands of the Pacific be added to it ; of the value of the possible acquisition of the Spice Islands it was hardly needful to speak.   These two choices then were very sensible, but Aranda's choice of the third patron for his company was more than sensible : it was a stroke of sheer genius. The third was the Most Noble Bishop Fonseca of Burgos, and Aranda brought the project of Magellan & Co. to his notice because when Columbus had offered his services to Spain, after Portugal had refused them, with his programme of finding a new world across the Atlantic, Bishop Fonseca, instead of supporting it, had pooh-poohed so delirious a design, declaring it to be the fantastic dream of a lunatic Italian.   But the Italian had turned out not to be so lunatic, and now the fruits of his delirious design were pouring into Spain in the gold-laden ships from Nombre de Dios.   Bishop Fonseca therefore, recalling his own unfortunate pronouncement and the sequel to it, would be the least likely of all Spanish magnates to err in that direction again.   He was all for exploration now, and was indeed the Chairman of the Board of India House ; so Aranda came to him, as a member of that Board, feeling sure of an attentive hearing, and like a wise man he said nothing to the Bishop about Magellan's scheme having been already turned down by his colleagues.

The fourth of this new Board of Aranda's forming, which he hoped would reverse the judgment of India House, was His Eminence Cardinal Adrian of Utrecht : he also was a Netherlander, and had had a hand in the young King's education, and it seems clear that Aranda was getting private and personal influence to bear on the King, in case India House protested against the scheme they had already disapproved.   But, with the Chancellor, Bishop Fonseca and the personal advisers of the King in support of it, India House might be considered harmless. Again without attributing super-human sagacity to Aranda, he probably weighed the fact that Cardinal Adrian was a likely candidate for the Papacy (he eventually wore the tiara as that most inconspicuous Pontiff, Adrian VI) and that if, as Magellan believed, the Spice Islands rightly belonged to Spain it would be useful, should trouble arise with Portugal, to have a Pope who would be inclined *ex cathedra* to support Spanish interests. Not a single one of these most eminent personages knew anything whatever about geography, but it was impossible to make a wiser choice (could their support be secured) of men who would have the ear of the King. The only one of them who had pronounced on geographical questions was the Bishop of Burgos and, since he had been so lamentably at fault in turning down the ideas of the last explorer who had been brought to his notice, it was almost certain that he would vote for backing up the next. Of the four he was the only one of Spanish birth, and his advocacy on such an affair, as Chairman of India House, would carry immense weight with the King. Aranda was certainly doing his very best to render his eighth share in the profits of the firm a valuable property.

To all of these in turn the admirable Aranda took his two Portuguese, and to each of them Magellan expounded his scheme of sailing west to arrive at the East, and Enrique said a few words in Malayan, and Faleiro twirled the globe to show how far east of Spain the Spice Islands lay, so far east indeed that in truth they could more accurately be described as lying west of Spain, and that made a great impression : poor geographers as these great magnates were, they could see what that meant. But even now the strait was not shown on that globe ; though the strait was mentioned, it was more prudent not to mark it, for fear that one of these high lords might

take it into his head to equip an expedition himself and
leave Magellan & Co. out in the cold, even as the perfidious King John II of Portugal had turned down
Columbus's project and then fitted out three ships himself to look into it.   For at present the position of the
strait (and that only conjecturally) was known to those
alone who had studied the story and chart of the voyage
of Christopher Jacques, which was deposited in the
library at Lisbon ; and it was news to the Spanish that
such a corridor into the great South Sea existed at all.
But granted the existence of such a means of access, the
prospect opened for Spanish expansion in the west of
America and in the ocean beyond was almost limitless.
Already Spain had contemplated the digging of a canal
through the Isthmus of Panama in order to reach the
coasts and islands beyond, but the survey of it had shown
how immense that undertaking would be.   But, if
Nature had already provided this access, there would be
passage for Spanish ships to the huge uncharted lands
and seas that lay in her dominion, and crowning all these
expansions came Magellan's assertion, as demonstrated
on the globe, that the Spice Islands were anchored in it.
Moreover, the route lay in Spanish waters : their ships
might explore westwards without giving Portugal the
smallest justification for remonstrance, whereas the only
known route at present to that coveted and fragrant
group lay eastwards, and any attempt of Spain to reach
them through the passage by Malacca would at once
arouse a proper opposition.   As soon as they had
heard Magellan's exposition, each of Aranda's selected
audience, Sauvage, Croy, the Cardinal and the Bishop
of Burgos, gave the scheme their support and promised
to recommend it without delay to His Majesty's Government and to the King himself.   But far the most valuable
of these allies was the Bishop of Burgos.   He was a man
of grinding force, he was the Chairman of India House,

La Tr

and he was not going to repeat the error he had made with regard to Columbus.

✓ By the prestige and the energy of Aranda so much was accomplished within a day or two of the arrival of Magellan & Co. at Valladolid, and it is said that he immediately obtained an audience for Magellan with the King. But this is not very probable, for the whole object of these diplomacies, which were proceeding so admirably, was to get the scheme put before the King by just such weighty counsellors as Aranda had selected, and by his Government. The next step, then, was that these counsellors and the Government should jointly hear about the project, and Magellan and Faleiro were summoned to appear before this combined committee. So, still without disclosing the supposed position of the strait, Magellan repeated the arguments which had already proved so convincing, and added that even if he found no strait he would sail on till the continent of America came to an end, even as Africa had proved to do, and pass by open sea into the Pacific : he would be the Diaz of America. Then came that lure to which no Spaniard could fail to flutter, namely the rightful ownership of the Spice Islands. To colour his sketch he read the letters from his friend, Serrano, about the wealth that exceeded that of India, and produced Christian Enrique, who had returned with him from Malacca.

The Government debated on the scheme, and once more Aranda's sagacity in getting hold of the Bishop of Burgos was justified. Largely owing to his insistence it was resolved to recommend it to the King as meriting his favour and support. Magellan and Faleiro were recalled and ordered to draw up a statement in writing, such as they had just delivered, to be laid before him. It began to look as if King Manuel would have good reason to regret that he had been quite so contemptuously ready to allow the first navigator of the world to take his goods to another market rather than give him another shilling a month. There is nothing so expensive as economy.

In these preliminary steps for getting the Royal assent and support for this gigantic scheme of two penniless Portuguese adventurers, there is nothing more surprising than the speed with which the affair was bustled along. Two of its sponsors, Aranda and the Bishop of Burgos, were certainly possessed of that indefinable quality called " drive," which compels others to work for them, but to get a job of this kind through the various rings of officialdom which surrounded His Spanish Majesty it was usually necessary to bribe heavily and repeatedly, in order to secure any progress at all. Yet, though Magellan and Faleiro had not left Seville till towards the end of January, 1518, with a scheme that had failed to secure the favour of India House, February was not yet over before they were drawing up a proposition regarding the voyage which the Government had pledged themselves to recommend to the King. This briskness is the more remarkable when we remember that Magellan had produced no evidence to prove or even render probable the existence of the strait : he had not disclosed where he believed it to lie ; his mere assertion that it would furnish a short cut, and that through Spanish waters, into the ocean beyond, where lay the undiscovered treasure-grounds of the Spanish Hemisphere, was sufficient to set the wheels of the Government turning for him without stay or stoppages. We may reasonably infer that he, and perhaps the irritable astronomer as well, had the gift of inspiring confidence which marks off the men who lead from those who follow.

Though the sponsors of the scheme whom Aranda had manipulated so successfully knew nothing of geography, there came to Valladolid during February, while Magellan & Co. were employed in drawing up the dossier for the King, a man who of all others in the world could most convincingly endorse Magellan's assertion about the existence of the strait ; his arrival, in fact, just then was one of those strokes of luck which always seem reserved for the strong and the competent. This was Christopher de Haro, who sixteen years before had been a member of the syndicate which financed the Portuguese expedition under Christopher Jacques to the coasts of South America. That expedition, as we have already noticed, had gone far south along the shores of Brazil and beyond, and the account of its exploration, translated from the Portuguese into German, had caused Johann Schöner of Nuremberg to mark on his globe a strait leading from the Atlantic into the Pacific. As one of the syndicate which furnished this expedition, Haro must certainly have known that Jacques had conjectured or claimed to have found this strait. Nothing therefore could have been more fortunate for Magellan than the arrival at Valladolid just now of this very solid and respectable Spanish trader who believed in the strait as firmly as Magellan, and whose opinion, for these reasons, was bound to carry weight. He also considered it certain that the Spice Islands lay in the Spanish Hemisphere, and at the interview which he and Magellan were given by the King told His Majesty that he thought it quite possible that Malacca might prove to belong to him also. The notion of Portugal being deprived of the richest of her possessions and the Eastern gate to it must have been very entertaining and pleasant to Haro ; for, like many others who did business with King Manuel, he had lately suffered from the King's intolerable meanness over money matters, and had been treated by him in the scurviest manner over some trading contract. Like Magellan, who had similarly suffered, he had left Portugal and sought fairer treatment in Spain, and thus his support of Magellan fitted in most conveniently with his desire to get even with King Manuel.

But the chief stimulus which hurried on the official Spanish authorization of the voyage without delays and payments at every official toll-gate was the immensity of the prospect which the scheme disclosed, and the urgent necessity of getting it put through and on its way before Portugal could get wind of it and raise the opposition which would inevitably ensue. The Government were the first to appreciate the paramount importance of haste, and for once a petition passed through the avenues of Royal approach without paying blackmail to the crowd of noble middlemen who surrounded the King. For if maritime access to the islands and coasts of the Pacific, and, to crown all, the sovereignty over the Spice Islands, depended on the plans of Magellan & Co., the sooner they set sail from Seville the better. When once they had found their proposed route there by Spanish waters, and verified their claim, there would be pickings for everybody. Swarms of officials at suitable salaries would be needed, the Government would see that these gentlemen (largely themselves) who had recommended the scheme to the King, and opened for Spain the door into so vast an El Dorado, should not lack the due recognition of their services, and the sooner these just claims were registered for settlement, the more quickly would come to them their reward. Besides, there was the duty of patriots to urge them on : at present Portugal was reaping huge revenues from the Spice Islands which belonged by right, in virtue of the Papal disposition of the world, to Spain. He would be a traitor to his country who, for the sake of an immediate aggrandizement, kept Spain out of the patrimonies bequeathed her by Holy Father. It was amusing, too, to reflect that the paltry greed of poor King John of Portugal had caused the line of demarcation through the

Atlantic, as originally defined by the Pope, to be shifted further west, for it was that very alteration which, though it gave Portugal a larger slice of Brazil, might prove to have put the Spice Islands out of her hemisphere. That was humorous, though no one would expect King Manuel to appreciate it.   For all these reasons, and especially because Portugal would certainly put every obstacle in the way of the expedition sailing at all, as soon as she got wind of it, every facility was given to the petition reaching the King as soon as possible, and every support in its favour when it got there.   Let Captain Magellan and his partner make it ready with all speed.

CHAPTER V

KING CHARLES APPROVES

HE proposals which Magellan & Co. had been enjoined by the Government to draw up for the King's consideration stated the object of the expedition as already defined, and comprised two alternative schemes for its execution. The first was that the King should equip the expedition, furnishing all the costs of it, and grant the originators of it certain royalties or percentages on its fruits ; the second that it should be privately financed, and that the King should grant the syndicate a ten years' lease of the countries and islands discovered by it and lying in the Spanish sphere, and that in return for the granting of this privilege he should receive a fifth part of the revenues derived from them. At the end of ten years these dominions would become Crown property. This second proposal, which had been out of the question when first Magellan brought his scheme before the Board of India House, was possible now, because wealthy and influential men in Spain, and especially Haro, who was at the head of an enormous trading-business, believed in it and were ready to back it. Monarchs of the sixteenth century, when so much of the surface and the wealth of the world were in process of discovery, were accustomed to extend their territories and finance their treasuries by either of these systems of contract, and Magellan & Co. in submitting

these alternatives to His Majesty were following the ordinary course of procedure. It was at the King's pleasure to adopt whichever he preferred. He chose to equip the expedition himself, and on March 22nd, 1518, a courier arrived from the Palace bearing a packet for Captain Magellan, now naturalized a Spaniard, and the King's most loyal servant. It contained the contract as between King Charles of Spain and Magellan & Co. in the matter of this voyage, and it bore the signature of the King.

Considering the strong support the scheme had received, the King's choice was a most natural one. For his Government believed that the expedition would prove colossally remunerative, that it would result in the addition of countless islands and square miles of territory, and would bring into the Spanish Exchequer the immense revenues which Portugal now derived from the Spice Islands. It was therefore far more to the advantage of the Crown to equip the expedition itself, and after paying certain royalties, generous in their terms, to Magellan & Co., to reap the whole of the harvest. For, should the expenses of the voyage be furnished by private subscribers, they would naturally be entitled to the bulk of the profits, and the Crown only receive percentages. The King would doubtless have been advised to adopt this latter alternative had his Council thought that the expedition was likely to yield only moderate profits, or if they believed that its success was highly speculative, for in this case the King would not have been put to any expense in the matter, nor have lost the money he had spent on it, if it proved to be a failure.

Again the King's choice, as approved by his Council, to equip the expedition himself, shows that the fear of its leading to an embroilment with Portugal, which undoubtedly existed and had possibly been one of the reasons why India House had turned it down, was now considered not to be so very serious, especially if the expedition could be started quietly and speedily.   For, when the Council looked into this further, there really did not seem any reason to anticipate trouble until the expedition got back with the most welcome news that the Spice Islands really belonged to Spain.   For Magellan was about to sail west through Spanish waters, and being now a Spaniard he had every right, should the King of Spain entrust him with a few ships, to sail to America and do his business there, and the King had every right to send him there.   If he came back with the hoped-for news, then indeed Portugal might raise an outcry, but the Spice Islands were well worth a little un-pleasantness with a neighbour.   And yet even then the position of the Spice Islands was not the fault of Spain : Spain had not put them there ; and, if anyone was to blame for their proving to belong to. her, it was greedy King John II, who had been so urgent that Pope Alexander's line of demarcation should be shifted further west on this side of the globe and therefore east on the other.

This view, as outlined above, on the status of Royal and private expeditions of discovery and annexation, and on the reasons why King Charles decided to send Magellan out as on the service of Spain, is well illus-trated by comparison with English expeditions sent out under the auspices (or not) of Queen Elizabeth.   Many of these, like Francis Drake's voyage to Nombre de Dios, were frankly piratical, their object being to lay hands on gold-bearing Spanish convoys from Panama, or on treasure-ships returning with their cargoes.   They were exceedingly likely to give rise to trouble with Spain, and therefore Elizabeth did not send them out as national ventures, nor did she officially equip them.   She was thus able to state to the Spanish Ambassador at the

Court of St. James's that she was in no way responsible for them. Drake's voyage round the world which resulted in such amazing loot was another of these private ventures, and when, before his return, reports came of the Spanish ships he had sunk in the Pacific, and of the gold he had taken from them, Elizabeth declared again and again that she had nothing to do with that monster. Officially that was true, but actually it was very far from being the case, for though as Queen of England she had granted him no charter, and had not commissioned the " Golden Hind," as Miss Elizabeth Tudor she was a member, and an extremely greedy one, of the syndicate that had financed him. She even sailed nearer the line between Queen and private shareholder than that, for she leased him rather antiquated ships of her navy in lieu of cash, with which, like King Manuel, she was always loath to part, and valued them at an outrageously high figure, as her private subscription. These expeditions, moreover, which would certainly have caused international trouble between England and Spain if she had officially equipped them, could not possibly lead to such stupendous profits as the Spanish Government of King Charles expected to result from Magellan's voyage : no rich slice of the world's surface would be added to English territory, and so, both to avoid foreign complications and because there was no colossal enrichment of the realm in view, Elizabeth dissociated herself from them, though she extended a feverish shareholder's hand when they came back laden with King Philip II's gold. But Magellan's project promised territories and perpetual revenues, it was in no way piratical, and its ultimate object was to take careful observations as to the longitude of the Spice Islands. So King Charles openly godfathered it, and financed it out of his Royal exchequer ; but, though his conscience may have been quite clear, it must be admitted that he soon exhibited the greatest impatience to get it safely away, before Portugal had grasped the import of its destination. That very natural wish was not fated to be realized.

The crucial document which was delivered to Magellan at Valladolid on March 22nd, 1518, was prefaced by a short preamble defining in the most prudent and unexceptional manner the general object of the expedition to which the King now gave his assent and support, and may be detailed in full, since it gives evidence as to the imperial importance which Spain attached to the voyage, and to the correctness of the King's conduct in financing it. He was not going to make any trespass on the dominions assigned to his Brother of Portugal, and was only proposing innocently to explore in his own. The fact that the acquisition of the Spice Islands was the main objective of the voyage therefore need not be mentioned, for, if Magellan succeeded in proving that they were in the Spanish sphere, no trespass would have been committed on the territories of Portugal. . . . We may picture the Bishop of Burgos assuming his most prelatical and fatherly expression as he worded this clause, and Cardinal Adrian of Utrecht agreeing that it was very well put. The preamble ran thus :

The King :
Since you, Fernando de Magellanes, a Knight native of the Kingdom of Portugal, and the bachelor Ruy Faleiro, also a native of that kingdom, wish to render Us a great service in the limits which belong to Us in the ocean of Our demarcation, We order the following Capitulation to be established with you for that purpose.

The Capitulation (or contract) then follows ; it is rather an involved document, and for the sake of clearness may be split up into heads :

(i) Magellan & Co. are hereby empowered to make discoveries in the ocean (Pacific) belonging to the King of Spain. Since they are undertaking the labours of this voyage, the King covenants that he will not authorize any other person to proceed · on a voyage of discovery by the same route for a period of ten years, without first giving Magellan & Co. the option of fitting out another such expedition themselves. But Spanish explorers will have the right to sail in the same direction (south-west) by way of lands already discovered.

(ii) Magellan & Co. shall not pursue their discoveries or otherwise operate within the demarcation and limits of the most serene King of Portugal to his prejudice.

(iii) The King grants to Magellan & Co., in consideration of their services, five per cent. of the net revenues (after all expenses have been paid) derived from lands discovered by them. He also grants them the title of Adelantados or Governors of such lands. These titles are to be hereditary and borne by their heirs for ever so long as such heirs are of Spanish nationality, and marry Spanish wives. The patent will be executed and sent to them.

(iv) Magellan & Co. shall have the right to purchase at cost price, every year, a thousand ducats' worth of Spanish goods to sell in these islands and countries, and may bring back the produce (spices, &c.) which they purchase with them, without paying any duty beyond five per cent. of their value. This article shall not be held to apply to their first voyage.

(v) Should Magellan & Co. discover more than six islands, they shall have the privilege after assigning these six islands to the King, to choose for themselves any other two of the remainder, and appropriate from these one-fifteenth part net of all revenues and duties derived therefrom.

(vi) The King assigns to Magellan & Co. twenty per cent. of all profits resulting from this first voyage, after expenses have been paid.

(vii) For this first voyage of Magellan & Co., the King undertakes to equip five ships, two of one hundred and thirty tons, two of ninety tons and one of sixty tons. He will furnish these with paid crews amounting in all to two hundred and thirty-four persons : he will provide them with victuals for two years, and with artillery and all other gear needful. The King will order his India House at Seville to carry out this clause.

(viii) If either of the members of the firm Magellan & Co. shall die, the surviving partner shall carry out all the enactments contained in this Capitulation.

(ix) Accounts of all expenses shall be kept by persons appointed for that purpose.

A further Royal order bearing the same date, and signed by the King, the Chancellor and the Bishop of Burgos, conferred on Magellan the power of executing summary justice by sea and land. This gave him power of life and death over all his officers and crews. Magellan and Faleiro were also given the titles of Captains-General of the fleet at an annual salary.

Now this contract must certainly be considered not only fair but generous, and so it doubtless seemed to Magellan. Instead of being dumped down at Lisbon at the age of thirty-eight, under a master who in spite of his long and honourable services had refused to give him further employment, and had snubbed him with the utmost of unkingly contempt, he found himself, within six months of the day when he had left Portugal in search of service with Spain, entrusted with the supreme command of five ships, and with the King's charter authorizing him to set forth on an adventure as " brave and new " as that on which Bartholomew Diaz had started more than forty years ago from Lisbon. Indeed the scope of the two was somewhat similar, for just as Diaz set forth to find the way round Africa into the East and the Indian seas, so now Magellan was to sail round the unknown South of America, or through the strait which he believed existed there, to find a way westwards into the sea beyond ; but, whereas Diaz's voyage was over when once he proved there was a way round the Cape of Good Hope, this passage into the Pacific was no more than the first stage in Magellan's far vaster undertaking. So now, instead of mildewing his manhood away in idleness, he was in charge of an adventure far greater than could have been offered him in Portugal, even though he had enjoyed the highest favour of the King, for Portugal had penetrated to the easternmost limit of her assigned dominion, and had, so Magellan was convinced, gone far beyond it, and no conundrum of navigation in Portuguese waters could approach in magnitude and importance the task which he had been entrusted to execute for Spain. Instead, too, of being denied the paltriest of increases in a clerk's wage, he was promoted to a handsomely paid post as Captain-General in the career he loved, with the prospect of hereditary titles and immense dividends to be earned if he succeeded ; as for the rise in rank which King Manuel had scornfully refused him, King Charles dubbed him Knight of the Order of St. James. He had married the only daughter of a man of place and position in Seville, a countryman of his own, who, like him, had despaired of making a career under the niggardly and suspicious Manuel, and already he expected a child who should inherit the honours he hoped to gain.   Indeed, fate had looked on him luminously since the day when, stung to the quick with the whispered gibes of King Manuel's Court, he had limped out of the Presence discarded and despised : now the King of this country of his adoption received him with great honour, and gave him posts and emoluments and promises of which the brightness dazzled.

As well as being generous towards the partners, the contract showed considerable shrewdness, for though Magellan and his heirs were granted perpetual revenues from such islands as he might discover, and a hereditary Governorship over them, it was stipulated that those to whom these honours and emoluments might descend should be of Spanish birth, and marry Spanish wives. The condition was very reasonable, for otherwise a son or a remoter descendant of Magellan might revert to the original nationality of his family and thus draw revenues, and those perhaps of enormous size, from the Spanish exchequer.   As we shall see from the Will which Magellan executed before setting out on this voyage, being then the father of a son by Beatriz Barbosa, and expecting another child, he devised all estates and honours that might come to him from this voyage in accordance with the Capitulation, providing also for such future contingencies as the death of his children, in accordance with its spirit.   This clause perhaps throws some light on Magellan's marriage ; for, though one of his biographers tells us that it was a love-affair of passion and splendour, our complete absence of information about it must make us cautious in affirming that.   But now we see that this voyage was considered to be pregnant with immense wealth for its promoter ; a second Columbus had possibly arisen, and we can understand that Barbosa, who from the first believed in

Magellan's project, was not averse from his daughter marrying a man who, though for the moment a penniless Portuguese refugee, might easily turn out to be a very prince among possible sons-in-law. Again, on Magellan's side it was essential that he should marry a Spanish woman if his heirs were to enjoy such emoluments ; and thus the marriage was a very sensible one, and we can see the sense in it. It may, of course, have been a passionate love-affair as well.

Shrewd, also, was the framing of the clause that Magellan & Co. should not operate in Portuguese waters to the prejudice of King Manuel ; for, though the most lucrative object of the expedition was the acquisition of the most valuable of the Portuguese islands, the basic idea was to prove that they lay within the Spanish Hemisphere, and therefore no operations would be taking place in Portuguese waters at all, though nothing could possibly be more prejudicial to Portugal than what the King so fervently hoped would take place in Spanish waters. But, in a further document signed by the King on April 9th, he abandoned the discretion he had shown in the wording of his Capitulation and in its preamble, and gave specific instructions to his two new Captains-General that they should make those coveted islands of the Moluccas, the Spice Islands themselves, their first and foremost goal, to be reached without loss of time. For secrecy was no longer possible : Magellan, as ordered, had presented to the India House at Seville the Capitulation which charged it to equip the fleet, of which the King had appointed Sir Ferdinand Magellan and Sir Ruy Faleiro Captains-General, with all speed. The matter of the approaching voyage thus became public knowledge in Seville and in Valladolid, and Alvaro da Costa, Portuguese Ambassador to King Charles of Spain, instantly informed King Manuel what was on foot. Possibly His Majesty might remember a halting little man named Ferdinand Magellan whom, nearly three years ago, he had dismissed from his service : it was less likely that he should ever have heard of one Ruy Faleiro, a shady astrologer.   But these two obscure personages were now in the employment of the King of Castile, and were commissioned to command a fleet of five ships, and sail it by some westward route into the Great South Sea.   Their eventual destination was the Spice Islands.   Faleiro—Sir Ruy Faleiro of the Order of St. James—was a mere student, though learned in the sciences of the stars.   The person who mattered was Magellan.

Now King Manuel, it must be once more repeated, had told Magellan, with every circumstance of contempt, that he had no thought of giving him promotion or employment, that he had no use for his services and that he might take himself and them wherever he pleased. But when, in sequel to this permission, it appeared that his Brother of Spain was glad to avail himself of these services, and was intending to employ them on a very novel and important mission, the possible value of them seemed to change.   At first when King Manuel heard that the course of this proposed expedition was to steer south-west from Seville, and that its goal was undoubtedly the Spice Islands, he pooh-poohed the possibility of its reaching the Pacific at all : the only route to the Pacific was eastwards through Portuguese waters, the Indian seas and through the gate of Malacca.   But presently there began to dawn on him a most unpleasant uneasiness on the subject, based on some half-forgotten memory that there had once been some talk of a strait in the remotest parts of South America which was supposed to lead into the great South Sea.   Perhaps he had search made among the records of voyages in the Library at Lisbon, and there was the Portuguese pamphlet describing the voyage of Christopher Jacques, and the chart on which was marked the mouth of a strait. It is certain, at any rate, that at first King Manuel laughed at the idea of Magellan finding a strait there, and that soon he laughed no more, but took it very seriously, and did all that he could to stop the voyage. That the rediscovery of this pamphlet was the actual cause of his change of attitude is only conjecture, but it seems to fit the case. He gave instructions to Alvaro da Costa to seek audience with King Charles, and represent King Manuel's mind on the subject with great firmness. These instructions are not extant, but we can infer from Costa's report what they were. They certainly included an intimation that he should remind King Charles that a marriage between his sister, the Infanta Leonora, and King Manuel had only just been arranged and ratified. It would be a pity to bring discord into so happy and harmonious an alliance.

Costa accordingly had his interview with King Charles, and in a letter to his master dated the twenty-eighth of September, 1518, he reported what had occurred at it, and the sequel. He had spoken very firmly to the King, telling him that it was most unseemly for him to receive the subjects of another King who was his friend and who very much objected to his doing so. This was a peculiarly ungracious thing to do when His Majesty of Portugal was about to cement their ties of friendship by marrying his sister. He therefore begged King Charles not to employ these discontented refugees from Portugal whom King Manuel (who knew them) suspected would only do him a disservice. Neither Magellan nor Faleiro (so said Costa) wanted to serve King Charles, but asked leave to return to Portugal. Costa therefore begged the King to let them go.

Now these two statements, that King Manuel suspected that Magellan would do King Charles a disservice, and that Magellan and Faleiro had both asked leave to return to Portugal, were really remarkable lies. What King Manuel suspected was not that Magellan & Co. would do his Brother a disservice, but a service of the most immense value. As for Magellan desiring to return to Portugal, there was nothing in the world that he desired less, though King Manuel would have been very glad to get him there. The object of these two magnificent falsehoods, however, is clear enough, and was certainly clear to King Charles. Costa wanted to discredit Magellan with the King, and probably this pleasing device for so doing had been agreed upon between him and King Manuel. But it grievously failed in producing the desired effect, for (as Costa goes on to tell King Manuel) the King seemed so much surprised that he was astonished. He said that he wished on no account to annoy King Manuel, and was very polite, but he now closed the interview by referring Costa to Cardinal Adrian. The King, in fact, did not believe a word Costa said.

This interview then was not very successful : it handicaps a diplomatist, should he wish to tell the truth, to have been detected telling lies, for the chances are now against his credibility. But Costa hoped to fare better with Cardinal Adrian, for he had already talked matters over with him, and knew he was not very keen on this voyage : for this reason Costa informs King Manuel that the Cardinal " is the best thing here." Unfortunately for the interests of Portugal, the Bishop of Burgos was called in to confer, and that forcible prelate was in his most domineering. mood. He went straight off to the King when he heard Costa's business, and came back to say that His Majesty was behaving perfectly correctly. He was only sending out this expedition to operate within his own assigned dominions, and Manuel ought not to take it ill that he made use of two of his vassals, " men of little substance," while he himself employed many natives of Castile. Out he went again, and the faint-hearted Cardinal confessed that it was really no use. The King was completely under the thumb of these energetic people, who were in favour of the voyage.

Costa's letter cannot have brought much encouragement to King Manuel. He concludes by recommending him to get hold of Magellan somehow. . . . " That would be a great buffet to these people." Faleiro, he says, does not matter, he is next door to a lunatic : the man who matters is Magellan. . . . This depressing report was debated on by King Manuel's Council, and they decided that efforts should be made to bribe Magellan to return to Lisbon, as Costa suggested. Failing that, the best thing would be to get him assassinated. The Bishop of Lamego moved this pious resolution : he was a sensible, practical man, and was presently promoted to the Archbishopric of Lisbon.

Magellan and Faleiro meantime, after the signing of the Capitulation in March, and the delivery of the King's instructions to India House to prepare the equipment of the fleet, had been in attendance on the King for further conference and consultation. But India House, the Board of which had already rejected the scheme, was not being very zealous over the matter, and in July, 1518, the two left the Court, and went to Seville to superintend and hurry on the preparations. They carried with them an autograph letter from the King, which ordered that the instructions of his Captains-General, who delivered it, were to be carried out with precision and despatch. It mattered not at all to His Majesty what the honourable Board thought about it : they were to do what Magellan told them. This reminder was a well-merited rap over the knuckles, for the Board of India House, as we have seen, had disapproved of this expedition when Magellan submitted it to them on his first arrival, only a few months ago, at Seville, and this reversal of their decision by the King and the Ministers of the Crown, to whom a fuller exposition of it had been submitted, had been taken as a pointed and unfavourable comment on their judgment. So, though in March orders had been sent to them that preparations for the voyage should be put in hand at once, their zeal had been of the most tepid sort, and nothing particular had been done except to send minutes and queries to the Government. But the King's letter and the arrival of Magellan, that silent driver of men, briskened them up, for the King, no less than he, was in a hurry to get the expedition under sail as soon as possible, so that, in answer to the growing Portuguese remonstrances, he might reply with polite regrets that the voyagers were already on the high seas.

By the terms of the Capitulation (Clause vii) the King had promised his Captains-General five ships, and now, without further delay from India House, Aranda purchased them, and the necessary repairs and equipment of them began. These ships were the " Santo Antonio " of 120 tons, the " Trinidad " of 110 tons, the " Concepcion " of 90 tons, the " Victoria " of 85 tons and the " Santiago " of 75 tons. Though not quite coming up to the tonnage stipulated for in the Capitulation, they approached it very nearly, and Magellan selected as his flagship not the " Santo Antonio " which was the largest, but the " Trinidad," as being a handier and more seaworthy vessel. They were all old ships much patched up, and were at once beached for repairs. But it must be presumed that they seemed good enough to Magellan. All therefore appeared to promise well : the authorities of India House, wholesomely stimulated by the peremptory letter from the King, were now doing their best to speed departure, but not till their five ships finally cleared the bar of the river fourteen months later, in September, 1519, did a day pass on which some obstruction had not to be crushed or circumvented by Magellan. The storms and hazards which he encountered on the great adventure were not more difficult to weather than those which assailed him in his preparations to meet them.

The most menacing and dangerous of these were the gales that came bellowing out of Portugal. All this summer, ever since the destination of Magellan's voyage was known, King Manuel's Ambassador had been using the utmost arts of diplomacy and the falsehoods which were its usual weapons to dissuade the King of Spain from bestowing his patronage on Magellan, but these, the ill-success of which, as we have seen, was recorded in Costa's letter to King Manuel, were not the only means employed to procure the abortion of this expedition, which month by month ripened towards its birth. The direct appeal, however, to King Charles, which had failed, did not result in any rupture between the Kings, for in November of this year, 1518, King Manuel married the Infanta Leonora, a girl of twenty, and thirty years his junior, making her the third official partner of his bed, and the nuptials were celebrated with pompous cordiality. But King Manuel, who was notorious for never trusting anybody, did not see in this new tie with Spain any guarantee of her friendly relations, and he was as determined to stop this expedition as was his brother-in-law to proceed with it. Though he had laid down in Costa's representations to King Charles that it was a very villainous thing for a friendly monarch to employ the services of a denaturalized subject of his Brother, that had proved a fruitless argument. It was also quite unsound, for Portuguese were often naturalized as Spaniards, and Spaniards as Portuguese : the practice was quite common. King Manuel therefore began to work with methods less direct, and so more dangerous, and he gave private instructions to Sebastian Alvarez, his Factor (roughly equivalent to Consular agent) at Seville, where the fleet was being equipped, to watch for and take advantage of any opportunity for hindering the sailing of the expedition, which he now regarded and feared as a menace to his possession of the Spice Islands.   Alvarez became the hidden hand, and that hand had remarkably clever fingers.   From time to time he wrote letters to King Manuel acquainting him with the latest developments, and the King was diligent in reply, sending him comments and suggestions by an equerry.   One of Alvarez's letters, still preserved in the Torre do Tombo, tells us much of what was going on behind the efforts of India House to get the expedition started and on its way, and by its allusions to previous correspondence enables us to infer much of the methods of King Manuel.

Throughout these months of preparation the Bishop of Burgos continued to hurry matters on, and also extended his friendly protection towards the personal safety of Magellan himself.   News must have reached him of the kindly suggestion of his Brother of Lamego that the simplest expedient of putting an end to the scheme was to procure the assassination of Magellan, and we find that on one occasion the Bishop of Burgos provided the Captain-General with an armed guard to escort him, for the danger appeared real, though it does not seem that any actual attempt was made on Magellan's life.   But the Bishop could not provide against more subtle enemies, and disturbing incidents, contrived by Factor Alvarez, marked the course of the preparations now in full swing at Seville.   One morning of October, for instance, Magellan had given orders that his flagship, the " Trinidad," should be careened as she lay at low water on the sand.   As Captain-General he hoisted flags bearing his own coat of arms on the capstan, which was a perfectly proper proceeding, but by some mischance did not display the Royal flag of Spain on the masts. Alvarez, who had a sharp eye on all that was going on, noticed this and casually called the attention of the loafers on the quay to these other flags. " Surely," he said, " those are the ensigns of Portugal." The rumour was taken up, a crowd gathered and grew excited, and an official of the port suggested that, if they felt like that about it, they had better tear them down. A few loafers boarded the ship, with this official of the port among them, and on Magellan's coming up to see what was happening, the Alcalde told him to remove those Portuguese flags of his. Magellan replied that the flags bore his own arms, that they were properly displayed, and that this ship, under the commission he held from the King of Spain, was his flagship. As Captain-General of the King he would be obliged to the Alcalde if he would get off his deck at once.

Things looked ugly, and Don Sancho Matienzo, a high official of India House, came hurrying on to the " Trinidad " to see what this disturbance was. The excitement among the crowd was spreading, and he begged Magellan to take the flags down. Meantime the Alcalde left the ship, but presently returned with the Master of the Port and a posse of men, whom he ordered to arrest Magellan as a Portuguese who flew the ensign of the King of Portugal. Magellan, in fact, whose name was execrated in Portugal because he had become a Spaniard, was now being threatened with arrest in Spain because he was a Portuguese.

But the threat was not carried out, because Matienzo warned the Master of the Port that the matter would be reported to the King, and that he would have to explain why he arrested a subject of his whom he had commissioned to make ready his fleet for sea. So, instead, the Master of the Port threatened to kill Matienzo if he

interfered.   By now Magellan had removed the flags and
told him that, if he and the Alcalde did not instantly quit
his ship and allow the work for the King to proceed, he
would take his men off, and leave the " Trinidad " to
the rising tide.   The Master of the Port would then
doubtless account to the King for the damage done to
his flagship.   So work was resumed again.

This incident therefore, engineered by Factor Alvarez,
who really stage-managed it with high ingenuity, was
a sad fiasco : indeed, if anything, it strengthened
Magellan's position, for he at once wrote to the King
with admirable firmness and dignity, not as Ferdinand
Magellan but as " Your Highness's captain," and laid the
full facts before him : the effect of his letter was that the
Alcalde and the Master of the Port were both degraded.

As well as such oblique policies, others of which came
to light as the preparations for the voyage were pushed
on, Alvarez had more direct methods, and in this one
extant letter of his to King Manuel, written on July 18,
1519, he gives a most informatory budget of news from
Seville, and speaks of several interviews he had with
the renegade, Magellan, in which he tried to dissuade
him from conducting the expedition, which he believed
would fall through if only Magellan were out of it.
The letter is crammed with topics, for Alvarez had much
news of different kinds regarding the voyage to communicate to his master, and it requires a little re-arrange-
ment to enable us to get a clear and consecutive view of
its contents.   Though the date of this letter is some
months later than the events we shall subsequently
trace, it will add to our appreciation of them to realize
beforehand that they were all scrutinized by this secret
agent who was in constant communication with King
Manuel.

Alvarez describes how he had sought Magellan at
his lodgings for one of these interviews, and found him

packing boxes of dried foods for the voyage ; this looked as if the equipment of the fleet was nearing completion, and so he blew soft and sentimental, reminding the Captain-General of the pleasant and friendly conversations they had had on this subject and lamenting that this seemed likely to be the last of them. As that did not produce the melting mood Alvarez desired, he became more businesslike. " The road you are pursuing," he said, " has as many dangers as St. Catherine's wheel : you ought to leave it, and take the straight road home to your native country, where His Highness will shower benefits on you." This was exactly the suggestion that Costa had made ; we may suppose that King Manuel had passed it on to Alvarez as being a likely inducement to bring Magellan back to Lisbon. But the Factor must have found Magellan's reply most disconcerting, for he said that, if by any chance His Highness should omit to bestow on him His Royal favour, he would have to buy a serge gown, and fashion himself a rosary out of a string of acorns, and become a hermit. In fact, Magellan rated these rosy inducements at about their proper value ; and, indeed, if he had been unwise enough to return to Portugal at all, which was now yelling denunciations at him, it is extremely doubtful whether His gracious Highness would even have permitted him to make a hermitage for himself, unless a grave can be ranked as such. Magellan followed this up by asking what specific favours the King intended to bestow on him, for already one Nuño Ribeiro had spoken to him of such, and so had Juan Mendez, but he was puzzled, since Nuño Ribeiro's account of them did not agree with the other's. What then did Alvarez offer him on behalf of the King ? And Alvarez was obliged to say that the King had not told him that. So Magellan, we gather, with a slight smile, went on packing his preserves.

With much more to the same effect, all most elegantly expressed, did Alvarez try to seduce Magellan from his allegiance to Spain, but we cannot accept his statement that on the conclusion of his argument Magellan " made a great lamentation, and said he felt it all, but that he did not know of anything by means of which he could reasonably leave a King who had showed him so much favour." Our sense of what is possible and what is not recoils from such a picture : Magellan was now on the eve of realizing the dream of his life, and it is quite incredible that he should greatly lament that he could not throw it up. King Manuel had told him that he had no use for him, and in consequence of that he had come to Spain, where he was put in command of the adventure which was the desire of his heart. Costa, nine months before, had told King Manuel that Magellan had entreated the King of Spain to let him return to Portugal, which was evidently untrue, since Magellan was working night and day on the equipment of the ships, and Alvarez's repetition of the same falsehood only confirms the fact that King Manuel wanted grounds for telling King Charles that he was detaining Magellan against his will. But Alvarez, in spite of this promise of favours from King Manuel having failed, still trusted that the obstructions he was putting in the way of the voyage would succeed, but, should the expedition start, there was ground for hope that it would not go far. For he told the King that he had on several occasions inspected the ships which were being made ready, and that for his part he would be sorry to sail in them as far as the Canaries " because their ribs were of touchwood." There was a good chance then that the fleet would pleasantly founder long before it had made any embarrassing discoveries.

The whole of this budget of news written by Alvarez to King Manuel teems with interest. He, like Costa, considered Ruy Faleiro a negligible quantity : Magellan was the mainspring and the wheels of this abominable clock which might strike so ominous an hour for Portugal; once break the spring, the clock would stop. Faleiro, on the other hand, seemed to him " like a man deranged in his senses, and that this familiar of his has deprived him of whatever knowledge there was in him." As we have seen, Faleiro had been suspected of demonic possession while he was still a student in Lisbon ; he was " queer," and he was evidently getting queerer, and need not be reckoned with. Then Alvarez gives accurate information about the ships, their crews and their armaments, and enumerates for King Manuel's special information the names of all the Portuguese who are sailing. But there is nothing in the whole letter more significant, as revealing the Portuguese plots and counter-plots to hinder first the sailing and, if that could not be compassed, the success of the expedition, than the conclusion of Alvarez's account of his interview with Magellan as he packed his preserves. He told him that " he thought he was going as Captain-General, whilst I knew that others were sent in opposition, whom he would not know of except at a time when he could not remedy his honour." Here then was a threat, veiled but sufficiently explicit, that Magellan might expect mutiny, and it shows how utterly he disregarded all the arguments and persuasions and warnings of Alvarez, that he did not even ask who " those in opposition " were. Alvarez, we may guess, would not have revealed that, for it concerned the final and most desperate bid that Portugal was to make in order to stop the fleet from discovering and sailing through the strait into the Pacific. That warning was genuine enough, whatever the promises of the King might be worth, for already Alvarez had got hold of two of Magellan's officers, the one Juan de Cartagena, Controller of the fleet and Captain of one

of its vessels, the other Luiz de Mendoza, the treasurer
of the fleet, and with them he had hatched a conspiracy
of mutiny, which endangered the expedition more than
all the winds that blew from the frozen south.   All other
arguments, promises of King Manuel's favours ard
what not, had failed to influence Magellan, and now at
the end of the interview he put forward the dark, mysterious threat that there would be mutiny when he got
to sea, hoping thereby to shake his resolution to go.   It
had exactly as much effect on Magellan as the promise
that King Manuel would show him high favour if he
returned to Portugal.   With that, this " last talk " with
Magellan was over, and Alvarez left him to report to
King Manuel want of progress in that particular direction, and to try for better results in others.   How nearly
he succeeded in realizing the utmost of his aims the
narrative of the voyage will show.

CHAPTER VI

THE GREAT VOYAGE BEGINS

O go back then to the businesses above board, which, in this letter, Alvarez showed he had been so closely and intelligently watching, we find that early in 1519 King Charles and his Court had moved to Barcelona. The project had taken firm hold of the King's imagination, and throughout the spring a shower of instructions from him, all designed to hurry on the departure of the fleet, snowed incessantly down on Magellan. Endless difficulties were encountered, the most pressing being the lack of funds. The King had undertaken, in view of the immense importance to Spain of the hoped-for results of the voyage, to pay for the entire equipment, and thus be entitled to the bulk of its harvest, but the cash he had earmarked for the purpose, derived from the gold brought back from America by his West Indian ships, was exhausted long before the equipment was complete. It was necessary to raise further funds, and a subscription list was opened to the merchants of Seville : the expedition, in fact, became partly a syndicate which would have a share in the proceeds. But the general public had not much chance, for Christopher de Haro instantly subscribed for the whole of the rest of the money needed for the furnishing of the fleet and for a reserve required for the wages of seamen and officers.[1]   As we have seen, he had been

---

[1] If we go very accurately into the figures, we find that finally the merchants of Seville subscribed £120 between them.

in the syndicate for Christopher Jacques' voyage and
believed in the existence of this strait ; it was also
specially pleasant to him to finance an expedition about
which King Manuel, who had treated him so shabbily,
had such strong misgivings. He was to receive such
share in the profits of the voyage as corresponded to his
subscription, and this was one-fifth of the total estimated
cost. He also had the option of subscribing to subsequent voyages which were being already arranged to
follow that of Magellan. The first of these was to
consist of three vessels which would sail for the Isthmus
of Panama, carrying with them the finished pieces of two
other ships, to be transported by land across the Isthmus,
and put together on the shores of the Pacific ; the second
was to follow the track of Magellan. This planning of
two further expeditions before the first had sailed is
interesting, as showing what immense importance was
attached to the adventure now on hand.

Financial difficulties being thus overcome, instructions and advice continued to pour in from the King.
He had given Magellan a free hand to choose his crews,
but he seemed to have forgotten that, for Christopher
de Haro, now a large shareholder in the voyage, had
received different orders, and at his instance the officials
of India House sent for Magellan and demanded to
know why he had chosen so many Portuguese. Magellan
very properly replied that the selection of his crews was
entirely his business, according to the King's orders.
India House thereupon refused to pay any of the Portuguese whom Magellan had chosen, and both parties
appealed to the King, who withdrew from Magellan his
privilege of choosing his crews at his own discretion,
and ordered that out of the whole ships' companies only
five should be Portuguese. This was a drastic restriction, but there certainly was good sense in it, for it would
be an additional and a gratuitous annoyance to King

Manuel that the voyage whose ultimate aim was so disastrous for Portuguese dominion should be manned by
his own subjects ; moreover, from King Charles's point
of view it was only fitting that Spanish ships should be
handled by Spanish sailors. To revoke the free hand
he had given to Magellan needed but the scrawl of a
pen, and the King seems to have had not the smallest
perception of the amount of trouble this revocation would
entail on his Captain-General, who, after all, had only
used the licence the King gave him. But Charles was
busy too, for now his passion for writing orders and
memoranda to ensure the success of the voyage was
becoming a mania, and he concocted a portentous document which, the moment it was finished, was sent by
special courier to Magellan. This volume, for it was
nothing less than that, was an exhaustive dissertation,
by a man who had never been at sea, on every conceivable
matter connected with the handling of ships, the duties
of officers to their crews, the duties of crews to their
officers, and consisted of seventy-five elaborate sections.
Nobody apparently had ever been to sea before except
King Charles (and certainly he had not), so he told
Magellan that the Captains of his ships must be careful
to keep their pumps clean, and be sure that they were
not blocked with refuse, that they must inspect their
men's rations and pay kindly visits to those on the sick
list. If landing-parties had to be organized there was
a right way and a wrong way of manning the boats (so
the King informed Magellan) ; the same remark applied
to the dropping of an anchor ; and, indeed, there was
no detail in the due performance of a naval officer's
calling on which the King did not express his views.
With a similar thoroughness he discoursed on the duties
of the crew : he enjoined them not to swear, not to
assault women and never to gamble or grumble. On the
other hand they might all write home freely, though,

since they were bound for seas which no ship's keel had ever furrowed, the chance of getting these letters delivered might be held to be of the very smallest ; still they might write without restriction. . . ..

Whether Magellan, who was personally superintending every detail of the preparations, spare sails and cordage, provisions for two years (Alvarez had seen him packing preserved victuals with his own hands), clothes for his men in the Antarctic winter that was before them, canteen equipment, objects for trading with natives, such as red caps, looking-glasses, beads and balls and pairs of scissors, was supposed to master this exhaustive treatise himself, and then instruct all his officers and men in such sections of it as concerned them, was not apparent : probably the document may be taken to be merely a symptom of the King's feverish anxiety that the expedition should not, through any fault of his, lack any element of success.   But so detailed and voluminous an edict must have been very embarrassing to a man already working at full capacity in order to get to sea, as this series of Royal commands never ceased to insist, with the smallest possible delay.   Magellan was of the King's mind about that, and we may guess that he reserved the perusal of this treatise for the voyage ; the King with due pride of authorship had sent another copy to be kept in the archives at Seville.

There was another matter throughout these months which was a constant source of anxiety to Magellan. Ever since he had arrived at Seville in the autumn of 1517 he had had difficulties with his partner, Ruy Faleiro, and they were now equal in rank and authority as Captains-General of this adventure.   But Faleiro had no practical knowledge whatever of ships and sea-craft : his contribution to the scheme, invaluable in itself, was his unrivalled theoretical skill in the science of navigation and of taking observations : these he had embodied in a

treatise.   But it was clear that the whole practical side
of affairs, both in the equipment of the armada and in
seamanship when it was on its course, must be solely in
Magellan's hands, for he could not pretend to consult
his colleague on matters of which he was avowedly
ignorant.   Had Faleiro been a man of normal sense and
balance he would have recognized this, but he was, as he
had already repeatedly shown, of a jealous and furious
temper ;   he quarrelled with Magellan as to which of
them should carry the Royal Standard ;   he resented and
brooded over the fact that in any practical question that
came up for decision Magellan settled everything himself.   He now began to show signs of being mentally
deranged :   Costa had reported to King Manuel that he
was just a lunatic :   nobody paid any attention to Faleiro.
But the lunatic was, till a few months before the expedition sailed, not only a Captain-General, but Captain
of the " Santo Antonio " :   we learn this from Alvarez's
letter to King Manuel written on July 18th, 1519.
Then before the end of the month there came one of
those multitudinous edicts from King Charles that
Faleiro was not to sail with this expedition at all, but
stop in Spain to see to the equipment of that which
was already being planned to follow in Magellan's
tracks.

The King before giving such an order must certainly
have been advised from Seville that Faleiro was not a
fit man to be Captain-General or to be in charge of a ship,
and it is quite likely that Magellan was thus primarily
responsible for his removal.   Historians furiously rage
together over the incident :   it has been argued that,
since Faleiro was sufficiently *compos mentis* to be put in
charge of the preparations for the second voyage, his
mental derangement cannot have been so very serious,
and they have accused Magellan of having engineered
the deposition of his colleague in order to assume sole

command himself, and reap the royalties and rewards which had been jointly assigned to him and his partner. But this ultimate motive is merely a hostile inference, for Magellan seems to have had every reason to think that Faleiro was not fit to command or share responsibility with him, and in this case he was perfectly right to tell the King so.   Moreover, this appointment of Faleiro to superintend the equipment of the second expedition may only have been a device to make him give up his appointment as Captain-General without disturbance.   Again, it has been suggested that Faleiro feigned madness in order to get this post, which he really preferred ; that, however, is extremely unlikely, since nearly a year ago, before any arrangements for the second expedition were being made, Faleiro was feigning madness so successfully that Costa was convinced that there was no feigning about it.   Another pleasing and picturesque speculation is that Faleiro had cast his own horoscope and found, to his dismay, that he was doomed to meet his death if he sailed now.

Amid so many contradictory accounts it is impossible to know for certain what was the cause of Faleiro's dissociation from the voyage, and, if we make choice, it must be for that which on the whole is best supported by probabilities.   We know that Faleiro was " queer," that both Alvarez and Costa thought he was insane, and this is sufficient to account for the King's decision that he would not have a crazy fellow as one of his Captains-General.   It must also be admitted that, though there is no direct evidence that Magellan advised or demanded his removal, he must have been pleased to be rid of so difficult a co-dictator, and very likely advised the King in that sense.   But, though he did not want Faleiro, he very much wanted the results of Faleiro's work, namely his treatise on methods of determining longitude, and his solar and astronomical observations, which were his contributions to the assets of Magellan & Co. In order to obtain them he adopted a circuitous policy, for, thinking it unlikely that Faleiro would give them up, he asked that Francisco Faleiro, his brother, should be appointed in his place. Ruy might give them up to Francisco, and Magellan felt he could deal with Francisco. But Faleiro made no difficulty about handing them over to Magellan ; and we may, perhaps, conclude that though he was no longer Captain-General he retained his interest in Magellan & Co., which was therefore entitled to the work he had done for it.

Alvarez, as the spring and the summer of 1519 went by, was watching these activities, noting all the difficulties encountered in the preparations, helping to add to them himself, observing with chagrin that all were gradually surmounted, and keeping King Manuel informed of the slow but disagreeably steady progress. He was an exceedingly capable agent, for up till the middle of July, as his letter, already quoted, shows, he was on friendly terms with Magellan, and no doubt easily obtained information. A further point of interest, now to be noticed, is that, though King Charles had given orders that the number of Portuguese among the crews and officers who were to sail must be limited to five, the industrious Alvarez, some months after that, gives a list of them with their full names, fifteen in number, not reckoning Magellan himself and Ruy Faleiro, who at that date was still gazetted as Captain of the " Santo Antonio." This list includes Alvaro and Martin de Mesquita, who were blood-cousins of Magellan through his mother, and Duarte Barbosa, his brother-in-law. King Charles's limitation therefore on the number of Portuguese allowed among the crews of the fleet was not observed, and as a matter of fact Alvarez's list did not contain as many as half of the Portuguese who were actually among the crews when the ships left Seville.

The relaxation of this limitation was doubtless due to the difficulty of getting Spaniards to sign on ; for, though it was not yet publicly known in Seville (if we can trust the most reliable chronicler of the voyage) [1] that the fleet was to seek this semi-mythical strait, and penetrate into seas far beyond the confines of the known world, the very secrecy about its destination showed that a hazardous adventure was on foot, and the pay was considered to be unreasonably low.   No doubt, also, service under a Portuguese Captain-General, though now naturalized, was a reason why the expedition was unpopular among Spanish sailors, and we may be sure that Alvarez was busy encouraging such hesitancy.   He had deadlier business, too, than that, with Juan de Cartagena, who had now been appointed Captain of the " Santo Antonio," in place of Ruy Faleiro, and with Luiz Mendoza, Captain of the " Victoria " ; and the conspiracy, which he hoped would bring an end to the venture in bloody mutiny, was hatched and fledged long before the ships put to sea.   Mendoza's zeal, indeed, a little outran discretion, for he showed insubordination to the Captain-General while the fleet was still in harbour at Seville, and was favoured with some very peremptory advice from the King, to whom Magellan duly reported his conduct.   So Mendoza kept quiet after that till a finer opportunity presented itself.   Then Alvarez obtained information about the cargo the ships were carrying and the artillery they had mounted and, in general, proved himself a most valuable correspondent of King Manuel's : indeed, as much was known about the fleet in Lisbon as in Seville.

But, though the Portuguese Factor by his conspiracy with these two Captains had ensured that Magellan carried with him the bomb of mutiny which exploded at

[1] *The First Voyage Round the World by Magellan* (Hakluyt Society), p. 37.

Port St. Julian, all his machinations were powerless to prevent the fleet starting, and in August the last bale was embarked. A solemn Mass was celebrated at the Church of Santa Maria de la Vittoria in Seville, and, holding the standard of the King, Magellan pledged him his obedience and loyal service, and in turn his Captains pledged their loyalty to him. Three years later in that same church those who were left at the completion of that brave adventure gave thanks to God Who had brought them home again, and prayed for the soul of him who had been its architect and inspiration. Then on August 10th the fleet left the harbour of Seville and went down to San Lucar at the mouth of the River Guadalquivir, where it waited till the final tallies and receipts were made. It anchored in the port below the castle of the Duke of Medina Sidonia, and every day the men went to hear Mass in the church of Our Lady of Barrameda.

'Throughout these months of preparation Magellan's wife, Beatriz, had been living with him at Seville. In March, 1519, she had given birth to a son Rodrigo, and in August she was expecting another child. So now since all was ready for the final adventure, which crowned and ended his life, Magellan made his second Will. In the first, which he had drawn up before he started on his earliest voyage to India as a seaman under Almeida, he had bequeathed his family estate at Sabrosa in Portugal, from which country he was now alien, to his eldest sister and her husband and their heirs. He was unmarried at the time, and though in that first Will he had left Sabrosa to his son, should he have one born in wedlock, he evidently realized that by becoming a Spaniard he had forfeited his family estate in Portugal (for Rodrigo was Spanish born), and in this second Will makes no mention of it. But now there were his Spanish interests to dispose of : he was drawing pay as Captain-

General, which the King had agreed to remit to his wife, and beyond that there were the contingent interests granted him by the Royal Capitulation. For even if he never returned from this voyage it might easily happen that before his death he would have discovered certain islands of which his heirs would be hereditary governors, and would derive therefrom *in perpetuo* one-twentieth of the revenues they brought to the Spanish exchequer, as well as inheriting the other benefits bestowed on them by the Capitulation. Indeed, if this voyage yielded the most modest fraction of the financial results which King Charles and his Ministers expected of it, and King Manuel feared from it, the heirs of Magellan would be exceedingly wealthy folk.

In this second Will, dated August 24th, 1519, Magellan left to his son, Rodrigo, Spanish born, and to his heirs after him, all the benefits resulting to himself from the Capitulation. Should Rodrigo die without marrying or without legitimate heirs, his inheritance was to revert to the second child with whom his wife was now pregnant. If that should prove to be a girl, and she married and became a mother, her son was to take the name and the arms of Magellan, and live in the Kingdom of Castile. Should his direct line, through either of these descendants, fail, Magellan named his younger brother, Diego de Sousa, now a Portuguese subject, as heir to the property resulting from the voyage, with the provision (as stipulated in the Capitulation) that he should become a Spanish subject, live in Spain and marry a Spaniard. Failing him and the heirs of his body, Magellan's sister, Isabella, was to inherit, subject to the same conditions as those laid down for Diego. If either of these two came into this Spanish inheritance, they were to pay one-fourth of it, without duty or deduction, to his wife, Beatriz, if still living. Till his son Rodrigo and the child shortly to be born attained the age of eighteen, Magellan appointed Barbosa, his father-in-law, their guardian.

It is needless to go into the many minor details of these provisions about his heirs ; there is something pathetically futile about their extreme elaboration since none of the beneficiaries ever came into the enjoyment of one penny of the inheritance so carefully conveyed. Magellan's son, Rodrigo, now a baby of five months old, died in 1521 ; the child with whom his wife was now pregnant was still-born and Beatriz herself died in 1522, soon after she heard of her husband's death in the far-off islands of the Pacific. Nor did either his brother or sister inherit anything in default of direct heirs, for the voyage, though perhaps the greatest achievement in the whole history of navigation, was quite barren of such results as had been hoped for. Not less elaborate are the provisions of the rest of the Will ; but, though no less ineffective, they exhibit Magellan's extraordinary gift of attention to detail, which is in evidence in the inventory of the equipment of his ships, and that strong preoccupation with matters of faith and religion which emerges again and again in the chronicles of the voyage. Just as in his first Will he had left directions for Masses to be said for his soul at the altar of San Salvador in Sabrosa, so now with an infinitely greater meticulousness he devised as first charge on his estates a catalogue of religious vows to be performed. His body, if he died on this voyage, was to be buried in the church nearest to that spot which was dedicated to the Holy Virgin ; he left to the church in Seville where he had partaken of the Holy Sacraments (and where again he hoped to partake of them) a contribution to their funds ; he bequeathed a real of silver to the Holy Crusade, and another in aid of the ransoming of such faithful Christian men as may be captives of the Moors ; another to the Lazaretto for lepers outside Seville ; another to the hospital of Las Bubas within the city ; to the House of St. Sebastian another ; and another to the Church of St. Faith, beseeching from all of these an intercession for the peace of his soul. On the day of his burial, wherever and whenever that might be, he directed that thirty Masses should be said over his body, and that in the Church of Santa Maria de la Vittoria, where he had received the Sacraments on the day the fleet left Seville, thirty Masses, with offering of bread and wine and candles, should be said for him. And he willed that on that day three paupers should be clothed with gifts " of a cloak of grey stuff, a cap, a shirt and a pair of shoes," and that food should be given to the same and to twelve others likewise, with the request that they should re-member in their prayers the soul of Ferdinand Magellan, and also that a gold ducat be given for the sake of such souls as were now in purgatory.

These pious duties, so Magellan devised, were to be a prior charge on all Spanish property of his, before it came to his heirs, but one provision, 'and that a very strange one, took rank of them : " And I confess," so runs the will, " to speak the truth before God and the world, and to possess my soul in safety, that I received and obtained in dowry and marriage with the said Donna Beatriz Barbosa, my wife, six hundred thousand mara-vedis . . . and I desire that before everything she may be paid and put in possession of her dowry." The only reasonable conjecture that we can make about this is that Magellan had fraudulently pocketed his wife's dowry and concealed the fact. . . . Why, otherwise, should he have felt himself bound to confess the truth and make the restitution of it the first charge on his estate ?

He then deals afresh with his percentages on the revenues which might accrue to Spain as a result of his voyage. These, should the Spice Islands prove to belong to King Charles, might turn out to be colossal, and, with a renewed sense of his duty towards the Church, he bequeaths a further tithe of the whole to various religious bodies. Then follow certain specific bequests : the first to his page, Christopher Roberto ; the second to his slave, Enrique, whom he had brought with him from Malacca on his first voyage to India. Enrique had become a Christian, and so from the day of Magellan's death he was to be free " from every obligation of slavery and subjection," and his master begs Enrique to pray for his soul. Enrique, who accompanied Magellan on this voyage, survived his master, and soon after his death was guilty of as black a treachery to the safety of the expedition as it is possible to conceive. That sequel is the final comment of irony on Magellan's Will.

Magellan had now discharged all duties, actual and contingent, towards those he left behind him, he was free from the quarrels and intrigues, the jealousies and plots that for the last ten months had laid traps for his steps and threatened the accomplishment of his purpose, and in the terms of this Will there seems to emerge the man himself, who for the last year had been buried under the multiplicity of the tasks which he personally super- intended. With his genius for detail he was careful to provide for every possible situation that might arise in the succession to the inheritance he was going forth to seek, to repair the misappropriation of his wife's dowry (if such is the purport of that strange clause), but even more careful to remember in the disposition of his worldly goods the monasteries and churches where he had received spiritual succour and to make due thank- offerings to the Power that directed his destiny. There is an elaborateness and an earnestness about these which demonstrate a deep sincerity of purpose : they were by no means the formal bequests common in the use of that day, but expressive of his sense of direct guidance, and of his gratitude for it. Of the reality of this to him, the voyage itself gives ample and, finally, tragic testimony. For seven years, but for being ferried across to Morocco, he had been cooped up on land ; now, like some great sea-bird, he stretched his cramped wings for his last stupendous flight.

During the month when his fleet was anchored at San Lucar, Magellan was up and down between Seville and the port, seeing to final details, and on September 19th he finally joined his ship, on which he was to live till the day of his death. His first order was that every man sailing with him should make his confession and receive the Sacrament ; and this was done, himself the first. Next day the fleet put to sea on the westerly course that should bring it by way of the round world to the ultimate east of the Spice Islands, where Magellan's friend, Francesco Serrano, had been bidden to wait for his coming. Lame and little and swarthy he limped about the deck and saw the coast of Spain fade in the dusk of the September night.

CHAPTER VII

MAGELLAN ARRIVES AT
PORT ST. JULIAN

HERE had come to the Court at Barcelona, during the summer of 1519, in connection with the election and proclamation of King Charles as Emperor, a most vivacious and enterprising personage, one Signor Antonio Pigafetta, by birth a patrician of Vicenza, and a Knight of Rhodes. He was on the staff of the apostolic proto-notary and Ambassador of Pope Leo X, and Pigafetta had a very strong desire to see the wonders of the deep, or, as he calls them, "the very great and awful things of the ocean" which hitherto he had only read of in books and heard discoursed upon by the friends of his chief, Monsignor Francis Cheregato. There was naturally much talk at Barcelona about the armada nearly ready to start from Seville to find out the new route to the Spice Islands, and the Emperor Charles gave Pigafetta a letter of recommendation to his Captain-General, and permission to accompany him on this voyage. It is to the enterprising spirit of this Knight of Rhodes that we owe far the most complete account of the first Circumnavigation of the World, for, on his return among the remnant of those who had started on the voyage, the Grand Master of Rhodes desired him to write the story of the adventure. The value of his narrative therefore

has been discounted by certain authorities on the grounds that it was written up afterwards from mere notes.   This, however, is not quite the case, for Pigafetta at the conclusion of his narrative says that he went with the rest of those who had returned from the voyage to the Court of Emperor Charles V at Valladolid where " I presented to him a book written by my hand of all the things that had occurred day by day on our voyage."   Instead therefore of considering this account a mere subsequent compilation of notes, we see that it was founded on a regular journal, or perhaps was a copy of the journal itself, for Pigafetta tells us that he kept such a journal, and from start to finish of the voyage never omitted his daily entry.   Three copies of his narrative, written in French, are in existence, and there is good reason for supposing that the copy he presented to the Grand Master of Rhodes was in French also, but Pigafetta certainly also wrote a version of it in Italian, which was published at Venice in 1536.   For a complete account of these various manuscripts the reader may be referred to Lord Stanley of Alderley's introduction to his *First Voyage Round the World, by Magellan*, published by the Hakluyt Society, where the whole history of this is set forth in the most scholarly fashion.   Francis Drake when following Magellan's route through the Strait in 1577, and accomplishing the second Circumnavigation of the World, had with him Pigafetta's narrative ; this was probably the English translation by Richard Eden, published in 1555.   A comparison between Pigafetta's narrative and that of Francis Fletcher, chaplain on Drake's expedition, upon which *The World Encompassed by Francis Drake* is based, shows that Fletcher was largely indebted to Pigafetta.[1]

In addition to this narrative, which is far the fullest, we have also an account of the voyage written by a

[1] See Appendix, p. 249.

Genoese pilot of the name of Baptista, who piloted Magellan's flagship in the Pacific. It is written in Portuguese, and though no Genoese pilot appears in the list of the crew he may have been, though Genoese by birth, a naturalized subject of Portugal, which would also account for the language of his narrative. A third but very short narrative is that of an unknown Portuguese, accompanying Duarte Barbosa, who sailed on the "Victoria"; a fourth is the log-book of Francesco Alvo. This, however, consists almost entirely of nautical observations of latitude and longitude, and mentions but few of the events of the voyage : it does not, indeed, even record the death of Magellan, though it contains a couple of points of high geographical interest which are not given elsewhere.

In addition to these accounts which are contemporary and first-hand, written by men who accomplished the first Circumnavigation of the World and returned to Seville, we have another of almost equal evidential value, namely a long letter written by Maximilian Transylvanus to his father, the Cardinal Archbishop of Salzburg. Maximilian was in the secretarial department at the Court of King Charles when the "Victoria" came home after the voyage, and he took down from the lips of the survivors what they could tell him. Another account once existed compiled by Peter Martyr, who was on the Board of India House, and who, like Maximilian, received his information from the sailors who returned. It disappeared in the sack of Rome.

Of the five ships which on September 20th, 1519, set out from Seville, directing their course for the Canary Isles, three were commanded by native-born Spaniards. These were the " Santo Antonio " under Juan de Cartagena, who had taken the place of Faleiro ; the " Concepcion " under Gaspar Quesada ; the " Victoria " under Luiz de Mendoza. Magellan, Captain-General

H

of the fleet, commanded the " Trinidad," which was the flagship ; and the " Santiago," the smallest of them all, a ship of 75 tons, was under the command of Juan Serrano, with whom Magellan had served in India in 1506. It seems certain that he was brother of Francisco Serrano who was now waiting in the Spice Islands for his friend " coming by way of Spain." Magellan had long ago experienced the disastrous results of the units of a squadron not keeping in touch, in consequence of which two of the three ships returning from Cochim to Portugal had run ashore on the Padua Bank of the Laccadive Islands, while the third continued her course, and he had established a system of signalling of the most elaborate sort which was written out and given as an order to the commanders of all his ships. These signals were displayed on the flagship which led the rest, and each of the other ships must reply to them, to show that they were understood and being obeyed. All night a lantern or a flare of reeds or wood burned at the stern of the " Trinidad " visible to the watch on the other ships : this they must follow. The display of two lights indicated that the " Trinidad " was about to tack or take in sail ; three lights showed that the flagship expected a squall, and that the studding sail on all ships must be lowered, in order that the mainsail should be struck more speedily ; four lights had a further signifi-cation ; and to each and all of these signals an answer must be returned at once. The night was divided into three watches, the first from dusk to midnight, the second from midnight till towards morning, and the third called " La Diane," or the watch of the morning star, was kept till the advent of broad day. Every evening, also, each ship in turn must draw up to the " Trinidad " and, after saluting Magellan as Captain-General, ask if there were any special orders.

Six days' sailing brought the fleet to the Canaries.

There had been a Spanish settlement there from early days, and in the spring Luiz de Mendoza had been sent out by King Charles to deposit there certain stores which they now picked up. They anchored at Tenerife, and took in water and pitch for the ships, and Pigafetta records what we may regard as the stock conjuring-trick of the Canaries, for centuries ago Pliny had recorded this phenomenon of magic, and forty years later it much interested English mariners under John Hawkins. On one of the islands there existed no spring or stream of any natural sort, and the entire water-supply was derived from this remarkable vegetable, the Raining Tree. Once a day, at the hour of noon precisely, a cloud enveloped it, and so saturated it with water that a copious and perpetual stream flowed daily from it sufficient to supply the wants both of the human beings and of the animals, tame and wild alike, who inhabited the island. Oddly enough, the later English voyagers give exactly the same account of it, and yet we may be quite sure that there never was such a tree. Can they have blandly cribbed from Pigafetta ? But then there is Pliny. . . . Craven suggestions have been made that the legend is founded on fact, and that the mists on the Canaries are so thick that the trees get soaked to a most unusual extent. Pigafetta's version, being impossible, is far more credible.

But while Pigafetta was admiring this tree, and the crew was taking in supplies for the flight across the Atlantic, Magellan had more ominous business to attend to. A Spanish ship that must have started very soon after the departure of the armada put in to Tenerife, and there was delivered to Magellan, by letter or word of mouth, a message from Diego Barbosa. It warned him that there was a story whispered in Seville that his Captains were in a conspiracy of mutiny and murder against him, and that the ringleader in the plot was

Juan de Cartagena, Captain of the " Santo Antonio."
At that he must have bethought him of that dark threat
of Factor Alvarez, who, in his talk with him as he was
packing his preserved goods, told him that " others were
sent in opposition to him." He received this second
and more specific warning with the same apparent unconcern as the first, and sent back a message to his father-
in-law that he was the servant of the Emperor and his
life was dedicated to his business. But he took note of
it, just as he had taken note of what Alvarez told him,
and was quite prepared to act with all promptitude the
moment he thought that the occasion was ripe for so
doing. But that was not yet.

Pigafetta in his diary, which he subsequently tells us
he wrote up every day, concerns himself very little with
the politics and more serious matters of the fleet : " the
great and awful things of the ocean," as he told his
Grand Master, fish and birds and strange beings were
his chief preoccupation, and he chats about these with
the same picturesque zeal as Samuel Pepys. Probably
he never knew of this letter at all, and he makes no
mention of the first act in this drama of mutiny, on which
the curtain was so soon to rise. All the hint that he
gives of trouble brewing is that the masters and captains
of his other ships " did not love " Magellan : he sup-
poses that this was because he was a Portuguese. . . .

After leaving Tenerife Magellan set a more southerly
and less westerly course than had been given out in his
orders to his Captains, and Juan de Cartagena, bringing
the " Santo Antonio " up to the flagship for the evening
salutation, thought fit to ask why the advertised course
was not held. Magellan replied with one of the classical
naval aphorisms, " Follow the flagship and ask no questions." Cartagena answered with more than a hint of
insubordination, and told him that he should have consulted his Captains before changing his direction. But

the time for taking notice was not yet ripe, and Magellan did not answer, but held the fleet to its new course, leaving the Cape Verde Islands away to the west, and keeping close to the coast of Guinea. Why he held this course, when a more westerly one was the more direct towards the coast of Brazil for which he was making, is not clear : possibly Cartagena's advice to his Captain-General that he was going out of his way was sufficient reason. Continuing, they ran into a belt of calms, during which among the awful things of the ocean Pigafetta noted the presence of man-eating sharks with terrible teeth. The sailors caught some of these, and cooked pieces of them, but experiment taught Pigafetta that he was not a shark-eating man. Heavy storms succeeded these calms and, striking all sail, they drifted before the furious winds, in imminent danger of being pooped by the following seas. Then several times there appeared to them on the masthead the signal of salvation, the holy fire of St. Anselm, burning steadily there for the space of two hours, and that dried the tears of their despair, for the ships would now surely be saved. Before it vanished it grew to so great a brilliance that those who looked on it were blinded for a while by its splendour. Then, since St. Anselm had manifested his presence and protection, the wind dropped, and the fury of the sea abated.

Strange birds appeared : one a footless species (otherwise unknown to naturalists), of which the female laid her eggs on the back of the male ; another, Pigafetta records, pursued other birds, and ate their droppings. This piece of observation, though erroneous, can be accounted for : no doubt Pigafetta had seen Arctic skuas, which harry feeding gulls and terns till they drop the fish they carry in their bills, or disgorge what they have lately swallowed. The skua then swoops upon this morsel and eats it. Thrilled by the sight of these birds

" with their dirty diet," and of flying fish, in such dense flocks that they looked like an island, Pigafetta fails to record the second act in the drama of mutiny.

Among the instructions given to his Captains by Magellan was, as we have noticed, the order that every evening they should draw up to the flagship and salute him as Captain-General. It was the turn of the " Santo Antonio," and the quartermaster hailed him as " Captain." Magellan sent word to Cartagena that he and not the quartermaster should have saluted him, and that his title was Captain-General. To this Cartagena made an insolent reply, and for the next three days omitted to give the evening salute altogether. A sillier piece of insubordination can scarcely be imagined : it was just a rude gesture of a gutter-snipe. Probably Cartagena thought that he was introducing into the fleet the leaven of mutiny which he hoped would soon permeate it : he was beginning to show Magellan that " others were sent in opposition." It even seemed as if the Portuguese Captain-General felt himself powerless already, for no reprimand came from the flagship for his further impertinences. And therein Captain Cartagena made a singular error of judgment, for Magellan was not proposing to reprimand any more, but, when he thought fit, to strike.

So Cartagena was not long (following this course of tuition for his admiral) in setting him another lesson in docility. There had been a meeting of the five Captains on the flagship, and when their business was finished Cartagena again took him to task for changing their course without consulting them. That was just the occasion Magellan desired ; he rose and called for the guard, and told the man he was a prisoner. He was deposed from his captaincy and then and there put in irons. The mutinous spirit had not spread quite as far as Cartagena hoped, and it was quite in vain that he

called on the others to set him free.   Barbosa's warning
had not tarried long for its first fulfilment.

Soon after, the fleet crossed the line, and sailing west-
by-south first sighted the Brazilian coast at Cape St.
Augustine ; from there they coasted southwards and
anchored in the Bay of Rio, on December 13th, after a
voyage of eleven weeks.   This country, according to
Pope Alexander's disposition of the world, was, in consequence of the amended line of demarcation, in Portuguese territory.   Christopher Jacques had visited it in
1503 ; so, too, had Juan de Solis, who had been killed,
and probably eaten, by cannibal tribes further south, in
1508.   But Magellan's fleet was received in far friendlier
fashion, for the coast had been lacking rain for two
months till the very day when the fleet arrived.   The
natives thought therefore that the strangers had come
from heaven, bringing the rain with them, "which was
great simplicity," says Pigafetta.   Hitherto "they had
adored nothing, but lived rather bestially according to
Nature," but now, with this evident sign, they instantly
embraced Christianity.   Mass was celebrated twice
during the stay of the fleet, and many natives attended
it, behaving in the most reverent and devout manner
"so that it was pleasing and touching to see them."
Pigafetta, indeed, was in most Pepysian mood, eloquent
and enthusiastic over the singular lusciousness of pine-
apples and the wonderful bargains they obtained for the
objects they had brought for purposes of barter.   A
comb fetched two geese, a pair of scissors enough fish
to feed a mess of ten hungry men, and the most remarkable bargain of all (just as Pepys's would have been) was
his own, for the natives gave him five fowls for a king
from an old pack of playing-cards, and were afraid they
had cheated him.   They were a healthy people, for they
attained ages varying from a hundred to a hundred and
forty years, and they slept upon cotton nets which they

called " amache " (thereby surely supplying us with the derivation of " hammock "), and when they felt cold in bed they lit fires directly below them. They used knives made out of split flints, for iron was unknown to them, and Pigafetta records how a girl came on to the " Trinidad " and saw there a nail made of the unknown substance. So she stole it, concealing it in her hair, for being quite naked she had nowhere else to hide it : both Magellan and he " saw this mystery." A native was willing to part with two of his daughters as slaves in exchange for a knife or an axe, but no amount of agreeable objects would induce him to give up his wife. As Pigafetta had already noticed, they were simple folk, for when the ships' boats were launched they imagined that these were the ships' babies, and when they lay alongside they thought that their mammas were giving them suck. Simple, too, was their procedure when they killed an enemy : they kippered his body in the smoke and cut bits off him to eat when they were hungry, and this they did " in his memory." They did not care very much for human flesh, but this was their custom. Some of these stories Pigafetta heard from Juan Carvalho, who was pilot of the " Concepcion," and, escaping Solis's fate, had lived here for four years, and he concludes this lively account with a list of French words and their equivalent in the native lingo. He also must have assisted at some observations to ascertain the correct longitude and to determine whether this piece of the coast was certainly in the Portuguese sphere. These were made by Andres de San Martin, who had taken Faleiro's place as astronomer to the fleet, and who probably used Faleiro's treatise which Magellan had succeeded in obtaining. But these were a little outside Pigafetta's beat : all he can tell us about them is that the sun was " on the zenith, which is a term in astrology," and that the zenith is an imaginary point in the sky above the observer's head.

We gather that these observations were above Pigafetta's head likewise. Later on, however, he studied the subject to better purpose, and compiled a treatise on navigation.

Pushing on southwards again, the fleet encountered a violent storm when somewhere opposite the estuary of the River Plate. They ran into shelter of the land on the south bank of this, and there waited. So vague was Magellan's information about the position of the strait he was looking for that he thought that this estuary might be its entrance, and when the storm subsided he made an exploration of it. Here the " Santiago," since she drew less water than the other ships, acted as pioneer, but in a couple of days it became evident that there was no sea-strait ahead, for the water became fresh, and they knew that they were only pushing up into some great river-mouth. The ships were watered, but before they left the shore Pigafetta was in his element again, for now there appeared a company of giant-cannibals, one of whom with a voice like a bull came within ear-shot of the flagship and asked if he and his companions might approach : signs, we must suppose, were employed, for as yet Pigafetta did not know the language of giants. But panic seized these faint-hearted monsters, and they all ran away while their chief was parleying, to their castle inland. A party of a hundred sailors was landed in order to try to catch some of them, but, as the giants " did more with one step than we could cover with a leap," they were soon out of sight.

After leaving the mouth of the River Plate the fleet pushed on southerly again, hugging the coast as closely as it could, though once or twice bad weather and shoal-water drove it out to sea. A reconnaissance was made in the Gulf of St. Matthias, for no one knew but that any inlet might prove to be the entry of the strait. The whole coast was absolutely uncharted and unknown, and Magellan must search and scrutinize every reach of it, for fear of missing what he had come to seek. But St. Matthias, though it was his name-day, had nothing for them, and again the weary search went on. But for Pigafetta a veritable banquet of the awful things of the sea was in store, for presently they came alongside two islands covered with geese and ravening sea-wolves. These geese were black and unable to fly, and they had beaks like crows and were sumptuously fat ; the sea-wolves were legless but had terrible teeth, and Pigafetta saw that if only they could run they would be " very bad and cruel." The geese, of course, were penguins, the first recorded to have been seen by European eyes, and the sea-wolves no doubt were seals or sea-lions. All five ships were soon stocked with the skinned bodies of the geese, but the party who adventured after the wolves had a truly awful experience. They did not return to the ships that night, being unable to launch their boat in the rough water, and the search party which went to look for them next morning found them completely buried under the carcases of the sea-wolves they had slaughtered. After this happy rescue a violent storm sprang up, but now not only St. Anselm, but St. Nicholas and St. Clare made their luminous epiphany on the masthead of the " Trinidad," with the usual result.

It was already now towards the close of February, 1520, the Antarctic summer was fast on its wane, and soon it would be necessary to find some suitably protected bay in which to anchor, should the strait be still undiscovered, for the long months of winter darkness and storm. Once more the fleet put in at an inlet, which might be the portal they sought for, or, failing that, provide a winter harbourage ; but once again they drew blank, and rueful experiences caused Magellan to name it the Bay of Labour. They remained here for close on a week, but it would not serve for a long stay, since south-easterly gales made it a sorry haven, and Magellan left it again, still hugging the coast, with a watch kept for the entrance to the strait, which, if it existed at all, could not be now far off. But he was playing hide-and-seek for short hours of diminishing daylight ; frozen fogs blanketed the land, and search was difficult, for while the fleet was in shallow and dangerous waters the polar blasts came screaming out of the south, and they must beat out to sea again, for fear of wrecking on the shoals. Indeed, it seemed as if Nature, animate and jealous, was fighting to preserve from man's knowledge one of the great secrets about the face of the world which still eluded his questing spirit. King Manuel would have rejoiced had he known the perils which his Most Christian Brother's expedition was encountering, and the far more desperate hazards into which it and its scoundrel of a General were soon to be plunged : for these his thanks would be due to his very efficient Factor in Seville.

But at the head of the expedition was a man of in-domitable will, who seemed to have some reserve of determination to meet any emergency or obstacle. He was mysterious too ; none liked him, but all feared the stroke of that will of steel which flashed from its scabbard and pierced. For them, as well as for us, he was shrouded and withdrawn : they could scarcely do more than guess at what he was. Grim and taciturn he limped about on the deck, standing the cold better than any, and sundered from all fellowship with the Spaniards not only because he was of alien and rival race, but because he was not one who rated human companionship as comparable to the fulfilment of his own designs. Already mutiny had threatened, and he had made but one fierce and sudden and sufficient gesture when he told the Captain of the " Santo Antonio " that he was a prisoner.

By now he had given Juan de Cartagena his liberty
again, though we do not know the occasion of that, but
he had not been reinstated in his command, and was a
seaman on board the " Concepcion."   Antonio de Coca
had been appointed in his place ; but, as the ships
worked down the coast, he had been deposed also, and
the Captain of the " Santo Antonio " was now Magellan's
cousin, Alvaro de Mesquita, the son of his mother's
brother.   Events proved that this was not a very happy
appointment, for Mesquita seems to have been a weak,
unstable commander, and it was certainly unpopular,
and reasonably so with the Spanish section of the crews,
for Mesquita was a Portuguese.   It was a grievance
that gave food for grumbling in the groups round the
galley-fire, and Juan de Cartagena and Antonio de Coca
were among them.

CHAPTER VIII

THE MUTINY

ROGRESS had been slow with these contrary winds and that sedulous scrutiny of the coast, and it was not till the last of March, 1520, when the hours of daylight were far dwindled, that the fleet put in to the Bay of St. Julian. Magellan was still unwilling at once to lie up for the winter, for this bay itself might be the entry to the strait, and indeed it looked like the beginning of a channel, and he sent out a couple of ships instantly to explore it while the rest lay at the entrance. But they came back with the news that there was no strait here : the gulf was full of shoals and did not extend far inland. Further south the coast stretched interminably ; for the last fortnight the cold had been getting ever more rigorous and storms were frequent. He had hoped to find the entry to the strait, and, when found, to pass through it into the great South Sea before going into winter-quarters, but in this continued fierceness of the weather he now reluctantly decided to winter here until the return of lengthening days and the abatement of the Arctic cold : here at least there was a sheltered harbour, with shoal-water for fishing. But this would entail a longer period of inaction than he had intended, for when he set out he had hoped to be past the southern and unknown limit of his voyage before winter, and as a precautionary measure he at once gave the order that

the whole company, officers and crew alike, should be put on short rations. It is likely that he had already found out that, though the ships were supposed to be victualled for two years, the stores, either by mistake or some fraudulence on the part of the contractors, were very short, and, as was to appear later, contained little more than provisions for one instead of two years. As he himself had supervised the lists for the provisions and gear which he thought needful for the voyage, it seems hardly possible that he could have made so incredible a miscalculation ; the latter is the more probable alternative, and we must conclude that the stores had not been delivered according to the invoices. Perhaps, without being over-fanciful, we may see in this most serious shortage some further machination on the part of Portuguese agents at Seville to prevent Magellan reaching the Spice Islands even if, as King Manuel was justified in fearing, he found the strait. This order for short rations, made on the day of arrival at St. Julian, was naturally unpopular.

The crews, mostly Spanish, were already full of grievances and grumblings ; they disliked their Portuguese General, they had been through a long period of hard work and bitter weather, the strait was still to seek, and now, when they put into winter-quarters, and might expect more ease and greater comfort, they had no sooner got the anchors cast than there came round this damned order, curtailing their rations, which were already none too plentiful. Even their Captains, Gaspar Quesada and Luiz de Mendoza, sympathized with them, and there was much muttering that day and the next when it became apparent how exiguous the diet was to be. Groups collected round men like Juan de Cartagena and Antonio de Coca, who had once been Captains of the " Santo Antonio," and as they talked the voices sank to whispers, and men looked at each other, and half-promises of support were made. These groups formed and dispersed and formed again.

Easter Day in this year, 1520, fell on April 1st, and on the eve of the feast, the day on which the fleet arrived and anchored at its winter-quarters, Magellan sent word round the ships that all hands should attend Mass on shore next day, and he invited the Captains of the fleet to dine with him after Mass on the "Trinidad." Neither Luiz de Mendoza, Captain of the "Victoria," nor Gaspar Quesada, Captain of the "Concepcion," obeyed this order to attend Mass, nor did they come to the "Trinidad" afterwards to dine with their Captain-General ; and Magellan had only one guest at his table, Alvaro de Mesquita, his cousin, lately appointed to the command of the "Santo Antonio." Why Serrano, Captain of the "Santiago," who throughout was staunch to Magellan, was not there, we do not know : a possible explanation is that, since, immediately on arrival at Port St. Julian, Magellan had despatched two ships, of which the "Santiago" was one, to explore the bay, Serrano had not yet returned from his reconnaissance ; for, according to one account, this exploration lasted for two days. In effect, Magellan and his cousin, Mesquita, ate their dinner alone. When that was done, Mesquita went back, night having fallen, to his ship. Apparently all was quiet there, and he turned in.

After midnight, in the hours of the second watch, a boat-load of thirty armed men rowed across from the "Concepcion," and boarded the "Santo Antonio." Captain Gaspar Quesada of the "Concepcion" was at their head, and among the ringleaders was his servant, Luiz de Molino, Juan de Cartagena, seaman and once Captain of the "Santo Antonio," and Sebastian del Cano, who, in the decrees of destiny, is now immortally known as the Captain, when she came into port at Seville again, of the first ship that had been round the world. But to-night he was of the mutineers whose design it was to prevent any of these ships from going round the world, and to get back not to some Spanish port, but to Lisbon, and claim reward from King Manuel for their faithful services of mutiny and murder. . . . The second watch, which came on at midnight, was in the plot : the mutineers were expected, and no challenge was made to those who rowed so softly at dead of night ; the crew of thirty men came up the ship's side, and Antonio de Coca, seaman now on the ship where he had once been Captain, welcomed them. They were all armed, and before it was known, except to those in the plot, that they were aboard they had tiptoed into Mesquita's cabin and made him a prisoner. This was not done quite without disturbance, for the first mate, Juan de Lorriaga, hearing shouts from the Captain's cabin, came to see why he cried out in the night. There was his Captain, overpowered and surrounded by armed men, and already in irons. Lorriaga was thus in charge of the " Santo Antonio," and he ordered Quesada to leave the ship : for answer he was stabbed, and fell as one dead. Of the crew of the " Santo Antonio," many, like those of the second watch, had already declared for the mutineers, and the loyal men were helpless against the armed contingent from the " Concepcion." This surprise attack had succeeded to admiration, and Quesada did not even call upon the crew to declare themselves on this side or on that. The mutineers were in possession of the armoury, and the ship was in their hands.

Quesada remained on board the " Santo Antonio," for now he held the largest ship of the fleet, and it was his intention to conduct negotiations from here with Magellan, when the drowsy Captain-General awoke on the morning of Easter Monday. That was sufficient task for him, and he appointed Sebastian del Cano, an expert and skilful navigator, to be Captain of the " Santo

Antonio," and under his direction the ship was cleared for action, should that little limping Portuguese mean to show fight. He sent Juan de Cartagena back to the " Concepcion," to assure the mutineers there that all was well, and to take command in his absence. Probably Quesada mentally elected himself to be the new Captain-General of the fleet, and he might well tell himself that he had earned that distinction. The " Victoria," also, under the command of Luiz de Mendoza, was riddled with mutiny, and its Captain eager to get even with Magellan, who had caused him to receive so sharp a reprimand from King Charles. Out of the fleet of five, in fact, during those hours between midnight and day three ships had made mutiny : there remained faithful to their oath of loyalty to Magellan, sworn solemnly at the Church of Our Lady of Victory in Seville, only those aboard the " Trinidad " and the little " Santiago." So quietly had the *coup* been carried out that no hint by ear or eye had reached the watch on either of these ships that there had been aught astir.

The late morning dawned, and in the ordinary routine a party was required to fetch water for the ships from the mainland : wine and food were rationed, but there was plenty of water. Magellan, seeing to everything himself, as was his custom, sent off a party from the " Trinidad " to fetch other men from the " Santo Antonio " to share the job. They were approaching the ship, but not yet alongside, when they were hailed, and told that no orders were received here except those of Captain Gaspar Quesada. Back went the boat to the " Trinidad " to report, and Magellan knew that the curtain had risen on the last act of the drama of mutiny. Perhaps he had seen it a-quiver when yesterday his Captains had not come to dine with him, but he had said nothing, for he never spoke until the time was come to strike. He limped about the deck, staring with those wide, black eyes of his, with no word for any, while the boat waited alongside to know if there were any further orders, or whether they should proceed to their business of watering the ship.

The first step was to find out which of the ships had joined the mutineers, and the simplest plan was to send the boat across to the " Concepcion " and the " Victoria " to ask if they were for Captain Quesada or their Captain-General to whom they had sworn allegiance : there was no need to make such an inquiry of the " Santiago " (assuming that she was now back from her exploration of the bay), for she was under the command of Serrano, and there could be no question about her. So off the boat went again, and very soon it came back with the news, which did not surprise Magellan, that they both declared for Captain Quesada. That, for the moment, was all he needed to know, and the men could go off to their business of fetching water. They could do it without further hands to help, for now there were only two ships to water instead of five, and Magellan again stumped up and down the deck, silent and very dangerous. Before long he saw a boat put off from the " Santo Antonio," and it came across to the " Trinidad," which lay at the entrance to the bay. It brought a despatch from Captain Quesada of the " Santo Antonio " to the late Captain-General, to say that he was willing to open negotiations with him on certain terms : this order for putting the crews on short rations, for instance, must be cancelled, and there were other things. Captain Quesada therefore invited Magellan to step into the boat and come over to the " Santo Antonio " to discuss these matters. Magellan's reply to that was that the flagship was the headquarters of the fleet, and he the Captain-General ; he was willing to hear what Quesada had to say and awaited him here. Once more the boat returned from the " Santo Antonio " with Quesada's answer, which was merely a repetition of his first message, and expressed his willingness to interview Magellan on board the " Santo Antonio." He can hardly have hoped that so transparent a device for getting Magellan into his power on board the mutinous ship could have succeeded ; but it was worth trying. He was in an overwhelmingly strong position, with the " Concepcion " and the " Victoria " both mutinous, and both under the command of ringleaders, and perhaps Magellan on this display of firmness would recognize that, and come and make the best terms he could.

But Captain Quesada, with all his grasp of the situation, cannot have been prepared for Magellan's immediate response to this repeated invitation. With that Napoleonic attention to details which always characterized him, he seized the boat and made prisoners of the crew which rowed it. That was not much, but it was something, for the loss of the ship's boat would inconvenience Quesada ; and, what was more, it gained time. Quesada waited for the return of his boat, making no fresh move nor any new development of his plans till Magellan's reply came, for all depended on that. He did not want to attack the " Trinidad " and cause needless loss of life : the loss of one life, that of his late Captain-General, was all that was necessary. On board the " Santo Antonio " everything was very comfortable, for Quesada had broken into the stores, and served out full rations of food and wine to all hands. His boat would be back presently, perhaps with Magellan on board, and, as he finished his mug of wine and refilled it, he noticed that the short southern day was nearly over, and dusk was beginning to fall.

Magellan thought : the thread of thought was running strong and clear from his spinning. The centre and headquarters of the mutiny was the " Santo Antonio," and he obtained information of what was doing there from the boat's crew which he had detained, and decided at once that to make a direct attack on it with guns and armed sailors was to run an unreasonable hazard, for if the " Trinidad " bore down on the " Santo Antonio " and opened fire the two other mutinous ships would surely join in, and the " Trinidad," even if she called up the " Santiago," would have a very small chance. Besides, his business was to go to the Spice Islands, and not fight his own ships.   As yet, while Quesada waited for his answer to this Mrs. Bond invitation to come and be killed, the two other mutinous ships were waiting for instructions from the " Santo Antonio," and with inconceivable quickness Magellan planned and executed a lightning counter-attack on the enemy's flank.   An hour or two ago the " Victoria " had declared for Quesada, so now, as if to inquire into that mutinous message, he sent for Gomez de Espinosa, the master of his armoury, and told him to take a boat, manned with a crew of only five men, and row across to the " Victoria " carrying a written despatch to Captain Luiz de Mendoza ordering him to come back in the boat to the " Trinidad " and speak to the Captain-General.   If he came, good ; if he refused, and Magellan knew he would refuse (else he was not mutinous), Espinosa and his men had clear instructions what they were to do.   They all wore cloaks on this bitter evening, and all six of them carried arms below their cloaks.   Instantly they embarked, and paddled quietly off across the few hundred yards which separated the two ships.   The moment they had started a second boat was manned, and it held fifteen men, armed to the teeth, under the command of Magellan's brother-in-law, Duarte Barbosa.   Accurate timing was necessary for the success of this improvization of genius, and the crew of the second boat, concealed behind the " Trinidad," sat ready to strike the water on the word ; and Magellan watched from the deck.   He waited till the crew of the first boat, cloaked and armed, with Espinosa bearing the despatch for Mendoza, had gone on board the " Victoria " and then he gave the signal. The second boat foamed after it at top speed.

At the moment, then, when it started, Espinosa was already on board the " Victoria," and as it surged along he was presenting to Mendoza the summons which Magellan knew would not be obeyed. Espinosa gave it him, and his cloaked seamen stood by while Mendoza read the laconic message. He saw at once how transparent was this device to get him on board the " Trinidad," just as Magellan had seen how transparent was Quesada's invitation to go on board the " Santo Antonio." Mendoza laughed. " I am not to be caught like that," he said, and the words ended in a gasp. Out flashed Espinosa's hand from below his cloak, and his dagger was plunged in Mendoza's throat. Six men stood round him, and on the instant there came swarming over the ship's side Duarte Barbosa and his fifteen men all fully armed. Such an attack was utterly unforeseen, the crew of the " Victoria " were unarmed, and no word of command came from their Captain, and instantly it was plain that they were but half-hearted mutineers, with many loyal men among them. So sudden a flash of steel, and the sense of the grim and invincible will that had unsheathed it, sufficed to restore, without any further violence, a wavering allegiance. Mendoza was dead, and no traitor had ever more thoroughly deserved his, fate. And Quesada, watching from the deck, and now beginning uneasily to wonder why his boat had not returned from the " Trinidad," saw through the dusk the flag bearing Magellan's arms flutter up to the masthead of the " Victoria."

Magellan was watching for that signal from the flagship, and, when he saw his flag which had caused that well-engineered riot in the harbour at Seville stream out on the bitter wind that blew from the frozen void, he knew that he would carry out his will against conspirators even more dangerous. Perhaps he gave a sigh of relief, for this venture, supremely hazardous as was fit in countering the desperate situation disclosed that day at dawn, had succeeded, and the sequel to it, already planned, was in comparison but a corollary, sure as logic. He blew his whistle, rapped out his orders, and instantly all was bustle : arms were served out to the crew, and the flagship cleared for action. And now the " Santiago " could help, and a message was sent off to Serrano, who perhaps scarcely knew yet of the great peril, so quietly on both sides had the deadly work been done, ordering him at once to shift his anchorage and take his new station close to the flagship as she lay at the mouth of the harbour. This was done, and Quesada, still watching from the " Santo Antonio," but wondering no longer why his boat did not return (for by now any man could guess), saw that the " Victoria " had weighed anchor too : he must have known that these were the orders issuing from the flag. Two boatloads of men towed her, and she moved up, and, taking her station on the other side of the flagship, she anchored there. So now there were three ships, all loyal to Magellan, lying across the mouth of the harbour, closing the entrance, and the " Santo Antonio " and the " Concepcion " were imprisoned within : there was no hope of escape save by engaging and defeating the gaoler-ships. Boats passed to and fro between them, but none came across to the mutineers. Magellan, for the present, had no more to say to them, and Quesada and Juan de Cartagena on the " Concepcion " knew well how fruitless it would be to attempt a negotiation now. What they had done, they had done.

Night had fallen now, black and without a star, and the grip of the cold increased. The majority of the crew

on the two mutinous vessels had taken no part whatever
in the rising, though, unarmed as they had been when
the " Santo Antonio " was seized by Quesada, they had
made no resistance. But now in these hours of icy
darkness they had time and to spare to consider their
position, and all knew that t the entrance to the harbour
was the man who, still u seen and wrapped about by a
deadly quiet, was waiti   at the door of the trap, holding
the mutinous ships - n a grip as unrelenting as this
arctic night.

There indeed e was ; and he had thought of everything. It s   ed possible to him that the two im-
        ips might attempt to escape during the night ;
and so, not content with mooring his three ships across
the mouth of the harbour, he had served out arms and
good rations to every man on board, and in case of a
fight they were ready.

The wind from landwards blew stronger, the ebb-
tide ran swiftly, and soon after midnight the " Santo
Antonio " dragged her anchor ; she swung round and
came drifting stern-foremost on to the " Trinidad."
So dark was it that not till she was quite close did the
watch on the " Trinidad " get sight of her. Magellan
hurried up on deck, and Quesada was on deck too,
for he knew that his ship was adrift and moving out to
the mouth of the harbour where lay the other three.
Perhaps he still thought that he might drift clear between
two of them : if not he meant to fight. Then from the
deck of the " Trinidad " there came an order, her
grappling irons whistled, her guns belched fire, and
following that one discharge the crew of the flagship
leaped aboard, and up the other side of the " Santo
Antonio " there swarmed armed men from the " Victoria."
Before they struck, they hailed their comrades on the
" Santo Antonio " with the cry " On whose side are
you ? " and the answer came that they were the

sailors of King Charles and of Magellan. Quesada had about him those who had actively supported him the night before, but now they sheathed their swords, for where was the use of resistance when the crews of three ships were against them ? Irons were clapped on to them, Alvaro de Mesquita, imprisoned in a cabin below, was released, and the " Santo Antonio " was brought to anchor alongside the flagship. That morning three ships were in mutiny against Magellan, but at dawn next day the four ships that lay at anchor at the mouth of the port were flying his ensign again. Apart from them in the harbour was the " Concepcion," [1] still at anchor.

Next morning an armed boat-load of men rowed across to the " Concepcion " and demanded her surrender. Juan de Cartagena was in command, and he instantly tendered his sword and was taken to the flagship. Mendoza on the one side had been killed, on the other, the quartermaster of the " Santo Antonio," whom Quesada had stabbed, lay mortally wounded. Otherwise there had been no casualties, and though not forty-eight hours ago Magellan had been fighting against odds incalculably desperate he was now master

[1] Gaspar Correa in his *Lendes da India* gives a different account of the drifting of the " Santo Antonio " on to the " Trinidad," narrating that Magellan sent a sailor that night to cut the cable of the " Santo Antonio," so that she might bear down on to the flagship, as indeed happened not by design but by accident, luckily just missing her. But in spite of the alluring picturesqueness of the idea, it is impossible to accept it, for daring though Magellan was, it must be remembered that the " Santo Antonio " was the biggest vessel of his fleet, and to invite a collision between her, drifting on a night of strong wind and tide, and the smaller " Trinidad," riding at anchor, was to risk unconjecturable damage. Had other accounts confirmed this, or had Correa been otherwise reliable, we should have been obliged to accept it, but the incident is not recorded elsewhere, and Correa is constantly guilty of grave inaccuracies. For his account see *The First Voyage Round the World, by Magellan* (Hakluyt Society), p. 244.

of his expedition again.   The mutiny was over, and of
the three chief ringleaders two were in irons on the
flagship, and the third, Mendoza, was dead.

Magellan's next task, necessary and immediate, was
to deal with those who had incited the mutiny and those
who had been persuaded or coerced into joining it.   His
commission from King Charles gave him power of life
and death, by hanging or capital execution, over his
officers and crew, and if ever there could arise a case
where the extreme penalty was deserved it was here and
now.   This power had been given him for just such a
situation, and it was no less his duty to exercise it, and
punish the ringleaders, than it was his duty to secure
himself and those for whom he was responsible from
the repetition of such an attempt.   But the dead must
be dealt with too, and Magellan's first act, grim as
befitted the occasion, was to finish with Mendoza.   He
had already paid with his life for his part in the mutiny,
but now Magellan had his body brought ashore from
the " Victoria " to the place where he held assize,
and there slung it, head downwards, and, as if he had
been alive still, addressed him as traitor, and passed
sentence on him that his body should be drawn and
quartered, and the hacked pieces impaled on stakes for
all to see, both those who had been faithful and those
who, now heavily guarded, awaited trial and sentence,
what was the end of traitors.   From information collected from the crews of the three ships which but
yesterday were in the hands of the mutineers, there was
evidence that some forty men were implicated.
    Justice, to the uttermost indignity, had been done on
the dead, and now Quesada was set in the dock.   There
could be no extenuating circumstances : here was the
very head and front of the mutiny, and in his case no
clemency was possible.   He had stabbed with a wound

that was soon to prove fatal the loyal quartermaster of the " Santo Antonio," who at the outbreak of the rising had bidden him leave the ship, he had put its rightful Captain in irons, he was traitor in the first degree, and Magellan sentenced him to the full penalty, such as had now been executed on Mendoza. His servant Molino, according to evidence given, was no less guilty for his aiding and abetting his master, but his life was spared him on the condition that he should execute Quesada. Molino accepted the office, and the two men were taken back to the " Trinidad," the condemned man with his executioner.

Next came Juan de Cartagena : he was no less guilty of deliberate mutiny in the first degree than Quesada or Mendoza. Both he and Mendoza had been tampered with before the expedition left Seville by Alvarez, the King of Portugal's agent, and both had set out suborned, with the intention of causing mutiny in the fleet. And Cartagena had had his warning : he had been deposed from the Captaincy of the " Santo Antonio " for rank and repeated insubordination, and his case very remarkably resembles that of Thomas Doughty, who took part in Drake's voyage of circumnavigation in 1577. Like Cartagena, Doughty had been tampered with before the expedition sailed ; like him, he had been deposed from the command of his ship and made prisoner before the shores of South America were sighted ; and, like him, Doughty was tried by his General for inciting to mutiny at this very Port of St. Julian. But, unlike Drake, Magellan extended to Cartagena a bitter clemency. He had not, as Quesada had done, attacked and mortally wounded a loyal servant of the King, and instead of executing him, a fate which he had undoubtedly deserved, Magellan sentenced him to be marooned on the shore where now the trial took place, when the fleet started again to find the strait. Perhaps the sentence was not less terrible in fact, but the death-sentence must always rank as the extreme penalty ; anything short of that is a legal mitigation. Pigafetta attributes' this indulgence to the fact that King Charles had appointed Cartagena to be " conductor " of the fleet, and says that for this reason Magellan did not execute him. But it seems more reasonable to suppose that Magellan wished to draw a distinction between his guilt and Quesada's, for Quesada, no less than Cartagena, had been appointed Captain of a ship by King Charles.

There remained then thirty-eight men whose guilt in participating in the mutiny was duly established. Magellan passed sentence of death on them all, for such was their deserts, and then remitted it. While the fleet remained in winter-quarters they were kept as prisoners, and given work to do, but when the voyage was resumed they were released and went back to their posts. On April 7th, 1520, exactly one week after the fleet had dropped anchor in the port, Quesada was beheaded by his servant Molino, and his body drawn and quartered. The mutiny was over, and, considering the seriousness of it and the number of men implicated, the sentences passed by Magellan were those of a just judge, lenient rather than vindictive.

CHAPTER IX

THE FINDING OF THE STRAIT

HE great danger was past, the ring-leaders of the mutiny were gone, and those who had taken an active though subordinate share in it were prisoners, brought out to work under guard, and confined again. But plentiful causes for discontent were still in play : there was the prospect of this long winter ahead with its bitter cold and its endless hours of darkness ; there had been the long and fruitless search for the strait ; the men's hearts were sick with deferred hope and hardly one out of ten now believed that even when the winter was over they would find that mythical strait that led into the sea where lay the isles of summer, with the tropical luxuriance of their spices. But the greatest immediate cause for discontent sprang from those diminished rations : the darkness and cold would have been bearable on a bellyful of good food and a full draught of wine ; but, instead, there was just this bit of biscuit and dried beef and a sip that made them only long for more. For a few days the excitement of the mutiny and the judgments that followed kept the men's thoughts busy, but that faded, and there was nothing but hunger and darkness and cold. The grumbling groups began to form again, and, as always happens when men are of one mind, the grievances took shape. A deputation waited on Magellan petitioning that full rations should be at once restored or that the fleet should

set sail for home again. They had already forced their way into seas where no ship had sailed yet, without finding what they sought, and was not that sufficient ? At the least, would he not let them begone from this place of ice and of blood and run before this bitter wind from the south till they found some less cruel harbourage ? All the crews were of the same mind : this deputation represented the feelings of the men who had been loyal to him.

Magellan must have recognized a reasonableness in this view, and saw also the seriousness of the situation, for he did not dismiss them out of hand, as we might have expected, but tempered his ultimatum with appeal. He told them first of all, so that there could be no room for doubt on that score, that only death would cause him not to carry out his enterprise, for he had sworn to the King, whose commission he held, to go through with it, and thus he neither would nor could abandon it while breath was left in his body, and he would go on, when once the hold of winter relaxed, till he found open sea at the end of this weary coast,[1] or a strait through it which would give access to the ocean of the Spice Islands. As for their rations, there was plenty on shore to supplement the reduction which he had felt bound to make, and which he could not consent to restore : they must remember, too, that he himself was no better off in that regard than they. But on the shores of the bay there was abundance of mussels,[2] fish teemed in its waters, birds and beasts could be shot or snared for the pot, and the land was well timbered to supply fuelling. The

[1] It must not be imagined from this that Magellan had the smallest reason to suspect that there was open sea beyond Cape Horn : he only thought that, on the analogy of Africa, the continent would somewhere come to an end. Until Drake's circumnavigation of the world in 1577 the frozen and conjectured Terra Australis Incognita was believed to join on to South America and extend to the Pole.

[2] It is only fair to add that Pigafetta says they were uneatable.

biscuits and the wine in the ships' stores were sufficient, as now given out, for health though not for stuffing and guzzling.

So much for material needs, and now Magellan administered a tonic to their pride, with an eye, especially, to the Spaniards, who, so he rightly imagined, were the moving spirits in this petition. He reminded them that not every year only, but every day almost, the Portuguese ships, in their voyages eastward to India and beyond, went further south than they had yet penetrated : it would be a lamentable return for them, against which all in whom the splendid spirit of Spain was alive would revolt, if they crept back now to Seville with nothing achieved. But ample would be the compensation for the discomforts and weariness of these days when they brought back to their King the gift of a new world full of spices and of gold.

For a while this sensible and spirited speech, in which Magellan revealed himself as not wholly of steel stuff, but capable of sympathy, produced the effect he wanted. But within a few days the discontent began to simmer again, with ugly murmurs. Though Magellan had been naturalized as a Spaniard and thereby incurred the undying hatred of the Portuguese, it was because he was a Portuguese that the Spanish sailors spread mischievous gossip about him. All the cunning resources of King Manuel had been devoted to his undoing, but now these mutterings of his men credited him with the design of working the destruction of the fleet to pleasure Portugal. He had professed himself to be the loyal servant of the King of Spain, and to be set on adding the Spice Islands to his crown, but his real object (so ran these mutterings) was to fail in doing so, and by the story of the impossible hardships incurred to deter Spain from ever again embarking on such a quest. The course of the voyage already showed that : they were no nearer the Spice Islands for all their privations, but were still heading for the regions of eternal snow and night.   Such talk was utterly illogical, but none the less it was dangerous stuff, and the focus of it, the man who chiefly encouraged it, was the priest, Pero Sanchez de Reina.   He was doing exactly what Juan de Cartagena had been doing, and once more Magellan struck. The priest was arrested, and sentenced to be marooned in company with the other when the day came that the fleet should leave its winter-quarters.   We do not know how strong was his influence over the men, or how perilous his seditious talk, and are thus unable to estimate, as we can do in the case of the ringleaders, the justice of this very terrible sentence.

Pigafetta alludes to the mutiny in only the most cursory fashion : he did not much concern himself with such matters, however deadly and significant, for his business was to see the world and the awful things of the ocean, and even these months of midwinter at St. Julian supplied him with the richest banquet of remarkable phenomena.   At first, he confesses, there was nothing doing.   April and May passed without a single inhabitant of these regions appearing, but after that the giants made life an orgy of marvellous experience.   One morning one of these monsters was unexpectedly seen on the shore : he was dancing and singing, and for all the rigours of Antarctic midwinter he had not a rag to cover him, and as he danced he put sand on his head to show his humble disposition.   Magellan sent out a sailor to sing and dance too, and this evident community of tastes led to the establishment of friendly relations.   The giant was thus brought to see the Captain-General and he pointed to the sky.   Pigafetta opined that, like the natives in Brazil, he thought that they had all come down from heaven.   Such was his stature that the tallest Spaniards only stood as high as his waist, and his large face was outlined with red paint, and he had two yellow circles round his eyes, and two hearts painted on his cheeks, and his hair was painted white. He must hastily have put on his clothes when his dance was done, for, though just now he was stark-naked, he appeared before Magellan in a garment of skins sewn together and he had shoes made of skins on his feet, and he carried a thick bow and some Turkish arrows. He was given food and drink and was then shown a mirror, and at the sight of himself reflected there he was so startled (and no wonder) that he leaped backwards and knocked four men flat. He was presented with this mirror and a comb for his hair, and some other bright objects ; and this friendly reception so encouraged his fellow tribesmen that they came forward, men and women alike, all naked, and some plucked up courage to go aboard the Spanish ships. Then the singing and dancing began again, and the giants, whose wives came after them, laden with their belongings like donkeys, showed the sailors certain pots containing a white powder made from herbs, and by signs conveyed to them that they never ate anything else except this admirable and nutritious powder. There must, however, have been some slight misunderstanding over this, or, at any rate, they were capable of digesting more solid viands, for on a subsequent occasion two of these giants ate a basketful of biscuit (apparently Magellan did not ration giants) and quantities of rats without even skinning them, and washed down this curious repast with half a bucket of water at a single draught. For medicine, when they felt unwell, they adopted the drastic device of thrusting two feet of an arrow-shaft down their throats. This Pigafetta tells us (with revolting details) had the desired effect : two feet of an arrow-shaft was to a giant what a feather in the throat is to others. Maximilian Transylvanus, however, who also independently records this feat, says that all this arrow-shaft had no effect whatever : the giants merely did it to arouse admiration. Whenever a giant died, twelve devils appeared and danced round the dead man ; the name of the greatest of them was Setebos.

The women were not so colossal, " though quite big enough," [1] and " they were dressed like the men," says Pigafetta, thus elegantly conveying to us that they were not dressed at all. As well as being laden like donkeys with their husbands' belongings, they brought with them, coupled together like dogs on a leash, some guanacos, a species of small llama. The full-grown guanacos supplied them with skins, and guanaco-hunting, under the direction of the giants, became a sporting diversion to the fleet. The giants tethered the young guanacos out in the open, and then hid close by in the bushes ; so when the mothers came to play with their young, they were shot with arrows. Already eighteen of the giants were on friendly terms with the sailors, and now there appeared the best giant of all : he was " a gracious and amiable person " and so enormous that when he leaped in the dance his feet, where he landed, sank quite four inches into the earth. He became a real friend, and was presently baptized as a Christian and given the name of John. John could say his own name and the name of Jesus and repeat his *Pater noster* and *Ave Maria* as well as anybody, but his voice was appallingly loud. He told them of a horrible devil he had seen with two horns on his head, and the power of emitting fire from various parts of his person. Magellan gave him a shirt and a pair of breeches (how he got himself into them does not appear) and other agreeable objects. But after a while he appeared no more, and Pigafetta was afraid that the other giants killed him for being so modern.

[1] Opinions differed about the women : the Genoese pilot expressly says that they were very small.

Magellan seems to have hoped (to follow this truly Pepysian diarist) that John would become a permanent inmate on the ship, for he wanted to get a giant to take home to Spain with him, and on John's disappearance he adopted a trick that was more creditable to his head than his heart, in order to secure one. A loose giant on the " Trinidad," if detained against his will, might have been an embarrassing and dangerous inmate, and he had recourse to a very treacherous device. He loaded two young giants with presents, knives and forks and mirrors and bells, till their hands were full. He then showed them two pairs of irons, used to shackle the ankles of prisoners, which the giants thought very attractive, for iron was a substance unknown to them, and they wanted the irons too. But their hands were full, and Magellan intimated by signs that they could carry these on their feet, and the moment they were on he hammered in the bolt which closed them, and the giants were helpless to run away. They roared and foamed like bulls, and called on Setebos all to no purpose, and their wrists were likewise handcuffed. At this point, Pigafetta, feverishly scribbling down this inhospitable incident, descends into a bottomless pit of confusion, and it is really impossible to gather what happened next. We conjecture that somehow or other one at least of these victims of treachery got free, and some sort of fight ensued in which the giants killed one of Magellan's men with a poisoned arrow. Cross-bows and guns were of no avail against them, because they would not stand still while a man could take aim, and since they ran faster than horses pursuit was in vain, and they all got away. But from the narrative of the Genoese pilot we learn that one was kept prisoner and eventually was brought alive to Spain in the " Santo Antonio," while Maximilian Transylvanus tells us that, though one of them remained a prisoner, he died in a day or two because he would not eat anything.   Again from Pigafetta's subsequent narrative we learn that a most amiable giant called Paul was still on the flagship when it passed out of the strait into the Pacific, and that he died not because he would not eat anything, but because there was nothing to eat. . . . Those who are skilled in reconciling contradictory statements may perhaps make something of this tangle.   What is certain, however, is that Magellan called the giants Patagons, because of the size of their feet, and that the country still bears their name.

But, before these giants were making diversion for Pigafetta and us, the winter of the far south had closed in, and, though during April, when the mutiny and its attendant troubles were over, Magellan had thought to leave St. Julian and push on again in search of the strait, the incessant gales made it unwise in his opinion to risk moving the whole fleet.   One ship, however, under a man he thoroughly trusted, might be sent forward as a scout to prepare the way for the general movement when the winter was over.   She could at least explore for some little distance, and note some further harbourage in case of need ; she might even find the strait itself.   So, towards the end of April, he sent out the " Santiago," which had been used for reconnaissances before, under the skilled and trustworthy Serrano.   Prowling down the coast Serrano discovered an estuary and river-mouth which he named the Rio de Santa Cruz : there was good harbourage there and abundance of fish.   Leaving it to push on further yet, he was overtaken by a violent storm ; a wave smashed the " Santiago's " rudder, and she drove ashore and could not be got off.   But the crew, with the loss of only one man, scrambled to land, while the ship, pounded by the waves, began to break up. Their lives were all they had saved from the wreck, and they were without victuals of any sort, and somehow or

other they must make their way back to Port St. Julian
by land. But there were herbs of some sort which they
could gather, and shell-fish, and Serrano with a foresight
worthy of his Captain-General, remembering that the
River Santa Cruz lay between him and the base at St.
Julian, loaded his men with planks washed up from the
wreckage of the " Santiago," in order to make a raft when
they came to it. A raft was then put together, and on
it two of the shipwrecked crossed the river, and started
on their desperate journey. They slept out in the
bitter nights, and struggled on through the dwindling
days, keeping the life in them with meals of roots and
grass, and finally after eleven days they reached the
Spanish ships, emaciated beyond recognition. The
dogged determination of these two, whose names are
unrecorded, in the face of incredible exposures and
privations is truly a gallant episode, and reflects the spirit
of their inflexible commander. Magellan instantly
despatched a relief expedition, duly provisioned, to
rescue Serrano and his men who were still on the south
bank of the River Santa Cruz, and they, following the
same route as that gallant pair who had come like ghosts
into St. Julian, brought the remainder safely home.

The continued inclemencies of April had determined
Magellan to wait in Port St. Julian till winter was over,
and lengthening days and fairer weather made it possible
to push on with the quest of the strait, but Serrano had
brought back a favourable account of the harbourage
in the estuary of the Santa Cruz and of the plentiful
supply of fish to be obtained there, and Magellan
resolved to wait no longer at St. Julian for the coming
of spring, but to put behind him another sixty miles of
coast by finishing the winter at this harbour which
Serrano had found. But Serrano's ship, the " Santiago,"
had been lost, and there were Captains to be appointed
to the " Concepcion " and the " Victoria " in place of

Gaspar Quesada and Luiz de Mendoza : Magellan therefore gave the command of the " Concepcion " to Serrano, and of the " Victoria " to his brother-in-law, Duarte Barbosa ; Mesquita had already been reinstated as Captain of the " Santo Antonio." He had ascertained by the observations of Andres de San Martin that St. Julian lay in the Spanish sphere of dominion, as laid down by Pope Alexander, and he erected a Cross on the top of the highest neighbouring hill, as token that Spain had occupied this territory and claimed it for King Charles. But there remained one grim duty to be done, namely the execution of the sentence he had passed on Juan de Cartagena and the priest Reina for their part in the mutiny. Since then they had been prisoners on the " Trinidad," but now, while the fleet was preparing for sea, their chains were struck off them, and with a supply of bread and wine they were put on shore. Finally, before weighing anchor, Magellan gave the order with which he invariably preceded any fresh adventure, and after making their confessions all officers and men received the Sacrament. Then on August 24th, 1520, the fleet set sail and left the ill-omened port to nurse its dark tradition of mutiny and death, tragically to be revived when next ships of adventure followed the route of which Magellan was pioneer. For in the year 1578 an English fleet put in to this dark harbour, and here Thomas Doughty was tried before a jury of the crews and found guilty of inciting to mutiny. He was sentenced to death by his General, Francis Drake, and here he suffered the fate of Quesada.

The weather was reasonable when the fleet set out, but before it reached Santa Cruz a very violent and sudden storm nearly caused disaster. Maximilian Transylvanus attributes the loss of the " Santiago " to this tempest, and omits from his account Serrano's original adventure and the return of the rescued crew to

St. Julian. But the testimony of the Genoese pilot, as well as the detailed account given by Herrera of the arrival at St. Julian of the two men sent forward by Serrano, and Serrano's appointment to the command of the " Concepcion," make it clear that the " Santiago " had been lost while the fleet was still at St. Julian. All authorities are agreed that during the six or seven weeks that the fleet now remained at Santa Cruz much of the gear of the " Santiago " was recovered from the wreck. Then towards the middle of October and the advent of the Antarctic spring Magellan pushed southwards again, having revictualled the fleet with dried fish, still searching the coast for the entry to the strait, and on the third day of the voyage, the same being the Feast of St. Ursula and the Eleven Thousand Virgins, they sighted a great Cape that stood boldly out from the low shore, and beyond it was a wide stretch of water like the mouth of some big river. On the far side of that was land rising into peaks of snow-clad mountains, but this broad channel continued as far as eye could reach into the very heart of the continent. The strait, which Magellan had seen marked on that dim chart in the library at Lisbon, for the sake of finding which he had left his native country for Spain, and Spain for the perils of mutiny and shipwreck beyond the ends of the known world, opened out in front of him.

But he did not yet know that : this broad water might be only the mouth of one of those weary rivers which so often before had exalted and then cast down his hopes.

NOTE.—In the foregoing account of the mutiny, of the discontent over the rations which led to Magellan's speech to his men, and of the subsequent punishment of the priest Pero Sanchez de Reina, we have been following a chronology which has not hitherto been suggested. It is agreed on all hands that the fleet entered Port St. Julian on the last day of March, as specifically stated in the narrative of the Genoese pilot and the log-book of Alvo, and that Magellan immediately gave the order for reduced

rations.   But all later historians take that as being one of the main causes
which eventually culminated in the mutiny.   No doubt it contributed to it,
but the mutiny seems to have broken out immediately on the day after
the entry to Port St. Julian, and the discontent about the rations to have
followed.   For we learn that Magellan's speech to the deputation quieted
the discontent for a while, but it boiled up again, and for participation in
that the priest Reina was sentenced to the same fate as Juan de Cartagena.
But Juan de Cartagena was implicated in the mutiny itself, and for his
share in it was sentenced to be marooned when the fleet left the Port.
Reina's offence was clearly subsequent to this, and it was for attempting
to ferment mutiny a second time that he was condemned.   It seems
therefore necessary to place the whole business of the deputation and of
Magellan's speech after the mutiny instead of before.   This view, moreover, is confirmed by Pigafetta, who states that the mutiny and the
punishment of the mutineers occurred immediately on arrival at Port St.
Julian.

CHAPTER X

THE TRAVERSE OF THE STRAIT

HE anchors found no bottom, for there was deep water right up to the head of Cape Virgines (for so in honour of the day had Magellan christened it), and the " Trinidad " and the " Victoria " tied up to the shore while the " Santo Antonio " and the " Concepcion," commanded by Mesquita and Serrano, passed them by, and sailed into the bay to explore. From here, just within the headland the inlet seemed entirely landlocked by mountains, and the general opinion in the fleet was that this was but one more of those deep bays formed by a river from inland. But Magellan's hopes were high, and as he watched the two reconnoitring ships pass westwards up the bay he believed that at last he had come for certain to that broad water marked on the chart which led into the Pacific. They vanished into the night, and presently the wind rose, and the " Trinidad " and the " Victoria," slipping their moorings, beat out for safety into the bay. This gale blew out of the south-east : and before morning the " Santo Antonio " and the " Concepcion," which had anchored in shallower water for an abatement of the wind, tacked out again to get more sea-room, for they were near what looked like an unbroken stretch of lee-shore. It was morning now, and with some difficulty they weathered an outlying promontory, and there behind it was no continuation of

the shore showing a landlocked bay, but a channel. They passed up this, and it broadened out into a second bay, and still deep water burrowed into the heart of the land. A second narrows some fifteen miles in length succeeded, with a Cape terminating it on the south, and the two ships rounded this. Again the water broadened, and in front of them now was a channel twenty miles wide stretching due south without land visible at the end of it. Firmly convinced that the strait lay open before them, they put about to carry the great tidings to their Captain-General, who had never doubted that sooner or later they would find what they sought. Magellan had bidden the two Captains to return, whatever was the result of their exploration, within five days, and since their departure there had been rough weather, and, when the fifth day was passing without sight of them, there were many who feared that they must have been driven ashore. But now before that day was spent the watchers on the flagship saw them coming down the bay with all sails spread and a-flutter with flags. Their guns boomed out, and there was cheering aboard, and the "Trinidad" knew what this salvo and this shouting meant, and bellowed back her welcome, for they were come again with joy.

The two Captains, Mesquita and Serrano, went on board the flagship and justified the news which their guns had proclaimed. By no possibility could this passage up which they had penetrated be any great river-mouth, for, if so, on the ebb of the tide it must have grown brackish or fresh with the outpouring of the stream, and it was salt as the sea itself. And, had this been a river-mouth, the ebb would have been swifter than the flow of the tide, for on the flow the sea would be against the current, whereas on the ebb it would be moving with it. But this had not been so : the flow of the tide was as strong as the ebb, and the ebb as salt

as the flow.   Moreover, as they ascended, the channel
must have grown both less wide and less deep, whereas,
after passing through the two narrows, it had broadened
out again into a bay twenty miles across and shoreless
ahead, and it remained of great depth.   As surely as
this channel led from the sea, so it led to the sea again,
and that sea must be no other than the great Southern
Sea, which Balboa had looked on from the peak in
Darien.

Their report did no more than confirm Magellan in
the conviction he had held before this reconnaissance
started, that here at last was the Eastern gateway into
the Pacific which King Manuel had feared he would
find.   Mutiny and the perils of unknown seas, mountainous under the polar blasts, had been its Cerberus,
but those grim guardians had slunk away before his
inflexible will, and the gate was open.   What lay in
the corridors within was yet unknown, and now without
pause he hoisted sail again.

They passed through the first narrows, which to the
reconnoitring expedition had lain concealed behind the
Cape that seemed part of a landlocking shore, and into
the bay which Magellan now named after St. Philippo ;
the second narrows, lying S.S.W., succeeded, and they
rounded the Cape which, perhaps owing to its bold out-
standing cliff, Magellan named Cape St. Vincent, and
in front of him, even as Serrano had reported, lay this
wide channel as broad as the Straits of Dover, stretching
away to the south.   At the north end of it, adjoining the
western shore, was an island, now known as Elizabeth
Island, where for one night Magellan anchored.   Perhaps he was sponsor for it, but it must not be confused
with the group of islands further south which, sixty
years later, Drake christened the " Elizabethadæ."
Next day, October 29th, they started again to traverse
the Broad Reach lying due south.   Up till now there

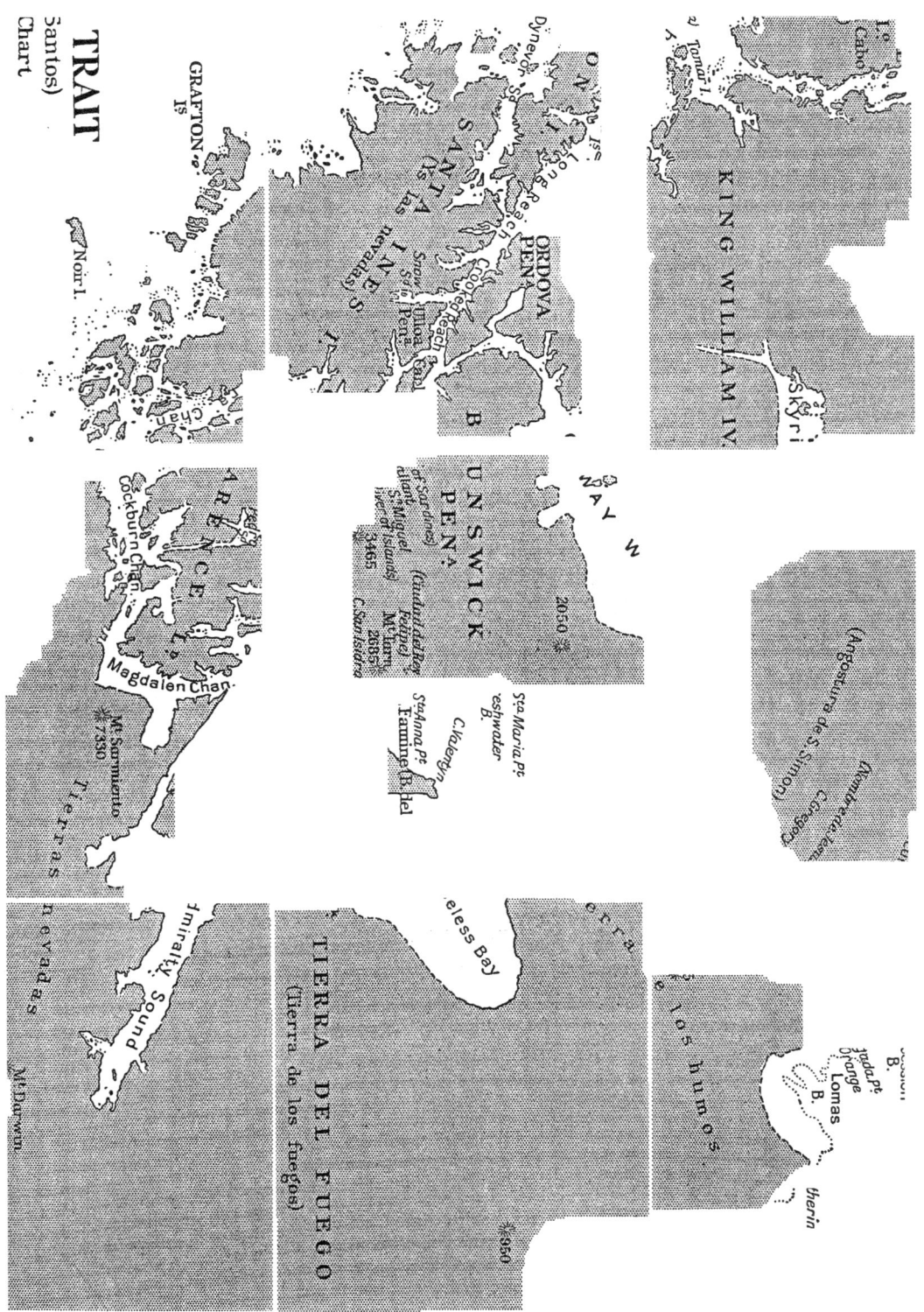

had been no choice of routes, for there was no other channel except that which they were following, but as they approached the southern end of the Broad Reach they came in sight of the headland of Cape Valentyn parting this single channel into two.[1] The one lay due south still, the other trended south-westerly and more directly towards the great South Sea. But these were now unknown waters, where no ship had ever penetrated, and it might prove that this south channel turned westwards, or that the south-west channel ended in some cul-de-sac. Magellan therefore determined to explore them both, and in order to save time his plan was to send the " Santo Antonio " and the " Concepcion " together again up the southern channel, while the flagship and the " Victoria " went to explore the channel to the south-west.

That evening, probably on the second day after leaving the harbourage behind Elizabeth Island, Magellan anchored off Cape Valentyn, where the Broad Reach bifurcated, and called a meeting of his Captains and officers on the flagship, and there asked them to give their opinion on a question that at first sight seems of the most amazing sort, namely whether they should continue the voyage at all. His own intention, as he was very soon to make manifest, was absolutely firm, and his resolve to proceed with it inflexible ; there could be no longer any reasonable doubt that he had found the strait, which was the key of the whole expedition, and which at this moment was turning in the

[1] It seems safer here to follow Pigafetta, who mentions two channels, rather than Herrera, who says there were three. For the only third channel must be the mouth of " Useless Bay," which they had passed on their way down the Broad Reach, and it could clearly not be the right one, as it led east, and if it had any opening at its far end must have brought them back into the Atlantic at some point south of the mouth of the strait.

lock. And yet he asked his officers if, in their opinion, it was wiser to leave it there and go home.

But though Magellan was confessedly, even to his contemporaries, a mysterious and withdrawn personage, it is not really difficult for us, even though we have to construct him from such shreds and fossilized fragments as remain, to understand why he did this : indeed, before this meeting was over he gave the clue himself. We must remember first of all that he had put the ships on short rations at Port St. Julian, though they had been at sea then only just six months, and the fleet was supposed to be carrying provisions which would suffice for a voyage of two years, and it is evident that he must then have known that there was nothing like two years' rations on board. But now this fact, hitherto known perhaps only to himself, was known to his officers also, and though, when he put this question to them, they all with one exception voted that they should continue the voyage, the one dissentient voice showed this. Estevão Gomez, pilot of the " Santo Antonio," spoke in favour of immediate return. Every step of their way before them now, he said, was uncharted and unknown ; a vast sea, when they were once clear of the strait, lay in front of them and, ill-supplied as they were, any further delay, through storms or calms, would end in their all dying of starvation. It was far wiser to turn back, now that the existence of the strait was proved, carry to the King the noble news of their exploit, and start again with a fresh armada. And Magellan answered him with that brevity with which he had told Cartagena to follow the flagship, that even if they had to eat the leather from the fittings of the yards he would go on. That was for Gomez alone, since all the rest were of his own mind, and then turning to the others he said that, if any of them let it be known to the men how desperate the shortage of food was, he should surely pay for it with his life.

His officers then, it is clear, knew of that, but not the crews.

Now Magellan must have guessed when he put this question to his officers what their reply was likely to be, for it was only a few days ago that the reconnoitring vessels, the " Santo Antonio " and the " Concepcion," had come back to the other two ships waiting at the entrance to the strait with their flags flying and their guns booming to announce their discovery. He had leavened the fleet with his own yeast, and it was not likely that, when every day since had added to the certainty that the strait did exist, they should have turned faint-hearted at the moment of triumph. In any case he meant to go on. But he clearly wished to be quite certain on that point ; and, had there been any considerable show of hands in favour of turning back, we must suppose that he had some plan to meet such an emergency, or he would not have asked the question. It seems possible that he would have sent one ship back to Spain with the malcontents and gone forward with the rest. This ship would, of course, have been short-rationed, but with summer coming on, with the course known, and with trade-winds favourable, it could have reached the Canaries, at any rate, with less bulk of rations than if it was to go forward with the rest : there would have been rations to spare for the remaining three. This is only conjecture, but it would have saved rations, and rid him of men whose hearts were not with him. Such a contingency did not arise, and he knew now that, with one exception, his officers were of his mind. They were aware how woefully short were the stores, but they were eager to run the risk with him, and the spectre of mutiny was quite exorcized, for in the days of starvation that were coming there was never a hint of its ill-omened presence. Whether any man has the right, by virtue of such unquestioned autocracy as Magellan now held, seriously to endanger the lives of all those under him in such a quest, is a matter of morals with which we are not concerned : it depends on the degree of risk as weighed against the chances and also the reward of success.   Magellan was playing for a huge stake— no less, he believed, than the acquisition of the islands of the Pacific by Spain ; he burned with the passion of the explorer, and success meant to him personally, and to his heirs after him, wealth and honour incalculable. He believed (or he would not have persisted) that he could carry the thing through, he would share in every privation which he inflicted on others, and he now knew that his officers backed him up.

Now this meeting is unrecorded by Pigafetta ; but Pigafetta, as we have already seen, did not much concern himself with such matters ; moreover, he was not an officer, and probably all he knew about it was that Magellan held a meeting, and immediately afterwards the fleet split up and set sail again.   A similar inter- rogation was put to the Captain and officers of the " Victoria " on November 21st, a week before the three ships that then alone remained emerged from the strait into the Pacific, but it is clear that there was as well this earlier meeting, as recounted by Herrera, before Magellan sent the " Santo Antonio " and the " Concepcion " to explore the channel leading south from the Broad Reach, and this he did as soon as the fleet arrived at Cape Valentyn, within a few days of his entering the strait. The reason why this is certain is that Estevão Gomez spoke at this meeting, and that immediately afterwards he piloted the " Santo Antonio " down the south channel, and never rejoined the fleet.   This meeting therefore must have taken place before the exploration of the south channel, for by November 21st, as we shall see, the " Santo Antonio " was well on the way back to Spain.

Next day the fleet split up again, and while the flag-ship and the " Victoria " explored the south-west channel, the " Santo Antonio " and the " Concepcion " went south. Where the rendezvous was to be, and when, is not explicitly stated, but from the fact that Magellan waited for these two to rejoin him at his anchorage in the south-west channel, and then turned back to look for them since nothing had been seen of them for five days, we may infer that they had been bidden to follow the southern channel for not more than two days, and then, whatever the result of their explora-tion, to turn and follow him up the south-west, where he would be waiting for them. This should give them ample time for determining whether the southern channel turned west and led into the Pacific ; for, as Pigafetta records, there was light now with the approach of the southern midsummer for twenty-one hours out of the twenty-four, so that the nightly halts could be of the shortest. It appears, indeed, a little later, that the ships were on the move continuously, for every hour was precious in which progress could be made, and mid-night itself was no more than a dusk.

The channel that Magellan followed after leaving Cape Valentyn lay south-south-west : at its narrowest it was ten miles across ; and for forty miles it lay straight before him. Then due south in front appeared a broken coast-line, with various small inlets, any of which might conceivably prove to afford a channel into the Pacific. But before reaching that there was a Cape to starboard, and when that was cleared the main channel was seen to turn sharply and run west by north. That was the desired direction ; for, though Magellan was ready to go further south yet to find the outlet into the new ocean, this seemed far the most promising route. He there-fore turned up this westerly channel, passing Cape Froward, and straight as a ruled line before him went on the broad water.   And now Pigafetta was in paradise again, for new wonders of nature poured in upon his thirsty eyes.   Instead of the starved and sombre shores between which they had passed in the earlier part of this penetration of the strait a fertile and wooded landscape spread itself.   Every half-league there was good anchorage with abundant water, and round the springs grew crops of celery ; the celery alone formed an admirable addition to their rations.   There was fragrant cedar-wood to burn, and shoals of sardines in the sea, and there were other fish as well, "amusing fish," Dorades, Albacores and Bonitos, which hunted a species that flew in the air when pursued : these the Spaniards called " swallow-fish," for their flights were like those of birds. But the clever Bonitos followed their shadows when they took to the air, knowing that they must needs take to the water again when their wings grew dry and would sustain them no more, and so they got gobbled up, which was " a thing marvellous and agreeable to see." . . . In fact, says Pigafetta, vastly content, " I think there is not in the world a more beautiful country or a better strait than this one." . . . He then adds as a sort of appendix to his treatise on giants a list of ninety-one words, almost all French, but with a few Italian words, and their equivalent in the language of the giants. These were given him by the giant who, he now tells us, was on the ship and who was infinitely intelligent.   If he wanted bread he said " capoc," if he wanted water he said " oli," and when he saw Pigafetta write these words down he understood what he was doing, and thus this large vocabulary was compiled.   It does not resemble that of any other known language, but for our further guidance Pigafetta tells us that all these words are " pronounced in the throat " because that is the way the giants pronounce them.   One day Pigafetta made a Cross and kissed it, and this remarkable man understood that worship was intended and said " Setebos," which was the name of the chief **Patagonian** devil.   He warned **Pigafetta** that if he made another Cross it (Setebos) would enter into his stomach and cause death.   Some sort of theological discussion must have followed, for when subsequently the giant was unwell he kissed the Cross too, and expressed a desire to become a Christian before he died.   He received the name of Paul.

So the " Victoria " and the flagship with happy Pigafetta on board went up this incomparable strait for a distance of some thirty miles from Cape Froward, and anchored at the mouth of a small river on its northern side, which for the most simple of reasons they called River Sardine.   Here Magellan waited for four days in order that the " Santo Antonio " and the " Concepcion " should join him after their exploration of the southern channel.   But in accordance with his procedure at St. Julian when a halt was necessary, he utilized it by sending boats provisioned for three days to scout on ahead.   Straight in front and close at hand was an island in mid-channel, but there was no longer any possible fear that there was a landlocked water beyond, for the flood-tide poured in strongly from the west, and it must come from the ocean which now could not be far off.   Direct as a canal, when the boats had passed this island, the deep water led on still, narrow but unimpeded.   By this time of the year, within a month of midsummer, there was no night at all, only a twilight that soon brightened again into dawn, and the boats could be sailed or rowed in relays from noon to noon. And then the narrow water broadened out into a bay, and on each side the shores retreated ; this bay ever widened, and they went on till land on the south was far away, and they could see a Cape standing out into the limitless expanse of the great ocean.   The strait was finished, the great unknown sea open to them ; and, with this now absolutely established by the evidence of their eyes, they turned and went back to the ships at River Sardine, and reported to the Captain-General what they had seen. At that the grim iron of him melted, and his eyes rained with tears, for the desire of his heart had been granted him, and he said that the Cape should be known as the Cape of Desire.

But the two ships that had gone south were still missing ; for four days the flagship had anchored, waiting for their return, and on the fifth Magellan weighed anchor again, and went back to look for them. Presently they sighted a sail ; and, since there could be no sails on these waters except those of his fleet, all no doubt was well, and they would soon be out and away beyond the Cape of Desire. This was the " Concepcion," but she knew no more than the flagship what had happened to the " Santo Antonio." The two of them, so Serrano now reported, had gone south according to the Captain-General's orders, and it had been settled between them that, if any promising channel opened out to port of their ships, Mesquita on the " Santo Antonio " was to explore it : but she was the speedier of the two, and he had lost sight of her at once. This south channel had soon bifurcated, and Serrano had sailed straight on according to plan, leaving on his port a broad and open water, trending eastwards, and now known as Admiralty Sound. Thereafter he had not seen the " Santo Antonio " again, and so in obedience to his General's order he had turned and followed up the western passage, where he was to rejoin the flagship. The " Santo Antonio," he thought, must have gone up the more easterly channel, and so Magellan on the " Trinidad " went and searched Admiralty Sound up to its head, in case she had been wrecked or met with some disablement, but there was no sign of her : the " Santo Antonio " was neither ashore nor afloat there. But in case, by some misunderstanding of the rendezvous he had appointed, she had sailed back up the Broad Reach he sent the " Victoria " to look for her.   But the Broad Reach was as empty of her as Admiralty Sound, and, in order to make a thorough job of this search, once more the " Victoria " threaded the narrows and passed out into the bay at the entrance of the strait eastwards.   Then at length she turned, without sight of the " Santo Antonio " ; but it was still possible that she had put into one of the numerous little bays to make good some damage she might have suffered, and so Captain Duarte Barbosa put up two signs on conspicuous hills, one at the northern entrance of the Broad Reach, the other at the parting of the ways into the southern and the western channels by Cape Valentyn, and placed at the foot of each an earthen pot containing an instruction to the missing ship that the fleet had passed up the western channel and was waiting for her.

Before the " Victoria " rejoined the fleet, the fruitless search of Admiralty Sound had been completed, and the flagship and the " Concepcion " were again waiting, after the lapse of precious days, at the mouth of River Sardine.   But before she came in sight Magellan must have been prepared for the unwelcome news she was bringing.   The " Santo Antonio " had been an unlucky ship from the very first : his partner, Faleiro, had been appointed originally to command her, and he had gone crazy ; then Juan de Cartagena, made Captain in his stead, had been deposed from his command before they had sighted the American coast for repeated insubordination ; Antonio de Coca had succeeded him, and had done no better ; and Magellan had appointed his cousin, Alvaro de Mesquita, in his place.   Then there had followed the mutiny at Port St. Julian, when Quesada had seized the ill-fated ship and made Mesquita prisoner ; then at Cape Valentyn, where the meeting of Captains and officers was held, Estevão Gomez, pilot of the " Santo Antonio," had voted for the abandonment of the expedition and an immediate return to Spain, and now the ship had vanished.   Magellan called his astrologer, Andres de San Martin, and bade him consult the stars, and the answer was that Mesquita was for the second time a prisoner on his own ship, and that the " Santo Antonio " was already out on the Atlantic, sailing back to Spain, but that the Emperor " would do them an injury."

Such was San Martin's interpretation of the stars, as Magellan waited for the " Victoria " to return, and indeed Faleiro himself could not have read the signs in the House of Saturn more accurately, as those who accomplished the voyage and came back home to Spain were to learn, when they reached Seville again.   For ever since the mutiny there had been many malcontents on board the " Santo Antonio."   Captain Mesquita, who seems to have been a bad appointment from the first, as he was also certainly an unpopular one, being a Portuguese, had no real hold over his men, while Estevão Gomez, a skilful pilot and navigator, was no less skilful in the arts of conspiracy, and had always been jealous of the Captain-General.   He must have been at work with his evil leaven before that meeting was held to take the opinions of the Captains as to whether the voyage should be persevered with or abandoned ; his vote that the fleet should turn homewards had found no backers, but the crew of the " Santo Antonio," he knew, were ready to rise against their inefficient Captain, and, like himself, eager to take the first opportunity to desert, though after the affair at Port St. Julian they had no stomach for another open mutiny.   But such an opportunity as they were ready to take immediately presented itself, for the next day the " Santo Antonio " and the " Concepcion " were despatched on their exploration of the southern channel, while Magellan and the "Victoria" sailed westwards. The "Santo Antonio" at once outsailed the other, and turned eastwards up Admiralty Sound as had been agreed with Serrano, and all was now easy. As soon as she was out of sight of her consort, Gomez gave the word, Mesquita was arrested and for the second time made prisoner on his own ship, and Geronimo Guerra appointed in his place. The ship was put about, and before Serrano had turned to rejoin her [1] she was being piloted up the Broad Reach by Gomez. Serrano hung about waiting for her, but, with such a start, she must have been clear of the strait and out in the Atlantic before the "Victoria" passed through the narrows and into the outer bay in search of her. Whether she called at Port St. Julian or not in an attempt to rescue the two mutineers who had been marooned there is uncertain; if she did, it is unlikely that she found them, for the balance of probability is against Cartagena having ever returned to Spain. The "Santo Antonio," however, reached Seville in May, 1521, but it does not concern us to enter into the embroilments and investigations that followed.

The news, then, that Captain Barbosa of the "Victoria" brought to Magellan at River Sardine confirmed, as far as it went, the readings of the stars by his astrologer. The "Victoria" had searched the strait back to its mouth without finding any trace of the missing ship, and unless she had been wrecked, and all on board had perished, it might be presumed she was nowhere in the strait. Considering that Gomez had lately spoken in favour of abandoning the expedition altogether, it was likely that San Martin had interpreted the stars correctly. She had disappeared anyhow, and this was a very serious

---

[1] Another account says that the "Santo Antonio" slipped by the "Concepcion" under cover of darkness. But this is scarcely possible, since at this time of the year there was no night at all.

matter, for the " Santo Antonio " was the largest ship of the squadron, and carried more of the stores than any of the rest, and thus the shortage of food, already grave, had become far graver.   The officers of the " Victoria " took a very gloomy view of the situation, and this reached Magellan's ears, for now on November 21st, after she had joined him again, he addressed an order of the day to Duarte Barbosa and his officers, bidding them once more to give their opinion, this time in writing, as to their continuing the voyage or turning back.   In this strange document, which fell into the hands of the Portuguese on the Spice Islands and has been preserved, Magellan states that he was still personally determined to go on, but that he was aware that since his handling of the mutiny at Port St. Julian, the death of Mendoza and Quesada, and the marooning of Cartagena and the priest Reina, his officers had been afraid of speaking frankly to him in matters concerning the fleet.   This should not be ; it was not in accordance with their loyal service to the King and with the oath they had made to himself, and now he commanded them (as speaking for the King) and charged them for himself to declare fully their reasons for and against going on, " not having respect to anything for which they should omit to tell the truth."   He in turn would state his views and announce his decision.

Now this order asking for the opinion of his officers in the " Victoria " was considered by Barros, who gives it in full, to have been only made in order to please them and make them feel that they had been consulted.   But Magellan's adjuration of them to open their minds frankly to him without fear, in accordance with their oaths of obedience to him and of loyal service to the King, is far too solemn to admit of such an interpretation : there is an earnestness about it which proves the sincerity of his desire to know what they really thought.

Perhaps during the "Victoria's" absence in search of the "Santo Antonio" he had consulted Serrano, but whether he had or not the document reads as if he now felt the crushing burden of his responsibility, and demanded that it should be shared by others ; as if, too, he was experiencing the terrible secret loneliness of men who are formidable, in whom no one will lightly confide, because they fear them. He had asked, it is true, for their opinion not many days ago, and with the exception of Gomez they had all supported him then, but now matters were far more critical : precious days had been wasted, and the "Santo Antonio" had carried off far more than her due proportion of the stores which were already scanty. But, sincere though his appeal undoubtedly was, he was formidable still : he scolds them for not being more open with him, he is infinitely grim even while he asks for their confidence. Whether he got their confidence, whether they did open their hearts to him, is unknown, for none of the replies for which he asked are recorded. But evidently Magellan again consulted his astrologer, who was on the "Trinidad," and whose reply therefore was not among those of the officers of the "Victoria," and San Martin, rather in the manner of the Delphic oracle, was not very helpful. He said it was doubtful whether there was any open channel ahead (though that had already been proved by the boats Magellan had sent on from River Sardine), but he advised an advance up till the middle of January while summer and long daylight lasted. What would be the advantage of going on for seven weeks more and then turning back, San Martin seems not to have explained ; perhaps he supposed that seven weeks would see them in the Spice Islands. But the officers of the "Victoria" duly sent in their replies, and Magellan gave them his answer, and his reason in full for deciding to continue the voyage, swearing by the habit of St. James, of whose

Order he was a Knight, that this appeared to him " to be for the good of the fleet." Anchors were weighed on November 22nd, 1520, and the ships left the harbourage to finish the traverse of the strait.

The remaining section had already been explored, for when first anchoring at the mouth of River Sardine, before the desertion of the " Santo Antonio " was known, Magellan had sent forward boats, which, as we have seen, had followed up the channel he now pursued, till the crew saw the open ocean and the Cape already named the Cape of Desire : we may gather therefore that the pronouncement of his astrologer had not much disturbed him. The sight he got now, traversing the final reaches of the strait, of the many inlets and channels opening to the south, combined with the report brought him by Serrano of his exploration in the south channel, convinced Magellan that there was no great continent here, stretching to the Pole, but a group of islands. But this Terra Australis Incognita, conjectured but never seen (since it did not exist), continued to be marked as such in charts, and positive proof that Magellan's surmise was correct was not arrived at till the second traverse of the strait was made in 1578 by Francis Drake. He, on emerging from the strait into the Pacific following Magellan's route, was carried far to the south by a storm that lasted for a fortnight, and undoubtedly discovered Cape Horn, for he saw the Atlantic and Pacific meeting " in a wide scope." Magellan was thus perfectly right in the conjecture he had always held that the South American continent would be found to end, like Africa, in a cape, beyond which there was open sea : he had been prepared, so he had affirmed, if he found no strait, to go further south yet, until he established that. But now having proved the existence of the strait, he spent no further time in exploration there, for the route into the Pacific which he had set out to find was proved, and the strait **was** passed.   Not an hour could he spend in any such detour, for he carried with him on board a danger of the deadliest, that phantom of famine which would daily grow more terrible.   Of mutiny there was no longer the slightest fear : that demon was indeed exorcized, for when once it had been agreed that the fleet should put out from **the** strait on its adventure westwards there can only have been one desire in officers and crews alike, namely to work with all singleness of purpose for the speedy accomplishment of the quest.   There was no turning back now, and the only hope of salvation lay in swift progress ahead.

CHAPTER XI

THE PHILIPPINES

N November 28th, 1520, the flagship, the "Victoria" and the "Concepcion," the three ships that now remained out of the five that had set forth from Seville, passed the Cape of Desire, and north and south and west stretched the illimitable sea. Unlike Drake, who on his emergence from the strait encountered a series of the most violent tempests, Magellan put out on to an ocean of calm waters and favouring winds, and for the next three months the Mare Pacifico justified his christening of it. The Spice Islands for which he was bound, where, with a hope that was already vain, he expected, " coming by way of Spain," to meet his friend Francisco Serrano, whom he had bidden to wait for him there, lay infinitely remote towards the north-west, though now in the same vast sea that his ships were traversing, but for three weeks from leaving the strait he headed due north, keeping within fifty miles of the coast. This was not the direct course, and time, he knew, with provisions so short, was at deadly war with him, but thus he advanced more rapidly into warmer weather, and the pinch of cold was relaxed. Then in the middle of December he changed his course to the north-west, heading, so he calculated, directly for the Spice Islands. Oddly enough, it was not till now that Pigafetta recorded the appearance

of the Southern Cross, but hitherto there had been so much doing both on land and in the sea—what with giants and Bonitos—that he had had no leisure ; he now also records that in the southern hemisphere the compass was less steadfast to the north, and allowances had to be made for this in navigation.

The fleet, already woefully short of food when it left the strait, had not been long at sea before the spectre of famine and of want of water began to take shape, and in the three and a half months that followed it assumed a monstrous aspect. Soon they had nothing left but biscuit that had crumbled into powder ; it crawled with weevils and was foul from the excrement of the rats that had nibbled it. The water had gone bad : it was yellow and stinking, and even that, as if it was the crystal water of life, must be measured out by the ounce. Chips of wood and sawdust were devoured, the very rats that had ruined the biscuits were eagerly sought for, and a man would willingly pay a half-ducat for one, and think himself fortunate to get it, for rats had grown scarce. And now Magellan's oath which he swore to Estevão Gomez that he would go on with the expedition even if he must eat the leather from the yards of the ship found accomplishment, for, says Pigafetta, ' We also ate the oxhides which were nailed under the main-yard, so that the yard should not scrape the rigging : they were very hard on account of the sun, rain and wind, and we left them for four or five days in the sea, and then we put them a little on the embers and so ate them." Scurvy broke out, and caused such swelling of the gums that the sufferers could not eat at all, and they had boils and ulcerations on their arms and legs. There were nineteen deaths on this section of the voyage from these disorders, among the victims was that gentle, intellectual giant called Paul, and very few remained healthy. In one thing only did luck remain with them, for the winds continued to blow favourably, so that they made fifty or sixty leagues a day, by the reckoning of the log at the stern.   Twice only during these weeks of drought and famine did they sight islands, where they hoped that fresh supplies of food and water could be obtained, but on landing that hope in both cases bitterly perished. There were trees on the first of these islands, but neither human life nor water, which now was their greatest need, nor anything of the nature of fruits.   The second island was as barren and, though the two were a couple of hundred leagues apart, they dubbed them both the " Unfortunate Islands " ;   the sea, too, was as inhospitable, for it had no life in its waters except sharks. " Indeed," says Pigafetta, " if Our Lord and His Mother had not aided us, in giving us good weather to refresh ourselves with provisions and other things, we should all have died of hunger in this very vast sea, and I think that never man will undertake to perform such a voyage."

But this admirable diarist continued cheerful and interested in whatever there was to be seen, though stars and compasses had to supply entertainment in this interminable voyaging over barren waters, and he thanks God that his health remained excellent.   He studied navigation, for that was interesting too, and made notes for his treatise.   Then at length, after having crossed the line, and still sailing west-north-west, there rose from the sea, to eyes weary with watching and dimmed with despair, the shapes of three islands ; the first land, with the exception of those two inhospitable rocks, that they had seen since the coasts of South America faded in their wake.

These islands, beacons of salvation to the starving crews, were doubtless of the same group as those which first broke the void of the Pacific to Drake and his sailors on the " Golden Hind " when in 1579 he crossed the Pacific from the coast of California. The coincidence, so far from being remarkable, is exactly what might have been expected, for both Magellan and Drake were steering for the Spice Islands, the one from the coast of South America, the other from that of North America, and it was perfectly natural that within so comparatively short a distance of their goal their routes should join here or hereabouts. Drake had been sixty-eight days out of sight of land, Magellan ninety-eight, but Magellan had come from far south of the line into the northern hemisphere, and had also first coasted northwards before striking directly across the Pacific ; making allowance for this, their respective rates of sailing were not very dissimilar.

These islands, at which Magellan arrived on March 7th, 1521, were the Ladrones, and "one Island," says Pigafetta, "was larger and higher than the other two. The Captain-General wished to touch at the largest of these three islands." . . . There is some confusion here, for the most northerly, Rota, has a considerable peak, whereas Guam, lying further south, is the largest. Alvo, however, in his log-book records that they turned south-west on approaching them, and left one island to the north-west : it seems most likely therefore that they landed at Guam. Their reception in any case was not encouraging, for while they were lowering sail in order to anchor and go ashore, the islanders swarmed about them in their canoes and sailing-vessels and " with much address and diligence " stole the skiff that was towed behind the " Trinidad." This enraged Magellan, and with quite unwarrantable savagery he landed forty armed men, burned forty or fifty of the houses on the island, as well as some of their boats, killed seven men and recovered the skiff. This was mere slaughter, for the natives had no weapons except stones and sticks, and were even unacquainted with bows and arrows, for if a man was wounded he drew out the arrow in astonishment at having been struck by something that came from a distance.

Pigafetta went ashore with the troops, and he records that the sick who were left on the ships begged them to bring back the entrails of any islanders who were killed, for they believed that these would cure them. Whether this gruesome prescription was tested he does not tell us ; in any case it failed to cure Master Andrew of Bristol, chief gunner on the " Trinidad," the only Englishman aboard, who died before they left the island. But while the fighting went on Pigafetta was busy with his notebook : there seemed to be no chief among the islanders, and they had hitherto believed that there were no other men in the world except themselves : signs conveyed this curious information. The men went naked except for small hats, and they were tall and well-made : the women were " beautiful and delicate " with black hair reaching to the ground, and they were fairer than the men, for they never left their houses where all day they made cloth out of palm-leaves and plaited baskets. The boats, which they handled with such dexterity, were pointed at the stern as well as the bows, and they had sails, made of palm-leaves sewn together, and of the shape of lateen-sails. Magellan therefore inserted these islands in his chart as the Isles of the Lateen Sails, but the thievish habits of the natives earned them the more usual name by which they are still known, the Ladrones, or Isles of Thieves. After this one encounter the shore party replenished the larders with the fresh vegetables they so sorely needed, sweet potatoes and bananas, a store of flying-fish and some pigs, and the ships made ready for sea again. These ill-behaved islanders gave them a send-off similar to their reception, for a hundred of their boats followed them offering them more fish and then throwing stones at them. So nimble were they with their craft that they passed between the sterns of the ships and the boats that were towed behind them : it was a wonder to see them. There were women among them, Pigafetta tells us (though immediately afterwards he says that the women never left their homes), who " wailed and tore their hair " and this was " certainly for love of those whom we had killed." . . Chaplain Fletcher, on whose notes the account of Drake's voyage is based in *The World Encompassed*, must be suspect of plagiarizing from Pigafetta in his narrative : he even claims that it was on this English voyage that these islands were christened the Isles of Thieves, though Pigafetta expressly says in his diary, which we know that Drake had with him, that they had been so named by the Spaniards sixty years before.[1]

The fleet had stayed for three days at the Isles of Thieves, and, with the wind still favourable, a voyage of seven days brought them at dawn on March 16th, 1521, within sight of an island to the west. Whether Magellan thought that this was one of the Spice Islands has been disputed. He knew he had crossed the line, and that the Spice Islands (some of them, at any rate) lay south of the Equator, and it has been argued from a passage in the narrative of the Genoese pilot that he was aware that this was not one of them. This passage runs as follows :

" They ran on until they reached the line, when Fernan de Magellan said that they were now in the neighbourhood of Maluco : as he had information that there were no provisions at Maluco, he said he would go in a northerly direction as far as ten or twelve degrees."[2]

[1] For further comparisons between Pigafetta's journal and Fletcher's narration see p. 249.

[2] *The First Voyage Round the World, by Magellan* (Hakluyt Society), p. 9.

This seems explicit, but there are other points to be considered before we can accept it.   In the first place how could he know that he would meet with any islands at all on the new course ?   These were unknown seas, his crews were already decimated by disease and starvation, and if (as the Genoese pilot affirms) he knew he was near the Moluccas it seems unthinkable that he should not have headed there, instead of taking a course which, as far as he knew, was as barren as the Pacific plain he had traversed.   Mr. Guillemard suggests[1] that he was making for the coasts of China, but in the dire straits to which illness and starvation had reduced his crews he must surely have been making for the nearest inhabited land.   In the second place, how had Magellan got the information that there were no provisions at the Spice Islands ?   He had now been eighteen months at sea, without any communication with the outside world, and he must therefore have got such information before he started.   Mr. Guillemard states that it came out of the letters of Francisco Serrano,[1] but Serrano, on the contrary, had written to him that " he had found yet another new world richer than that found by Vasco da Gama."   In the third place, King Charles had given him orders to go straight and before all else to the Spice Islands,[2] and we cannot believe that with that imperative instruction he sailed intentionally wide of them on the chance of finding other islands or the Chinese coast.   Moreover, Alvo's log-book shows that Magellan was almost incredibly wide of his correct reckoning when they did arrive at these islands.   All these considerations, taken together, give strong reasons for believing that, in spite of the narrative of the Genoese pilot, Magellan thought that the island sighted on March 16th was one of the Spice Islands for which he was making.

[1] *The Life of Ferdinand Magellan* (F. H. H. Guillemard), p. 222.
[2] See p. 83.

Next day he was off the southern cape of this island, which in his intercourse with the natives that presently followed he learned to be Zamal, now known as Samar. Hard by to the south was a small uninhabited island, called Humunu, on which he landed and found a good supply of water. Here, in order to avoid any possible collision with hostile islanders, he moved his sick for a few days' recuperation while he watered the fleet, setting up a couple of tents for them ashore, and killing for their refreshment one of the pigs he had brought from the Isles of Thieves. But his ships had been observed, and next day after dinner there was seen approaching a boat with nine natives from the neighbouring island of Suluan. While their friendliness was still in doubt, Magellan was resolved that no provocation should be given them, and gave the order that no one should speak or move till he had met them. But no such precaution was necessary : the head-man advanced with gestures of joy at their appearance, and friendly relations were at once established. Magellan, "seeing they were reasonable," gave them food and drink, and presented them with bright and agreeable objects such as red caps and looking-glasses and bells, but they had come unprovided with a suitable return for such pleasant gifts. What they had, they gave, fish and palm-wine and bananas, large and small, and two coco-nuts ; they intimated by signs that they would return, and bring worthier gifts with them. It was clear by now that these were not the Spice Islands, and, since it was the day of St. Lazarus when he first sighted them, he subsequently called the group the Archipelago of St. Lazarus, and the Philippines were thus added to the maps of the world.

The attainment of one of the main objects of the voyage, namely the discovery and acquisition of new islands in the Pacific, was now actually being realized.

The discovery and traverse of the strait, by which
Magellan's name was to attain a supreme place among
the explorers of the world, and the ninety-eight days of
starved and barren voyaging across the Pacific, which
ranks as high as any feat of Polar exploration for hardi-
hood and iron endurance, were, from the practical point
of view, only heroisms of the route which should lead
to this guerdon of discovery, of which the crown, it was
still hoped, was the demonstration that the Spice Islands,
with their fabulous wealth now pouring into the exchequer
of Portugal, belonged by right of Papal disposition to
Spain.   That diadem was not grasped yet, nor indeed,
if Magellan had ever laid his hand on it, would its possession have proved to rest on a solid title, but already
the contracts set forth in the Capitulation made by King
Charles with Magellan and Co. were coming into force.
For it was therein stipulated that if more than six islands
were discovered in the Pacific, lying within the Spanish
sphere of dominion, one-fifteenth part of the revenues
derived from the profits of trading with two of them
should pass into the pockets of the firm, and that (among
other benefits) Magellan and Faleiro should receive the
title of Governor of all such islands that they discovered,
the said titles being hereditary and passing to their heirs.
Whether Faleiro had forfeited his partnership when,
by reason of his mental unfitness, King Charles had pro-
hibited his sailing on this voyage, is not known, but for
Magellan at any rate those contracts were fast maturing.
Without reckoning the " Unfortunate Islands," which
were clearly worth nothing to anybody, Magellan had
already, before arriving off the Philippines, discovered
the Ladrones, about which there could be no dispute
that they lay in the Spanish sphere.   He had not got
much out of them ; vegetables and pigs were all that he
had taken away from there ; he had found no spices
there, the inhabitants were savage barbarians and he

had made no trading contract with them.   Possibly he considered them as worthless as the Unfortunate Islands, but, in order to estimate how far the Capitulation he had entered into with the King was passing into the concrete, it would certainly seem as if they must be reckoned among the discovered islands, and that, though the revenues derived therefrom seemed likely to be derisory, he had earned the title of Governor, and that such title would pass when he was dead to his son, Rodrigo, whom he had left in Seville a child of six months old.   But now prospects were beginning to look far more substantial : he had discovered the Philippines for Spain, where the natives seemed friendly, and it was presently to appear that the spices were beginning to flow.   A situation was coming into existence, islands were multiplying, and in these thick-sown seas would swiftly multiply further, but of this situation neither Pigafetta nor the Genoese pilot makes any mention whatever. Probably they knew nothing of it, for Magellan was certainly not the man to chatter about the Capitulation, and he never lived to carry home the reckoning of his islands, and the percentages due to him.

But Pigafetta had regained his earthly paradise ; never had he much busied himself with great matters ; he had dismissed the mutiny and the desertion of the " Santo Antonio " in a few sentences ; and now the imperial significance of the discovery of the Philippines, and the approach to the ultimate goal, the faery Spice Islands, where Magellan's friend, Francisco Serrano, had gone, travelling eastwards from Malacca to the El Dorado which, it was hoped to prove, lay in the Spanish sphere ; the diminishing latitudes which lay ahead before the complete circumnavigation was accomplished—all these tremendous issues went over the head of our cheerful diarist, who had borne the rigorous privations of the voyage with unimpaired patience and health.   He was back, after that dreary desolation of the Pacific, among amusing and novel and entertaining experiences again, and with inimitable gusto he launches into an inspired panegyric on the virtues and properties of the coco-nut palm. The two nuts which the natives had brought set him scribbling again.

Whereas, he tells us, the less fortunate inhabitants of Europe must seek their bread from the wheat, their wine from the grape, their oil from the olive, this truly comprehensive tree supplies bread, wine and oil out of the exuberance of its unique richness. First comes the wine : you bore a hole at the summit of the tree deep into the heart of its trunk, and therefrom wells out a liquor like white sweet must, but with a touch of the bitter in it. With hollow canes, thick as a man's leg, you draw off this wine which oozes out from morning till night, and from night till morning again. Then this wonderful tree produces fruit as well, about as large as a man's head, the husk of which, fibrous and stringy, can be made into rope. Inside this husk is a hard shell which can be burned and made into a " useful powder," but Pigafetta omits to mention what it is useful for. Below the shell comes a white marrow, almond-flavoured, to be eaten with meat or fish ; if dried and reduced to flour you can make bread of it. Then in the middle of the marrow there is a " clear sweet water, and very cordial," which, when it has " rested a little and settled, congeals and becomes like an apple " ; it is of the " consistency of honey." But the marrow is not finished with yet : it can be allowed to rot, and then it becomes oil, thick as butter, and the cordial water within it, if exposed to the sun, becomes vinegar in the manner of white wine. Furthermore the marrow and the cordial can be pounded up together and mixed with water ; then you filter it through a cloth, and there drips out a milk like that of goats. Two of these trees give all needful nutriment for a family of ten persons, and if they are not both drained for wine continually, but take it in turns, they will live for a hundred years. . . . Admirable trees, whose bounty and novelty were fit to be celebrated by the spiritual ancestor of Pepys !

Pepys's ancestor, however, like Pepys himself, could be sometimes enticed by his very exuberance into strange inaccuracies, and immediately after this epical dissertation on the coco-nut palm he is caught in one of them. These friendly strangers from the island of Suluan, who returned as they had promised, and unfolded the lavish mysteries of the coco-nut trees, were now invited on board the " Trinidad," and to astonish them Magellan fired off some of his guns ; their astonishment was tragic, and out of terror they wished to jump into the sea. And then Pigafetta becomes quite inexplicable, for he tells us that, in order to do them greater honour, Magellan showed them his cargo of " cloves, cinnamon, pepper, ginger, nutmeg, mace and gold." But whence, so we vainly ask ourselves, could Magellan have got these treasures ? He had called at the Ladrones, and from them had come straight to this uninhabited island in the Philippines where he was nursing his sick. There could not have been an ounce of any of these desirable commodities aboard : it was to seek them and to carry them back to the ports of Spain that he was traversing the world. We must, in fact, reverse all Pigafetta's pronouns in this passage,[1] and read instead that it was the friendly strangers who showed these treasures to Magellan. Only thus can we make sense out of the narrative : they showed him these things, and then (running smoothly again) we accept that it was they who by signs conveyed to him that there was abundance of these aromatic wares in the islands to which he was going. As for gold, the

[1] *The First Voyage Round the World, by Magellan* (Hakluyt Society), p. 73.

voyagers had already discovered traces of it on this island where the convalescents were being nursed and, with the passion of explorers for suitable nomenclatures, they called it " The Watering-place of Good Signs."

For eight full days the fleet of three ships remained anchored off this hospital-island where the sick were being nursed ashore, and every day Magellan tended them, performing the duty of an officer to his invalid hands, as defined by the King of Spain in his voluminous memoranda, and he administered to them the cordial water of the coco-nut, which they found very comforting. Remarkable visitors came to pay their respects to the master of the loud bombards : there were men with such large holes in their ears that they could pass their arms through them ; others were tawny and fat with long black hair reaching to their waists, and their daggers and knives were inlaid with gold. Here, too, Pigafetta, who had been proof against so many perils and privations, nearly came to an end which would have been a sad anti-climax to his adventurous spirit, for on March 25th, the feast of the Annunciation of Our Lady, so he piously informs us, he went to the side of the ship to fish, and slipping on a spar, wet from recent rain, he fell into the sea. There was no one by who saw the accident, and he was near drowning when he found close to his left hand the sheet of the mainsail, to which he clung, shouting for help, until a boat came and picked him up. This salvation, he tells us, was in no way due to his own merits, but to " the mercy and grace of the fountain of pity," the Holy Virgin. So Pigafetta got safely on board again, and the fleet with its convalescents started that afternoon on a south-westerly course, passing four small islands, of which Pigafetta gives unidentifiable names, where no landing was made. Evidently they were not to " count " in the tale of discovery : we gather that they were uninhabited.

Now all these summer seas, and every rock that jutted from them, belonged, so Magellan believed, to the dominions of the King of Spain, and by virtue of his discovery of them to the fruits of his expedition, and there were signs already, in the spices they had seen and the gold that damascened the daggers of the islanders, that the richest reward of all, the fragrant fabled isles themselves, where Serrano was waiting for him, were drawing close. For three days more they held their course, but that night they were driven by a northerly gale past the coast of Seilani, and saw lights on an island to starboard. The wind abated, and he cast anchor by the shore of Massava in the morning. Enrique, the Christianized slave, whom he had brought with him to Portugal many years before, from the taking of Malacca in his Indian campaigns, was on board, and now Magellan knew that his own circumnavigation of the world was nearly rounding to its full circle, for Enrique could understand the lingo of the islanders who came out in a boat alongside the " Trinidad," and could render their remarks in his own Malayan tongue, which was also intelligible to them. But, in spite of this kinship of language, the islanders were afraid of venturing quite close to the great ships, and so Magellan enticingly decked out a plank with those popular red caps and other brightnesses and launched it towards them. They grabbed eagerly at them, and paddled away to the shore to show what pleasant objects had been bestowed on them. Confidence grew, and soon the King of Massava himself put out in his state canoe with its canopy of mats, and Enrique conversed reassuringly with him from the " Trinidad." He would not himself come aboard yet, but he directed some of his men to do so, and they returned to him with " all sorts of things." The King paddled off to take stock of these presentations, and then sent Magellan " a rather large bar of solid gold " and a basket full of ginger.   Magellan thanked him for these, but would not take them.   However, the situation now promised well, and he moved his ships closer inshore and anchored for the night.

Next day was Good Friday, and in the morning, advancing matters by another stage, Magellan sent friendly messages to the King by the mouth of Enrique, who could make himself perfectly well understood, with money to purchase provisions for the ships.   Pigafetta revels in recounting with full and delightful details the cordialities that followed, not omitting to confess to his diary that though it was Good Friday and a fast-day he indulged himself with meat.   Back came Enrique with the King himself, who now hesitated no longer but came on board with a few men, carrying rice and fish on china dishes.   In return Magellan gave the King a red cap, extra fine, and a smart Turkish robe, and knives and looking-glasses to the others.   Then he and the King embraced and both declared that they desired to be brothers.   They went together over the ship, and saw the wonders it contained, cloths and linen, and the ship's compass, and Magellan told him how that magic box had pointed his way through the strait and across the landless ocean for four months' voyaging, and the guns were fired and produced the usual astonishment. Then he bade one of his men put on helmet and steel cuirass, and three others stabbed at him with swords and daggers and could do him no hurt ; one man thus accoutred, said Enrique the interpreter, was a match for a hundred unarmed islanders, and the Captain-General had on board two hundred of these invulnerables.   Astonishment was piled on astonishment ; the King had no more spirit left in him at the contemplation of these marvels, and all that this master of magic wanted of him was that he should allow two of his men to go ashore and see his home and his country.

Pigafetta was deputed to be one of these : no ambassa-dorial appointment can ever have given greater satis-faction to the recipient. They went without Enrique to interpret, but Pigafetta did not fail to take his note-book, and he used it extensively during that day of marvels. The King took him by the hand and led him under a canopy erected on a boat eighty feet long, and there, surrounded by the Royal guard, they ate pigs' flesh with high ceremonial (which Pigafetta knew was a wicked thing to do on Good Friday) and drank full cups of wine, with no heel-taps, at each mouthful. One slight misunderstanding occurred, but that was quickly cleared up, for when the King seemed to threaten Piga-fetta with his closed fist he thought His Majesty intended to strike him, but he quickly perceived that this was a sign of friendship, and did likewise. Then out came his notebook, in which he wrote down what the King and others said, and created great astonishment by being able to read and reproduce their speech. It was then supper-time, and rice and pigs' flesh with sauce and gravy were eaten with the same ceremonial. After that they went to the King's palace, which was built like a hay-loft, raised on big timbers high above the ground, and accessible only by ladders. There, for half an hour, they sat cross-legged on mats, and after that a second supper was served, consisting of roast fish and ginger newly gathered, and more wine. They had hardly finished this when the King's eldest son came in, and, in order that they might eat with him, more fish and rice were brought and so they had a third supper. This was indeed a change from the soaked leather and foul biscuits of those ninety-eight days of traversing the Pacific, and was too much for Pigafetta's companion, who got tipsy. So the King thought it was time to go to bed, and retired ; the two others slept with the prince. . . . In the morning the King came back and taking

Pigafetta by the hand led him off to breakfast, but Magellan sent a boat to fetch him away. So they kissed each other's hands, and Pigafetta took the King's brother off to the " Trinidad," where he stopped to dinner.

This brother of the King of Massava was King of Caragua, and had territory also in the island of Suluan ; he had come to Massava on a hunting expedition. There were gold mines in his domains, and ingots as big as an egg were found there. The eating-vessels in his house, as in that of King Solomon, were all of gold, there were gold plaques or panels on the walls, and he was the handsomest man they saw in all these islands. This magnificent creature had thick black hair down to his shoulders, and large gold rings in his ears, and the handle of his dagger was of solid gold, and his loin-cloth was embroidered with silk, and he was scented with storax and betel-nut. His skin was tawny, he was painted all over his body, and each of his teeth had three studs of gold. Indeed Caragua and Suluan were worth counting among the islands of the King of Spain.

Next day, Sunday, was the last of March and the feast of Easter. Exactly a year ago by calendar reckoning, Magellan's fleet, then numbering five ships instead of three, had cast anchor at Port St. Julian of tragic memory. The spectre of famine already menaced them, for on that day the Captain-General had put crews and officers alike on short rations, and mutiny was imminent. Magellan had sent word that his Captains were to attend Mass on shore next day, and dine with him on the flag-ship, and none had dined with him but his cousin, Mesquita, from the " Santo Antonio," who that night had returned there to be made prisoner, and mutiny had flamed. The strait was yet to seek and few believed in its existence ; even when Magellan's faith was justified, it was still to be traversed, and, when that was accomplished and the Cape of Desire had faded eastwards, the huge plain of the Pacific, across which no ship had ever been navigated, lay between him and the islands to which now he had won his famished way. Not yet, indeed, had he come to the Spice Islands, where he still believed his friend, Francisco Serrano, was waiting for him in territory that should soon be Spain's, nor was it his destiny ever to reach them and find that Serrano had already passed to a shore infinitely more remote than the frozen ends of the world. But of his own destiny, so near now to its earthly accomplishment, and of Serrano's death he knew nothing. Up till to-day, through the winter of desperate hazards and incredible privations, God had given him the fulfilment of his inflexible will, and he was on the threshold of the complete realization of his heart's desire. It was very meet and right to give thanks in the sight of the heathen for these unfailing mercies.

Early then on that Easter morning, Magellan sent his Chaplain ashore, with Enrique as interpreter, and charged him to tell the friendly Kings that he was not coming to dine with them on shore that day, but only to hear Mass. The Kings did not know what manner of feast that might be, so they each sent a dead pig as contribution. The Chaplain made a shrine with spare sails that had been brought from the ship and of woven boughs for framework, and in it he set up, an altar. Then at Mass-time the Captain-General came ashore with fifty men all dressed in the finest of their sea-stained clothes, and they carried no arms (for this was the feast of love), except only the swords which were part of the gala-habit of Spanish gentlemen ; and as the boats neared the shore the ships fired six guns. The Kings met Magellan on his landing, and went with him to where the altar had been made ready. Before the Mass began he asperged them with rose-water, and at the offertory they, too, kissed the Cross. At the Elevation the whole artillery of the fleet saluted the miracle of grace, and the Kings knelt in adoration of the Body of the Lord, and all humbly received it.   After Mass was done, Magellan showed them a wooden Cross and the nails of the Passion and the Crown of thorns, and told the Kings this was the sign of the Emperor, and he gave it them for their profit, so that when Spanish ships sailed here again their Captains would know that they had come to a friendly and allied people.   They must now set it on the highest mountain in their country, so that all seeing it should adore it, " and if they did this, neither thunder nor lightning nor storm would do them hurt."   The Kings did reverence and promised to set up the Cross, as Magellan had bidden them.

This celebration of the Mass followed by the adoration of the Cross had then a double significance : the Cross was primarily a sacred symbol, but its erection here served also as a token of amity and alliance with Spain, and the brother of the King of Massava, as well as he, was sharer in that, for now Magellan asked him whether there were any islands that were hostile to him ; if so, he would make an expedition against them with his ships, and reduce them.   The King said there were two such islands, but this was not the time to attack them.   Magellan promised that if he returned here he would perform this service for him, as an ally of Spain equally with his brother. . . . Then after dining on the ship Magellan went ashore again with his men in their best clothes, and in company with the Kings they carried the Cross up to the top of the highest mountain in the island, and all recited the *Pater noster* and the *Ave Maria*, and worshipped.   It could be seen from everywhere in the island and from the sea, a sign of Divine protection and of alliance with the King of Spain. Massava was formally claimed as one of the new lands which Magellan had come to seek.

It seems rather like Pigafetta that, while conversing after this ceremony, he inquired of the Kings which were the best ports to visit for victuals. Three places were recommended : Ceylon in Seilani (now the island of Leyte), Sebu and the district of Caragua. Magellan had now been four days at Massava, and he was wanting to add other islands to the tale of Spanish dominions. He asked the Kings if they could give him a pilot to Sebu (" for there," says Pigafetta, " his ill-luck led him ") and he promised to leave one of his men on Massava as hostage for the safety of the pilot. This is a most important indication, not yet noticed, as to what Magellan's future plans were. It is clear from it that he meant to visit the most important of the Philippine group, which would then, by virtue of discovery, belong to Spain, to make friendly alliances there as he had done at Massava and then return here. The King of Massava said he would himself pilot him in his own ship, from which we gather that a very complete confidence had been established, but he begged Magellan to wait for a couple of days more, while he got in his rice-harvest, and that would be more quickly accomplished if Magellan would lend him sailors to work in the fields. The Captain-General agreed to this, and, though the rice-harvest took three days instead of two to gather, everyone was ready on Thursday morning. Pigafetta was busy again with his notes, recording that the men of Massava were gentle and naked and great drinkers ; that the women had hair reaching to the ground and gold rings in their ears. Everyone chewed areca-nut all day, which made their mouths very red, and led to copious spittings. The climate was so hot that they would not have been able to live without this refreshing habit.

With the King conducting them, the fleet sailed from Massava northwards, and without calling at Leyte touched at an unidentified island called Satighan or

Gatighan.   It was probably a mere rock, and without
inhabitants, for Pigafetta only noted beasts and birds.
There were tortoises and parrots and black birds like
hens, which laid eggs as large as those of a goose ; they
buried these a good arm's length in the sand, and left
the heat of the sun to do the hatching.   And there were
bats as big as eagles ; they killed one of these only,
because it was late when they landed, but they cooked
it, and found that it tasted like chicken.   From Satighan
they sailed westwards, but their pilot-King in his canoe
could not keep up with the great ships, so when they
found themselves among intricate channels they waited
for him.   He was astonished at the speed of the Spanish
vessels, and thereafter he piloted them from the
" Trinidad," till they arrived off Sebu.

They coasted down the island to the capital-town,
where they anchored, with flags flying, on the first
Sunday after Easter.   All the guns of the fleet were
fired, which produced more than the usual conster-
nation, and Magellan sent Enrique ashore, with a boy
from Massava to assist, to explain that this horrible
noise, which had frightened everybody so much, was a
signal of peace and friendship and in honour of the King
of Sebu.   This reassured them, and Enrique went on
to explain that Magellan was a Captain of the greatest
King in the world and was sailing by his command
to visit the Spice Islands.   He had made this formal
call on the King of Sebu because everybody (and especially the King of Massava who was on board) had told
him what a fine gentleman he was.   The Captain-
General had also got merchandize in his ships, which
he wished to barter in exchange for victuals. ·

Enrique, we may observe, was most tactful, and
the King of Sebu was pleased to see him, but the
mention of the greatest King in the world had little
effect, for he told Enrique that every ship which called

at his port paid dues, and he did not make any exceptions.

" Only four days ago," he said, " there came a junk from Siam, bringing gold and slaves, and it paid dues. To prove what I say, here is the Moorish trader himself, and he will tell you."

But Enrique knew that this would not do for Magellan and he was firm. He told the King that a Captain of the Emperor of Spain would pay tribute to nobody. Those guns just now had spoken of peace and friendship, but if the King did not like peace they had another music.

Then came the most dramatic moment in all Magellan's voyage, for now Portugal, pushing east by India and Malacca to the Spice Islands, came definitely face to face with Spain, which had arrived at the same rich lands of dispute by sailing away to the west. The Siamese trader, who knew the might of Portugal, intervened, and spoke for the King's ear in his own language.

" Look well, O King," he said, " what you will do, for these people are of [akin to] those who have conquered Calicut, Malacca and all greater India : if you entertain them well and treat them well, you will find yourself the better for it, and if ill, it will be so much the worse for you, as they have done at Calicut and Malacca."

East and West had met : it was as if Magellan was crossing swords with his old Admiral, Albuquerque . . . Enrique, being of Malacca, understood all that was said for the King's ear, and he interrupted, saying that the King of Spain, his master, was far more powerful by sea and land than the King of Portugal, of whom the Siamese trader spoke : he was Emperor of all Christendom, and if the King of Sebu did not treat his subjects in a friendly way he would doubtless send great hosts for his destruction. This produced its due effect, and the King said he would hold a Council and give his decision next day.

Meantime, to show a hospitable and benevolent neutrality, he provided a repast to be served to the deputation on porcelain dishes from China, and large quantities of wine. They then returned to the ship, and the pilot-king of Massava, who, after His Highness of Sebu, was the most puissant of these island monarchs, went ashore to tell his Brother what a polite and agreeable man Magellan was. . . . So, even as King Manuel had feared, Magellan had sailed the ships of Spain westwards till ultimate West had become furthest East, and the two were side by side as, on the other side of the world, were Lisbon and Castile.

The leaven of Enrique's words worked well, and Pigafetta, once on the staff of the Papal Ambassador to the King of Spain, records with acute and vivid pen the diplomacies that followed. He had faced with gusto and serene health the hardships and hazards of this unique voyage, just to see with his own eyes the " very great and awful things of the ocean," he had rapturously recorded the prodigious storms and fishes and giants which he had encountered and the astonishments of adventure, but clearly he is more at home now, and his diary becomes the writing of an expert in reporting these conferences. Next morning he went ashore with Enrique and others, and was received by the King of Sebu, who, in the interval, had consulted his advisers. The King wished to know, first of all, whether Magellan was plenipotentiary, and whether he himself was expected to pay tribute to the Emperor. He was reassured on these points : Magellan's authority was unquestioned, and all he asked on the Emperor's behalf was monopoly of trading. That satisfied him, and in token of his agreement he sent Magellan some drops of blood drawn from his right arm, and hoped that the Captain-General would return the compliment. It was also customary that presents should be exchanged, and he was assured that

Magellan would meet his wishes. But it was for the King to begin.

It is noticeable that throughout these preliminary negotiations Magellan never appeared in person before the King at all, and it is not fanciful to see in this correct aloofness the traces of his long years at Court. Drake in his dealings with natives always pursued the opposite course : he conducted such businesses personally, with geniality and much enjoyment. But Magellan in these matters observed the etiquettes : he represented the King of Spain in the imperial affairs of alliances with these newly discovered islands, already seen to be rich in gold and spices and promising far more yet, and he remained secluded and invisible until the proper formalities had taken place between the deputations from this side and that, after which he would be prepared to receive the Emperor's vassal. Next day, accordingly, the King of Massava came back from his visit to his Brother with the Moorish Siamese trader, bearing the salutations of the King of Sebu. He was busy himself at the moment preparing his present for Magellan, but after dinner he would send two of his nephews with other state-officials to the flagship to conclude an alliance. Magellan said they would be welcome, and again exhibited to the Moor a man dressed in armour and impervious to swords and daggers (a sight that had already so much impressed the King of Massava) and told the Moor that, if there was to be any fighting, all his men fought like that. This was very astonishing, but he must not be afraid, " for," said Magellan, " our arms are soft to our friends, and rough to our enemies ; and as a cloth wipes away the sweat from a man, so our arms destroy the enemies of our faith." . . . The Moorish trader was more intelligent than the others, and he would tell what he had seen and heard to the King of Sebu.

The interviews that followed must be given in full as
Pigafetta wrote of them, for neither omission nor comment are needed in this lucid and vivid narrative.   Often
in his pages hitherto, as in the matter of the mutiny at
Port St. Julian, we have found him omitting the most
crucial happenings : the mutiny did not really interest
him, and he wanted to get on with the voyage and see
more of the wonders of the world.   Often again he
records facts or fancies about birds and fishes which are
wholly trivial, though his intense preoccupation with
them gives a Pepysian charm to his diary.   But here
he is absorbed in matters of the highest interest, for now
the great project was being realized, islands yet unknown
were being added to the dominions of Spain in the most
picturesque of manners by the man who had sailed
through fabled straits and polar waters, through mutiny
and starvation, to reach this political arena.   Hitherto,
also, Magellan has been an influence rather than a man,
a force inhuman, inflexible and invisible, which has been
felt but not seen, as it lay coiled, like the steel mainspring of a watch which, hidden from view, causes the
wheels to revolve and the pointers to record hours never
yet marked on the dial of time.   But here Magellan
suddenly appears in his habit as he lived, for though in
every step of the voyage we have been aware of him,
the glimpses we have hitherto actually had of him have
been those of something cloaked and shadowed.   We
have deduced his inflexible will, his personal fearlessness,
and, above all, though the indications have been unmistakable, his passionate devotion to his religion.   Now
Pigafetta in this inimitable narrative, turns the full light
on him :

"After dinner, the nephew of this King, who was a
prince, with the King of Massava, the Moor, the governor
and the chief of police and eight of the principal men,
came to the ship to make peace with us.   The Captain-

General was sitting in a chair of red velvet, and near him were the principal men of the ships sitting in leather chairs, and the others on the ground on mats. Then the Captain bade the interpreter ask the above-mentioned persons if it was their custom to speak in secret or in public, and whether the prince who had come with them had power to conclude peace. The Captain spoke at length on the subject of peace, and prayed God to confirm it in heaven. Those people replied that they had never heard such words as these which the Captain had spoken to them, and they took great pleasure in hearing him. The Captain, seeing that those people listened willingly to what was said to them, and that they gave good answers, began to say a great many more good things to induce them to become Christians. After many other subjects, the Captain asked them who would succeed the King after his death. They answered that the King had no son, but several daughters, and that this prince was his nephew, and had for a wife the King's eldest daughter, and for the sake of that they called him prince. They also said that when the father and mother were old they took no further account of them, but their children commanded them. Upon which the Captain told them how God had made heaven and earth and all other things in the world, and that He had commanded that everyone should render honour and obedience to his father and mother, and that whoever did otherwise was condemned to eternal fire. The people heard these things willingly, and besought the Captain to leave them two men to teach and show them the Christian faith, and they would entertain them well with great honour. To this the Captain answered that for the moment he could not leave them any of his people, but that if they wished to be Christians his priest would baptize them, and that at another time he would bring priests and preachers to teach them the faith. They then answered that they wished first to speak to their King, and then would become Christians.

"Each of us wept for the joy which we felt at the goodwill of these people, and the Captain told them not to become Christians from fear of us, or to please us, but that if they wished to become Christians they must do it willingly, and for the love of God, for even though they should not become Christians, no displeasure would be done them, but those who became Christians would be more loved and better treated than the others. Then they all cried out with one voice, that they did not wish to become Christians from fear, nor from complaisance, but of their free will. The Captain then said that if they became Christians he would leave them the arms which the Christians use, and that his King had commanded him to do so. At last they said they did not know what more to answer to so many good and beautiful words which he spoke to them, but that they placed themselves in his hands, and that he should do with them as with his own servants. Then the Captain, with tears in his eyes, embraced them, and, taking the hand of the prince and that of the King [of Massava], said to him that by the faith he had in God, and to his master the Emperor, and by the habit of St. James which he wore, he promised them to cause them to have perpetual peace with the King of Spain, at which the prince and the others promised him the same."

It is impossible to over-estimate the political importance of this treaty now formally concluded. The two most important Kings of the Philippine group were allied to Spain, and a glance at the map reveals an even greater significance than appears on the surface. For if these islands in the Pacific, newly discovered, were Spanish, then, according to the disposition of the world as devised by Pope Alexander VI, so also were the Spice Islands, for the Spice Islands lie east of Sebu, and, *a fortiori,* must be in the Spanish sphere : Portugal had undoubtedly pushed her eastward penetration too far, and had trespassed on her neighbour's hemisphere. As a matter of fact, proved by subsequent observations, that was not the case : Magellan in his Pacific voyage had pushed too far west, and this Spanish alliance with the Philippines was trespass according to the Papal definition. The whole matter had yet to be thrashed out, and a compromise, some years later, was arrived at. But as matters stood on this Tuesday, April 9th, 1521, the Moluccas were in the Spanish sphere.

After the alliance had thus been concluded, the ceremonial compliments and presents were exchanged : large baskets of provisions were given by the prince to the Captain-General, on behalf of his uncle and father-in-law, the King of Sebu, who sent a message of regret that they were not " as fine as was fitting." Cloth and the invariable red cap, and glass vessels, much prized in these islands, and a cup of gilt glass, were given in return by Magellan to the prince, and he sent Pigafetta off again ashore to bear gifts to the King, a Turkish robe of red and violet silk, a special red cap and more glass in a silver dish. Pigafetta describes this interview with his usual gusto and glories in picturesque detail. No more vivid sketch was ever penned by a descriptive writer :

" When we came to the town we found the King of Sebu at his palace, sitting on the ground on a mat made of palm, with many people about him. He was quite naked, except that he had a cloth round his middle and a loose wrapper round his head, worked with silk by the needle. He had a very heavy chain round his neck, and two gold rings hung in his ears with precious stones. He was a small and fat man, and his face was painted with fire in different ways. He was eating on the ground on another palm-mat, and was then eating tortoise-eggs in two china dishes, and he had four vessels full of palm-wine, which he drank with a cane pipe. We made our obeisance, and presented to him what the Captain had sent him, and told him through the interpreter that it was not as a return for the present he had sent to the Captain, but for the affection which he bore him. That done, his people told him all the good words and explanations of peace and religion which he had spoken to them. The King wished to detain us to supper, but we made óur excuses and took leave of him. The prince, nephew of the king, conducted us to his house, and showed us four girls who played on four instruments, which were strange and very soft, and their manner of playing is rather musical. Afterwards he made us dance with them. These girls were naked, except from the waist to the knees, where they wore a wrap made of the palm-tree cloth, which covered their middles, and some were quite naked. There we made a repast, and then returned to the ships."

The ceremonials were finished, and these islands of the Philippines, which Magellan had discovered, were allied to Spain.

CHAPTER XII

THE DEATH OF MAGELLAN

A SAILOR on the fleet died that night, and next morning Magellan, who had not yet landed from the " Trinidad," sent Pigafetta on shore again with Enrique to ask the King for a plot where he might be buried, with permission first to consecrate the ground, and set a Cross there. The King replied that he and his people were now vassals of the Emperor of Spain, and that therefore the soil of Sebu was his also ; as for the Cross that was to be set there, he would adore it himself. Accordingly, the most honourable site in the market-place at the centre of the town was given, the ground was consecrated and, since another man died on the same day, both bodies were buried there with Christian rites. A further step had thus been taken in the Christianizing of the island.

But not yet had Magellan been seen by his blood-brother the King ; this is rather puzzling, and we may reasonably ask ourselves what was the cause of this continuance of the mystery in which he still shrouded himself. The alliance had been concluded yesterday, he was the accredited Viceroy of the Emperor of Spain, but he had not visited the King, nor had the King come on board the flagship ; was it perhaps some personal diffidence which made him still withhold his presence ? He was small of stature, he was lame ; unless a man

looked intently in those eyes, sad and stern, he would
discern nothing that should fitly represent the Majesty
for which he stood.   On some such account as this he
may, perhaps, have thought it better to remain unseen
till trade had been definitely established, and the King
had made up his mind to be received into the Christian
faith.   But a mart could be set up at once, and as soon
as the two burials were done, a quantity of merchandise
was brought from the ships, and placed in charge of the
King, till a regular store could be opened for its display
and barter.   A big shed was speedily furnished ; wooden
scales such as the islanders used were set there, similar
to those used in France, with a basin suspended from one
arm and balancing weights from the other, and in two
days all was ready, and the shop opened for business.
Gold was given by the natives in exchange for iron,
fourteen pounds of iron was assessed at fifteen ducats-
weight of gold ; other merchandise such as cloth and
beads was exchanged for provisions, no doubt at an
equally advantageous rate.   But still that watchful eye
of the Captain-General took note of everything, and he
would not allow his sailors to sell their own belongings
too cheaply for gold, for thus they would spoil the
market for the merchandise he had brought.   This
stuff, it must be remembered, was the property of the
King, and though Magellan had twenty per cent. interest,
as laid down in the Capitulation, on the profits of the
voyage, we must acquit him of personal greed, for the
cargo was not his, and it was perfectly right that he
should control the market.

Some time during this week, so eventful in itself, and
so huge in promise, the King had signified that he would
embrace Christianity, and unless we choose to interpret
with the cheapest cynicism all these evidences of
Magellan's devout sense of religion, already noticed,
and to view in the same light all that now followed, we

are bound to conclude that this Christianizing of the island was as dear to his soul and as essentially precious as any adventure and achievement. Without doubt he saw in Christianity a humanizing and a civilizing force ; it would forge a strong link between Spain and these islands, but there was far more than that. The zeal of the missionary was his, he had baptized Patagonian giants, natives of Brazil and Kings of the newly dis- covered islands had attended Mass, and this zeal of the missionary was presently to flame into the fanaticism of a miracle-worker and into the faith that, secure in its reliance on omnipotent protection, disregarded all reason- able prudence. He had braved innumerable perils and weathered hurricanes of disaster to add new dominions to the crown of his King and, having reached these, he was a voice crying in the wilderness of their heathendom, adding the isles of the Gentiles to the Kingdom of the Lord of Hosts.

The ceremony of the King's baptism had been arranged for Sunday, April 14th, and on the day before the pre- parations were made for it. In the market-place in the centre of the town where the two sailors had been given burial in consecrated ground there was erected a dais, draped with Spanish tapestries from the ships, and decorated with branches of palm ; there the King's baptism was to be performed, and an altar was erected for the Mass that should follow it. On the dais were two chairs, for Magellan and the King, one covered in crimson, the other in violet velvet, and in front of it were cushions for the officials of the island, and mats for the general congregation. The King was warned that when Magellan landed for the ceremony on Sunday there would be a salvo of artillery fired from the ship ; this must not alarm him, as it was perfectly harmless.

So on Sunday morning Magellan came ashore for the first time ; forty unarmed men marched in front of him,

of whom two were knights in armour carrying the standard
of King Charles, which had been consecrated when the
fleet sailed from Seville, and was now for the first time
displayed on this new Spanish territory.   The great
bombards of the ships roared the salute, and the King,
who was prepared for this, stood his ground, but the
people ran away in all directions.   The King and the
Captain-General then embraced, and were escorted to
the dais, and the congregation reassembled.   Magellan
then addressed an exhortation to the King, with Enrique
to interpret, " to incite him to the faith of Jesus Christ
and told him that if he wished to be a good Christian,
as he had said the day before, he must burn all the idols
of his country, and instead of them place a Cross, and
that everyone should worship it every day on their
knees, and their hands joined to heaven : and he showed
him how he ought every day to make the sign of the
Cross."   The King and all the people signified their
assent to this, and with Magellan as sponsor the King
was baptized, and his godfather gave him the name Don
Charles, after his sovereign lord, in place of his pagan
name of Humabon.

Next were baptized the King's nephew, who was called
Don Ferdinand, after the Emperor's brother, and the
King of Massava, who was named Jehan, and the Siamese
trader, who was named Christopher.   Others of the
chief men of the island followed, fifty in all, and Magellan
stood godfather for each, giving them such Christian
names as he fancied.   All the new converts then attended
Mass, and Magellan went back to the flagship.

" After dinner," continues Pigafetta, " our chaplain
and some of us went on shore to baptize the queen.   She
came with forty ladies, and we conducted them on to
the dais : then made her sit down on a cushion, and her
women around her, until the priest was ready.   During
that time they showed her an image of Our Lady, of

wood, holding her little child, which was very well made, and a Cross.   When she saw it, she had a greater desire to be a Christian, and, asking for baptism, she was baptized and named Jehanne, like the mother of the Emperor.   The wife of the prince, daughter of this Queen, had the name of Catherine, the Queen of Massava, Isabella ; and the others each had their name. . . . The Queen was young and handsome, covered with a black and white sheet ; she had the mouth and nails very red, and wore on her head a large hat made of leaves of palm, with a crown over it made of the same leaves, like that of the Pope.   After that she begged us to give her the little wooden boy to put in the place of the idols.   This we did and she went away."

A strange and romantic future awaited the image of the Christ-child now given to Queen Jehanne.   After the death of Magellan and the departure of the ships Christianity lapsed, and this image was placed among the pagan idols which had been temporarily deposed : Pigafetta describes these as monstrous-faced with four large teeth like those of a wild boar.   It was found among the heathen hierarchy by Miguel Lopez de Legaspe when he came to Sebu in 1565, and continued to be worshipped as such until, in 1598, Spanish mission-aries again discovered it.   The island was then re-converted to Christianity, and the *bambino* was restored to its original significance in the church they built in the town they now named the City of Jesus.[1]

On that Sunday eight hundred islanders were bap-tized, and during the week that followed the total number of converts was raised to over two thousand.   Magellan's seclusion of himself on board the flagship was now over, and he came ashore every day to hear Mass, and in the

[1] *The First Voyage Round the World, by Magellan* (Hakluyt Society), p. 93. *The Life of Ferdinand Magellan* (F. H. H. Guillemard), p. 242.

rôle of missioner expounded the dogmas of the Christian
faith : the Queen attended in state with a procession
of her women, and her attendants carried three of her
hats.   She bowed to the altar, Magellan asperged her
with rose-water, and bade her turn out all her idols, and
put in their stead the image of the Holy Child.   But,
though there can be no doubt about the burning sincerity
of his zeal for his religion, he also saw very clearly that
the bond of Christianity would be extremely useful as
a consolidating force to unite the whole of Sebu, in
which were certain villages more than half independent,
under the sovereignty of the Christianized King, who
was individually the most powerful of the Rajahs in the
islands.   But he must first be established securely in his immediate territory, and Magellan bade him come to Mass
one day in state, and summoned his two brothers, one
of whom was the father of Prince Ferdinand, the heir-
apparent, with others of his chief men.   After Mass they
all swore obedience to the King, and kissed his hand.
Then Magellan asked the King in his turn to swear on
the image of the Virgin that he would be the faithful
servant of the Emperor of Spain, and instructed him as
to the sacredness of such an oath, telling him that it was
far better to die than to break it.   The King duly took
the oath and Magellan bound himself by the same.
The chiefs had thus sworn obedience to their King and
to the Emperor, and Christianity was established as the
State-religion.   After the solemn ceremony presents
were again exchanged : Magellan gave the King a
velvet chair, and the King gave him gold rings for ears
and arms and ankles, all set with precious stones.   He
also promised to prepare a gift of jewels to be rendered
to the Emperor from his new vassal when the Captain-
General returned to Spain.
      Magellan was draining the intoxicating draught of
fiery success.   These new islands of the Pacific, which

he had set out to seek in the service of his Emperor, were won, the Spice Islands would soon follow. He was realizing the utmost of his perilous emprise ; he had traversed, through a welter of incredible dangers and difficulties, the fabled western passage to the Orient ; he had already proved himself, in the teeth of mutiny and famine, the greatest of all the noble adventurers on the kingdoms of the sea. God, Whom he so grimly and devotedly served, had been with him, and we, who have followed the hidden love of that silent and religious soul, outcropping here and there into quartz gleaming with the royal metal, scarcely need comment to enable us to appreciate what the miracles of grace during this last week had been to him. Daily had he heard Mass, and expounded to heathen folk the surety of the Christian faith, daily had he seen the troops of pagans pouring in to seek baptismal regeneration, and though thereby he had been serving the noble mammon of patriotism, the glory of God had been his inspiration and it was as if his piety had been blessed by some Pentecostal week of the outpouring of the Holy Spirit. Pioneer and Empire-maker he had been for Spain, and he had also been like some prophet of the older dispensation, serving his King in righteousness, but accounting that allegiance as subsidiary to that of his service to God. It was no wonder that now his faith flowered into fanaticism : he was ready, like Elijah on Carmel, to manifest the power of the Lord with mighty signs that should confound, the prophets of Baal.

The opportunity which he was eager to embrace soon came. The new converts, who had been strictly enjoined and had promised to burn their old idols, had not all obeyed : Magellan learned that some of them still worshipped these images and made offerings to them. He reprimanded them for this, and they replied that they no longer worshipped them on their own behalf,

but for the sake of a certain sick man who was not a
Christian, and was therefore under the protection of
the ancient deities.   This man was a brother of Prince
Ferdinand, and he was highly esteemed for his bravery
and wisdom : there was no one so wise in all Sebu.   But
his sickness was sore on him, for four days he had lain
unable to speak, and we may suppose that this illness
was the cause of his not having embraced the new faith
like the rest of his family.   And then Magellan showed,
if further demonstration was wanted, that his faith was
no matter of lip-service or of ritual or of imperialism,
but of firm and practical conviction in the power of God.
" He was seized," says Pigafetta, " with zeal for religion,
and said that if they had a true faith in Jesus Christ,
they should burn all the idols, and the sick man should
be baptized, and he would be immediately cured, of
which he was so certain that he consented to lose his head
if the miracle did not take place.   The King promised
that all this should be done, because he truly believed
in Jesus Christ.   Then we arranged, with all the pomp
that was possible, a procession from the place to the
house of the sick man.   We went there, and found him
unable to speak or to move.   We baptized him with
two of his wives and ten girls.   The Captain then asked
him how he felt, and he at once spoke, and said that by
the grace of Our Lord he was well enough.   This great
miracle was done under our eyes.   The Captain, on
hearing him speak, gave great thanks to God. . . . On
the fifth day the convalescent rose from his bed, and as
soon as he could walk, he had burned, in the presence
of the King and of all the people, an idol which some old
women had concealed in his house.   He also caused to
be destroyed several temples constructed on the sea-
shore, in which people were accustomed to eat the meat
offered to idols.   The inhabitants applauded this, and
shouting ' Castile, Castile,' helped to throw them down,

and declared that if God gave them life they would burn all the idols they could find, even if they were in the King's own house."

Now this miracle is described at length by Pigafetta, and also by Maximilian Transylvanus to whom it was narrated by the survivors of the voyage who returned to Spain, and it was witnessed by a considerable number of people. Whether we accept it now as being super-normal, or give some rationalistic explanation of it, assigning it to some hypnotic or mental stimulus, or whether we reject it altogether, does not matter at all ; its bearing on the story of Magellan is all that concerns us, for the islanders saw in it a direct manifestation of a power which far transcended that of the idols they had hitherto worshipped. The God Who was incarnate in the mystery of the daily Mass had by this sign given evidence of His omnipotence, and the news of it, spreading through the neighbouring villages, confirmed their loyalty to the King : it was only wise to give allegiance to one under the protection of a Captain who not only had ships with bellowing guns, but was the administrator (so the miracle must have represented itself to the native mind) of such superior magic. The old idols could do nothing for the sick man, who had been for four days in the very shadow of death, but the moment that this spell of baptism was laid on him he recovered.

The effect, then, on the native mind was immense : they routed out the idols which would be an offence to the God of healing, even as the Israelites destroyed the groves of Baal, and came flocking in not from the villages of Sebu alone, but from neighbouring islands, to be enrolled by this same rite of baptism into the faith of so great a God, as expounded by Magellan. To him the great hour of his life had come, the supreme, the ultimate triumph. Devout and fervent Christian he had always been, with a faith that never wavered, and just as his belief in the existence of the strait he had come to seek had its moment of fulfilment when he saw the Pacific open out illimitably beyond the Cape of Desire, so now the omnipotent protection of God opened out to him in visible demonstration. He had staked his life that baptism would bring instant healing to the sick man whom all else had failed to cure, and the miracle had happened. Henceforth he knew himself to be the chosen Captain in this crusade that he was waging for the glory of God, in redeeming from the darkness of heathendom these islands of the Pacific. "The people that sat in darkness had seen a great light," and he, in the hands of his Master, had brought it them.

But, under God, he served the Emperor of Spain, the head of the Catholic Church of the land of his adoption, and his temporal fealty, consonant with the spiritual, must engage his wits and his energies. It was not sufficient to present Sebu alone before the altar of God, nor were Sebu and the island of Massava the only jewels he meant to bring home to Spain to set in the crown of his King, and now, in this state of spiritual exaltation, he planned to include in these newly won dominions the other islands of the group, subjecting them to the rule of the King of Sebu, which was to be the capital and sovereign state of this Christian and Spanish confederation. Close by, across a strait only a few miles in width, lay the island of Mactan : this should be the first to be brought under the sceptre of the King. Converts had already come from there, but there was a district whose Rajah, named Silapulapu, refused to recognize the sovereignty of Sebu, and Magellan sent over one night a couple of boats with armed crews who burned one of the villages and set up a Cross there. Some ten days later, he sent again to Mactan, demanding from a neigh-

bouring village, which had given allegiance to Sebu and
to Spain, a tribute of provisions for the use of the fleet.
Instead of the full toll of three goats, three pigs, and
three loads of rice and millet which had been asked for,
there came only a couple of goats. But Zula, the chief
of this village, sent with them his son, bringing a message
to the Captain-General to say that he had not furnished
the full quota, because Silapulapu prevented him from
doing so. He suggested that, if Magellan would send
across next night a boat manned by armed Spanish
sailors to assist him, he would be able to attack and
defeat this rebellious chief.

Magellan laid this proposal before the King of Sebu
and the Captains of his two other ships, Serrano and
Barbosa. But his own determination was already made :
he was Captain-General in these wars for the glory of
God, and here was an opportunity of furthering that
and of adding another island to the diadem of Spanish
Empire. The King was opposed to making an attack
on this scale : the one boatful of armed sailors which
was all that Zula had asked for he knew was quite in-
sufficient for the purpose, for the disaffected district was
large, and they would certainly encounter a very numerous enemy. If Magellan insisted on the raid, he would
supplement his force with a squadron of his war-canoes,
and native troops to the number of one thousand men.
Serrano was against the expedition altogether, for on
the King's showing this would be no trifling raid, but
a serious affair ; instead of one boat of armed Spaniards,
at least three must be furnished with crews of twenty
men each, and if any disaster occurred the ships would
find themselves very short of hands. But Magellan
was neither to bind nor to hold : let each ship, then,
furnish a boat with an armed crew, and let the King
order out his score of war-canoes. They would start
that very night as Zula had suggested, and to-morrow

Mactan would fly the banner of Spain.   He would take
command of the expedition himself.[1]

There was no resisting that indomitable will which
had ploughed its way through mutiny and famine and
the bitter storms that came from beyond the ends of the
world.   He would not listen to Serrano, and vainly did
his Captains try to persuade him not to take part himself
in this hazardous expedition.   They would do all his
bidding, but let him remain on the " Trinidad," to
await their triumphant return.   But he, says Pigafetta,
" as a good shepherd would not abandon his flock,"
and he ordered that all should be ready for the start at
midnight.   A strange portent now happened nightly
towards that hour in Sebu, for there perched on a house-
roof in the city a black bird like a crow which till dawn
continued croaking, and set all the dogs howling.   That
was no mere native superstition, for the Spaniards had
heard it, and with that ill-omened noise which none
could explain sounding dolefully in the darkness,
Magellan, for the last time, bid his men put out to sea,
on this midnight of Friday, April 26th.

The strait between Sebu and Mactan was but a few
miles in width, and the three Spanish boats, carrying
sixty men armed in helmets and cuirasses, spearmen,
bowmen and musketeers, and twenty to thirty of the
King's war-canoes with himself, Prince Ferdinand and
a thousand men with bows and arrows arrived off the
shore of the island three hours before daylight, that is
to say about two o'clock of the morning.   Enrique, the
interpreter, and the Christianized Siamese trader were
on board the Spanish boats, and Magellan at once
landed the trader with orders to go to the camp of the
Rajah, and tell his adherents that if they would recog-

[1] There are many divergences and discrepancies between the various
accounts of this expedition to Mactan : the above adopts the line of least
resistance among them.

nize the King of Sebu as their overlord, under the sovereignty of the Emperor of Spain, and pay their tribute, it was peace ; if not, they would see how shrewdly Spanish lances bit. The answer was returned that the Rajah's men had lances too, and that though they were only made of reeds and wood the fire had hardened their points. But the Rajah begged that the Spaniards would not attack them now before daylight, for they expected reinforcements in the morning.

Now this message was palpably absurd : to ask an enemy to delay an attack until you are better equipped to meet it presupposes an amiable desire on the part of the enemy to give you every possible chance of defeating him. Pigafetta, who was with Magellan, fancied that he saw through this, and states that the Rajah's troops had certainly dug ditches between the beach and their camp, and that the Rajah hoped that Magellan, thus considerately warned that he would find a bigger force to oppose him in the morning, would attack instantly, and fall into these ambushes. This message, in fact, was a trap and ludicrously obvious, and Magellan, interpreting it as such, did not land his men until morning. But it seems far more likely that there was a trap within the trap : any commander receiving so silly a message must know it was a ruse, and, suspecting some such trenches and ambushments as Pigafetta conjectured, would laugh at so transparent a device to entice him to attack in the dark. In all probability this conjecture about the ditching of the camp was absolutely wrong, for, if we consider the circumstances, it was impossible that the rebels should have known that any expedition was intended : the boats and canoes had left Sebu at midnight, under cover of the darkness, and the arrival of the Siamese trader with his olive-branch in the Rajah's camp long before daylight must have been the first news he got that a force had landed from Sebu.

By begging Magellan not to attack till daybreak when he would have received reinforcements, and knowing that any man of sense would instantly detect that this was a patent device to induce him to attack at once, the Rajah gained time to collect more troops ; and this he instantly did.

This delay did him another service on which no doubt he had calculated. The Siamese trader had been put ashore from the boats at about two in the morning without any difficulty, for the tide was high. But before daylight it had ebbed, and when Magellan prepared at sunrise to land his troops he found that the boats could not get near the beach, for the water was now shallow and sown with rocks. His men therefore had to wade in thigh-deep to reach land, and he led them. Once again, this time by the King of Sebu, he was entreated not to risk himself ; the King begged to be allowed to land his native warriors, for with his trained men, backed by some Spaniards armed with muskets, and protected by that magical steel armour that defied the thrust of spears, he would easily return victorious. But Magellan declined the assistance of these thousand men altogether : he told the King to remain with them in their canoes and see how Spaniards fought. An armed Spaniard, invulnerable in his steel accoutrement, was, as he had already said, a match for a hundred natives. Eleven of his men he left behind in charge of the boats, and he went ashore himself with the remainder, forty-nine in number.

The Rajah's men were waiting for them as they waded through the two hundred yards of rock-sown shallows without the support of the bombards on the boats, for they were out of range. He had by his ruse secured several extra hours for preparation, and he had been reinforced before daybreak, even as he had told Magellan, and by the lowest computation he numbered fifteen hundred men, while the account of the Genoese pilot reckons them as being between three and four thousand. One Spaniard would indeed have to show himself a match for nearly a hundred foes. But Magellan was still full of tragic confidence : he told his handful of men, among whom was Pigafetta, that Spanish soldiers had often faced greater odds ; besides, this day, April 27th, was a lucky day for him, he would have chosen it out of all the days in the year. . . . As they stumbled ashore the enemy charged down on them yelling their battle-cry, attacking them simultaneously on both flanks and in front. They were met with a random firing at too long a range to do any damage : the shots might pierce their wooden shields, but they were spent. Magellan called to his men to reserve their fire till it could prove effective, but they paid no heed to him and went on wasting the ammunition of their muskets and their arrows. And now the islanders, heartened by the harmlessness of their weapons, came on more savagely, until they were within range of their own spears, and from all sides came a shower of javelins, and wooden lances hardened in the fire, and of stones and even handfuls of mud. And in the war-canoes there were watching a thousand men of the King of Sebu, whom Magellan had told to wait there as spectators to witness the invincible might of Spain and of the Cross.

It seems impossible to account for Magellan's mad mismanagement of this raid, except on the supposition that some religious ecstasy possessed him. Under the protection of God he had brought his ships through mutinies and privations, through unknown straits and uncharted oceans, he had won Sebu for his Emperor, he had brought the great light of Christianity to disperse the darkness of paganism, and by the power of his Master he had wrought a miracle, snatching from the jaws of

death a prince of the Royal House.   He must, had his
sober judgment not been in abeyance, have seen that
this raging mob of savages was pressing close on his
disheartened men, and would overwhelm and annihilate
them, but he neither called up the thousand native
troops from the canoes nor ordered a retreat.   Another
miracle—God knew what—would surely be the response
to his faith.

Then he made another disastrous mistake.   He
detailed a few of his men to set fire to the native village,
hoping to make a diversion, and thereby he weakened
the small nucleus of those who remained.   This was
absolutely unsuccessful ; some of the islanders cut off
this party which was uselessly employed in burning a
few houses, and the rest, infuriated by the sight of their
village in flames, attacked with redoubled ferocity.
They could see now that, though their lances and
wooden spears had no effect on the steel helmets and
cuirasses of the Spaniards, their legs were undefended,
and they aimed at them.   Magellan had for years been
lame in his left leg, and now a poisoned arrow pierced
the other, and at last, and too late, he saw that no miracle
was coming.   Wounded himself, he could no longer
lead his men, and he gave the order to retreat, slowly
and in order.   But all discipline had perished, and the
panic-stricken Spaniards rushed helter-skelter to the
beach.

Six or eight alone stood staunch round their wounded
Captain-General, and among them was Pigafetta.   The
bombards in the boats were too far off to be of any protection to them, but still fighting, and assailed on three
sides by lances and showers of stones, this little band,
with Magellan in the midst, gained the shore and waded
out through the shoal-water towards the boats.   They
were half-way now, up to their knees in the water, but
still the islanders pressed close, throwing their lances,

and, as the Spaniards retreated, now no longer able to resist, picking them up and discharging them again. They had made out that Magellan was their Captain, and they aimed specially at him, and twice they knocked his helmet off his head. Then, wounded and exhausted, he could go no further, and for an hour the fight went on in the shallow water. At length he was wounded in the face, and with one final effort he pierced his assailant through the breast and left his lance in his body. A javelin struck him in the right arm, and he tried to draw his sword, but his strength failed him, and he could do no more than pull it half-way from its scabbard. Another islander dealt him a great blow with a scimitar on his left leg, and now both were helpless and he fell on his face in the shallow water and they stabbed him through and through. But even as the darkness of death closed round him he kept looking round to see if his Spaniards had got safe to their boats "as though his obstinate fight had no other object than to give an opportunity for the retreat of his men." So died Magellan, who, says Pigafetta, had been "our saviour, light, comfort and true guide." Those few who had remained with him to the end, and were covered with wounds, could now help him no more, and they got back to the boats.

CHAPTER XIII

THE SPICE ISLANDS

HE actual loss of life among the Spaniards was small, though many of them, among whom was the faithful Pigafetta, were wounded. Only eight of those forty-nine who had landed on the beach of Mactan at dawn that day had been killed, for their steel helmets and cuirasses had protected them from mortal wounds. But among the dead was Magellan, and instantly the visionary palace that he had been building here in Sebu for the glory of God and in the service of the Emperor began to quake and to crumble. He had come among them liké a prophet of God, preaching the invincibility of the Cross, and demonstrating it by a miracle of healing ; but to-day the Cross had withheld its power, and its prophet, who had bidden the new converts watch to see the victories which a handful of its soldiers would speedily win over the hordes of pagans, had perished miserably at their hands. Not less tragic had been the collapse of Spanish prestige : confident in their commander a bare fifty of them had gone ashore like the little band of Gideon to destroy the hosts of the enemy, and instead of routing them with their muskets and crossbows, invulnerable in that white armour of steel which made each of them a match for a hundred men, they had been unable to advance against the wooden lances of the enemy, and when told to retreat

216

orderly had simply run away, leaving their Captain to be butchered, while they looked on safe in their boats. Hardly, indeed, would they wait for those of their comrades who had not deserted the Captain to join them, and when, after Magellan was killed and further fighting hopeless, Pigafetta and those few others waded out to the boats they were already on the point of pushing off and leaving them.

The boats containing the Spanish sailors rowed back to the ships, and the war-canoes with their thousand men who had not been permitted to fight, since the Cross must prove invincible, returned to the beach with this disquieting news. The King had wept to see Magellan fall, and that afternoon sent a boat across to Mactan to say that the Spaniards would give the islanders whatever of their merchandise they might wish for in exchange for the bodies of their Captain-General and those of their company who had fallen. But the embassy was fruitless, the islanders refused to give Magellan's body up on any terms, for they intended to keep it as a memorial of their victory.

On board the ships the first business was to choose a new Commander, and it was voted that Duarte Barbosa, now Captain of the " Victoria," and Serrano, Captain of the " Concepcion," should be made joint-holders of the post of Captain-General, equal in command. Neither of them, we must suppose, had taken part in this disastrous raid, but had remained on their ships. Serrano at once confirmed Magellan's treaty with the King of Sebu, ratifying it by fresh gifts, and though he had been against the expedition to Mactan he now proposed that they should attack it again. But it came to nothing, and it is evident that there was mutual distrust already germinating between the islanders of Sebu and the Spaniards now that Magellan was not there to inspire and to drive, and his fanatical confidence in his God, his country and himself no longer inflamed all that felt its ardour. For as soon as his death was known the Spaniards in charge of the store in the town, where so brisk a trade had been going on with the bartering of Western goods, iron and cloth and glass for gold and provisions, instantly set about removing all their merchandise to the ships : they could not trust their new allies now that the Captain-General had gone. The stuffs were taken to the boats, the shop dismantled, and the islanders watched this going on, and the mutter of misgiving grew louder. Already their belief in the might of Spain and of the God Whom the Spaniards worshipped had been sorely shaken : He had done nothing for His servants that morning, and now they were afraid to leave their merchandise ashore.

Next day provisions were needed for the ships ; the business of bartering for them had always been done by Magellan's slave, Enrique, the interpreter. But he refused to go on his job ; he had been in the fight at Mactan yesterday, receiving a slight wound, and now he wrapped himself up in his mat and lay there all day, refusing to stir. Barbosa went to him, and told him pretty stiffly that he did not cease to be a slave because his master was dead ; and that unless he made an end of this malingering and went about his business, he would order him a sound flogging. Enrique got up at that, and made obeisance, and over the ship's side he went and so to shore. He was actually now a slave no longer, for Magellan by his Will had given him his manumission, and most likely he knew that, but he obeyed as if he was a slave still, and planned a black revenge for this treatment. First he did his business in the market, and, that finished, he asked audience of the King of Sebu. That was granted, and Enrique told him that the Spaniards were intending to leave Sebu, but that, if he had a mind, he might seize their ships and all that they contained. There was an easy way to do that, and Enrique expounded it.

Now the King's faith in Magellan and in what he stood for was already tottering. True, he had worked a miracle by some very superior magic, but that success had been largely discounted by the dire failure which had followed. The Captain-General, relying on the might of God and of his Spaniards, had been butchered by the men of Mactan, his invincibles had turned tail and fled, his sailors had removed their merchandise back to the ships, and now they were preparing to steal away. Their pretended friendship had collapsed like a pricked bubble ; their arms and their faith had proved themselves powerless, and Mactan was gloating over its victory. But the Spaniards had got some splendid ships which he greatly coveted, and the ships had considerable gold on board which his people had given in exchange for the wares of the West, and those wares of the West were now on board too. These were all very desirable possessions. So, when they had talked, and Enrique had unfolded a very practicable plan for obtaining them, the slave went back to his ship, and the King sent for his chiefs. Next day and the next Enrique went about his old duties : the threat of a flogging seemed to have sharpened his wits and he was uncommonly attentive and intelligent.

Wednesday was the 1st of May, and that morning the intelligent Enrique came back from his marketing with a hospitable bidding for the two Commanders from the King, and he interpreted to them the message with the meaning of which he was quite familiar, for the idea had been his own. The jewels, he told them, which His Majesty had been getting together as a present for his lord the Emperor of Spain, were now assembled, and he wished formally to hand them over to Captains Serrano and Barbosa for conveyance to him. He therefore begged the two Captains to dine with him that day, and bring with them " some of their most honoured companions " ; after dinner the King would give these jewels into their keeping. This invitation was accepted, and in all twenty-six or perhaps twenty-nine of the ships' officers and others went ashore. Among them was the astrologer, San Martin : perhaps he had not troubled to consult the heavenly bodies, or surely they would have warned him ; and there was the priest who had lately received practically the whole of the islanders into the Christian fold. Pigafetta was not among the guests, no doubt to his great regret at the time, for a wound he had received in the forehead from a poisoned arrow at the disaster of Mactan four days ago had invalided him. But the good fortune which had attended him through-out the voyage had never looked after him better than now, and that swollen wound preserved for us our most valuable record of Magellan's voyage.

So the party landed from the ships' boats, and was welcomed and escorted to the place where the King had prepared his banquet. Among them was Juan Car-valho, now pilot of the " Concepcion," an intimate friend of Serrano, and he with one or two others, in-cluding Serrano, had been a little doubtful about the friendly intentions of the King. Now, as he stepped along to the feast, walking with Espinosa, chief police-officer on the ships, he saw the prince who had been miraculously healed when the old idols could do nothing for him detach the priest who had baptized him and take him off to his own house. That seemed an odd thing, and Carvalho's misgivings increased. He and Espinosa considered it : it was as if the prince, out of gratitude, was saving the priest from a fate that awaited the rest. Neither of them liked it, and they turned back, got into the boat, and were rowed across to the " Trinidad," and told Pigafetta why they had not gone to the King's dinner. They had scarcely spoken, when from the shore there arose a tumult of shouting and of cries. The islanders who had welcomed the unarmed officers had closed up behind them as they went to the feast, and were butchering them.

Instantly the " Trinidad " got her anchor up, and was towed in closer to the beach, and Carvalho began firing her guns at the native houses. But already the massacre was nearly done : two only out of those who had gone ashore were left, and now one of these appeared on the beach, Juan Serrano, bound and bleeding, and surrounded by natives. He shouted to Carvalho to cease firing, or else he would surely be killed also, but his captors were willing to take a ransom of merchandise from the ships and give him his life. All the others who had landed were done to death, except him and the interpreter. Enrique was uninjured, and in high honour, for he had done his work well.

The ship was close in to the beach, Serrano's appeal was heard and was understood, and he saw looking over the bulwarks the face of his friend, Carvalho, who must now be in command. They were countrymen, and they had faced a thousand perils together, they were knit in a bond of intimate friendship, and Carvalho had but to order a boat to row ashore with parcels of the Western merchandise which the islanders coveted, and Serrano would step into it and be rowed back to the safety of the ship. And then Carvalho turned away, and gave some order to the sailors on the deck. He was Captain-General now, for all his superior officers had been murdered, but if he sent this ransom for Serrano he would be his subordinate again. Serrano saw a boat manned, but it did not come ashore. It vanished behind the stern of the ship, and a rope was thrown to it, and made fast, and there came the splash of oars and the " Trinidad " began to sidle away, and her sails were hoisted. For a while Serrano continued to cry out to his friend; but his friend answered him not. Then at last he saw that the infamous, the incredible thing was happening, and that his friend was leaving him to be slaughtered like the rest. Once more he raised his voice and he prayed God that on the Day of Judgment He would ask Juan Carvalho what he had done to Serrano. Within a few minutes, the islanders, seeing that no ransom was coming, did to him as they had done to the rest, and with his dying cry in Carvalho's ears, and for his eyes the sight of the Cross in the market-place being torn down and demolished, the new Captain-General set a course southwards from Sebu.

There was never a more complete collapse of what had promised so fair, nor from the loom of destiny had there ever been woven a fabric so rich in splendour and so shot now with tragic failure and treachery. It was little more than a fortnight ago that Magellan after a voyage unique in the annals of naval enterprise had enrolled Sebu in the dominions of the Emperor of Spain, and the King had rendered himself and his people his loyal vassals. This was the first-fruits of Magellan's adventure, the earliest of the sheaves to be garnered from a harvest of incalculable wealth. He had Christianized the island, its inhabitants had flocked in to be baptized, he had set up the Cross as a symbol of the spiritual kingdom of which they were the eager citizens and had demonstrated the power of its gospel by that miracle of healing, which, whatever rationalistic explanation we may give of it, had convinced its witnesses. Then he had committed that one fatal mistake which had caused all the structure he had raised to totter and finally to fall in ruin. Trusting in the valiance of his Spaniards under divine protection, he had landed a handful of men to defeat a horde of savage islanders on Mactan, and in an hour he had lost not only his own life, on which the conduct of his voyage depended, but, in the inevitable sequel, all the fruits of his adventure. Spanish dominion over the Philippines and that which would ensue, which had promised to be as noble a jewel in the crown of Spain as the new world of America itself, had crumbled into nothingness, the Cross was stricken from its eminence, and, after an act of desertion more monstrous than the treachery of the King of Sebu, the fleet, with its officers defencelessly murdered at the feast, and its crews now reduced to half the number of those who had embarked eighteen months ago at Seville, was in empty-handed retreat. In his own burning zeal for his Christian faith, Magellan had practically guaranteed that a miracle should be done on the shore of Mactan, for he would not let those thousand native warriors be more than spectators, and it had not happened ; also in his own almost fanatical faith he had imagined that the islanders of Sebu from the King downwards, who had formed queues for baptism, had felt the living force of the creed that inspired himself. Blinded by the very clarity of his own convictions, he had believed that his religion was real to them, and that their hearts were turned from heathendom by the power of God. That was as tragic and pathetic a mistake as the other, for Christianity in those few days during which they drank of it had, as the event proved, been to them only a novel kind of idolatry, worth trying, since its apostle demonstrated its efficacy, and since, as Captain of the Emperor, he recommended it. Their own idols had shown themselves of limited potency : the sickness of their prince had been beyond them, but it had yielded at once to the spells of this Spanish hakim. So they gave the new treatment a trial : it was a prescription that seemed successful. But on the shores of Mactan that prescription had utterly failed, and the old idols had scored a signal success over the new. So they smashed up

the symbols of the new quackery and massacred its
students.

At this moment, then, the whole purpose for which
Magellan and Faleiro had worked, and for which the
expedition had sailed, had come to nothing. For the
amazing adventure which Magellan had already accomplished, the discovery of the strait, its negotiation in the
teeth of tempests and of mutiny, the famine-stricken
traverse of the Pacific, the all-but complete navigation
of the unknown seas of the world, had not been in any
way "the object of the voyage, but only the means by
which that object could be attained. In itself it was
to add to the dominions of Spain all islands which the
explorer might discover in the Spanish half of the world,
as bequeathed to her by Pope Alexander, islands, it was
believed, of fabulous wealth in gold and in spices, and
finally on arrival at the Moluccas to prove that they lay
in the Spanish sphere. It was for this that the Emperor
had financed and patronized the expedition, risking
thereby a serious quarrel with Portugal; for this that the
fleet had been driven inflexibly on under the iron will
of its Captain-General through a windy Pentecost of
woe; and of this imperial programme no jot or tittle had
at this moment been realized. A few days ago a group
of new islands rich in gold had sworn fealty to Spain,
and now that fealty had expressed itself in wholesale
massacre of Spanish officers. Other visions of Magellan's
own had also been shaken into a rude awakening, for
his unofficered ships now hastening to vanish over the
sea-horizon of Sebu had left behind no Christian King
with a population of pious islanders, but a savage company, hot from massacre and busy with the reinstallation
of the large-faced, boar-tusked images which Pigafetta
described. Doubly perished, too, was Magellan's long-
cherished dream of meeting Francisco Serrano again
in the Spice Islands, coming not from Portugal but

from Spain, for even if he had come to the goal of his voyage he would have found that Francisco had already been killed by the perfidy of the King of Tidore, even as Francisco's brother had lately met his death by the perfidy of the King of Sebu and the desertion of his friend.   And the ruin of all these hopes, the sacrifice of all these lives, the bitter inutility of all these brave adventures must be laid to the charge of Magellan himself when in some fatal spiritual intoxication he had invited the disaster at Mactan.   It was primarily due to that, that his fleet, lacking its officers and short of provisions, set forth on the last lap of the great voyage without him.   *Sunt lacrimæ rerum* . . .

The subsequent adventures of the fleet, now that Magellan was dead, do not claim, in a history of the great Commander's life, much detailed attention, but since the voyage was his they belong to a sequel that cannot be completely omitted.   After the massacre at Sebu there were not sufficient hands to man the three ships, and on arriving at the island of Bohol the " Concepcion," which had traversed the strait and the Pacific under command of Serrano, was emptied of her stores and burned, crew and cargo being distributed between the " Trinidad " and the " Victoria," which now alone remained.   Thence sailing south-by-west, they touched at the island of Mindanao, where a local King came on board with friendly gestures.   Pigafetta had now recovered of his wound, and, inimitably chatty again, describes how he went all by himself to return this visit and see the island.   It was two leagues from the mouth of the river, where the ships had anchored, to the King's house, but there was singing to beguile the way, and on arrival he found a couple of chiefs and two "rather handsome ladies " who drank heavily of palm-wine while supper was being prepared. The prudent Pigafetta had only one drink, and after supper the King and the two handsome ladies withdrew. Next morning he took an early stroll, and paid several calls on natives, in whose houses he found many utensils of gold, but very little to eat. He guessed that neither of these handsome ladies was the Queen, so after breakfast with the King he indicated by signs that he should like to see her. So they went together to a house on the hill, and there she was. She was a musical lady and played tunes for Pigafetta on four metal drums each of which struck a different note. They then dropped down the river again, observing on the way three malefactors who had been hanged on a tree. Gold in this district was " more abundant than hairs on the head," but the natives were lazy about mining for it. . . . A thoroughly Pepysian visit.

The Spaniards' knowledge of the position of the Spice Islands was certainly very vague ; for though Magellan had received in the Philippines some sort of information about them,[1] and though they were still the destination of the two remaining ships, Carvalho after clearing the westernmost point of Mindanao did not sail south-by-east, which was the right course, but went nearly due west, touching at Cagayan, and from there north-west, that is to say in exactly the opposite direction from where the Spice Islands lay. They had left Sebu at a moment's notice, and they were now so short of provisions that there were thoughts of abandoning the ships altogether and settling on some island. But their new course brought them to the island of Palawan, and Palawan was full of flesh-pots. " We found this island to be a promised land." Cock-fighting was the national sport : there were prizes for champion birds and betting

[1] *The First Voyage Round the World, by Magellan* (Hakluyt Society), p. 105.

on them. Then with renewed stores, but still heading away from the Spice Islands, the ships struck across to Borneo, and coasted down its north-western shores till they came to the principal harbour at the mouth of the River Brunei.

Here they were well received : the King sent out a state canoe adorned with gold and peacocks' feathers, and eight of his chiefs, came on board the " Trinidad " bringing presents and a remarkably intoxicating wine made from rice, which had its due effect on many of the crew. He permitted them to trade with the islanders, and presently Pigafetta with six others went up the river to his city, to pay their respects and make a sumptuous present : there was a chair covered in violet velvet, packets of paper, a gilt pen and ink, and for the Queen slippers and a box of pins. Elephants were sent to carry them to the palace, and they were informed of the high etiquette that must be observed. It was impossible that they should speak directly to the King ; they must give their message to one of the chiefs, who would pass it on to a higher official, who would communicate it to a brother of the governor, who would breathe it through a speaking-tube to the King's personal attendant, who would tell the King, who, it was to be hoped, would understand it. The message was that they came from the Emperor of Spain, who wished to establish amicable relations with him, and to enter into trading-rights with his island ; and the message came back that the King was very pleased. They were then admitted to the Presence, and offered their gifts, and the King accepted each with a slight nod. In turn he gave them some brocade and cloth of gold and a strange collation of cloves and cinnamon. The King was a man of forty, fat and fond of female society and of hunting ; nobody ever spoke to him except through a tube.

The ships had spent a month of peaceful trading in

the port, when suspicions began to arise of the good faith of this magnificent monarch, which were probably correct. One day five of the crew who had gone ashore were arrested by his order, and there began advancing towards the ships three squadrons of canoes, over a hundred in all, with other smaller boats. Instantly Carvalho suspected some such treachery as had occurred at Sebu, and he put to sea, leaving an anchor behind. Next day he took a junk which contained a valuable hostage, for on board was a son of the King of Luzon, Captain-General of the King of Borneo, and with him three women. Carvalho accepted a heavy bribe to let his hostage go, and retained the women for his own enjoyment.

Discipline, it is clear, had gone to bits after the great Commander fell on Mactan. Never yet had a woman been allowed on the ships, and here was the Captain-General with his private harem. Mere negligence, unknown under Magellan's rule, led to other mischances : one of the ships from rank carelessness of handling went aground on a shoal ; a sailor, snuffing his candle, threw the smouldering wick into an open barrel of gunpowder, and it was only his nimbleness in snatching it out again that averted an explosion. The imperial mission on which the ships had left Seville degenerated into a series of small piratical raids : they took a junk here, a canoe there, pilfering them of their cargo and holding up the crew to ransom. All went awry with these slack ways, the men did their best when there was work to be done in repairing the ships, but there was none to direct and control, for the Captain-General was amusing himself with his women, or looking out for some other paltry prize to take. The ships were growing foul and needed fresh caulking, and in August, three months after they had left Sebu, they were still on the coast of Borneo, no nearer the Spice Islands than they had been when

Magellan died at Mactan. They put in to some harbour on this coast, to overhaul the ships, and it was probably now that the inefficient Carvalho was deposed and Gomez de Espinosa, who had escaped with him from the massacre at Sebu, was made Captain-General in his place, while Sebastian del Cano was given the Captaincy of the " Victoria." This was a strange restoration for one who had joined the mutineers at Port St. Julian and had been appointed Captain of the " Santo Antonio " by their ringleader, Quesada, that he should now be in command of one of the two remaining ships, and that, when out of the fleet of five that had left Seville one alone completed the Circumnavigation, it should be he who brought her home, and was loaded with honours. But now a man of authority and a skilful navigator, whatever his record, was necessary, and under the new command discipline seems to have been restored. Carvalho never saw the coasts of Spain again, but died at Tidore of the Spice Islands.

For six weeks the ships remained in this harbour, and then, thoroughly renovated, set forth again in quest of the great goal. In spite of Magellan's inquiries and the information they picked up from ships that they boarded, it was not till they were back again off the island of Mindanao, at which they had touched soon after leaving Sebu, that they found that their right course from here was due south. Soon after they kidnapped two pilots, of whom one escaped, but under the conduct of the other they at last sighted, away to the east, on November 6th, 1521, the peak of Tidore. For six months, since leaving Sebu, the ships under an inefficient command had wandered about with no real knowledge of where the Spice Islands lay : the traverse of the Pacific from the Cape of Desire to the Philippines had taken about half that time. But here at long last were the fragrant islands where Magellan had trysted

to meet his friend Francisco Serrano, coming, as he had
told him, by way of Spain. But Magellan did not
watch from the "Trinidad" to see those shores grow
clear, and Serrano was no longer there to see the flag of
Spain fly from the mast or to say "He has come."

It was on November 8th that the two ships entered
the port of Tidore and after casting anchor blazed forth
all their artillery in salute. Next morning the King put
out in his canoe, and was rowed round the ships, and
Pigafetta with some others went on board. He was
sitting under a silk umbrella, with his son carrying his
sceptre in front of him, and two men with gold vases
with water for his hands, and two more with gold caskets
containing betel-nut. Rajah Sultan Almanzor was his
name, and he was of a handsome presence and was a
very great astrologer. He had dreamed that ships
were coming to Tidore from very far off, and he had
consulted the moon to know if that was true, and to-day
he saw that these were the ships of his dream. He came
on board the "Trinidad," and all kissed his hand, but
His Royalty must not stoop, and so instead of entering
the cabin, where he was escorted, by the door, he got in
through the roof. Apparently the Portuguese had
made themselves thoroughly unpopular in the island,
for when he heard that they were Spanish he said that
he and his people were well content to be the friends
and vassals of the Emperor of Spain, and that hereafter
his island should not be named Tidore but Castile "in
proof of the great love he bore to our king and master."
The Portuguese, as Pigafetta soon learned, were keenly
apprehensive of the ships of any other nation coming
here, and with a view to deter them they had spread
abroad the report that these islands were surrounded
with shoals, and that navigation was not possible because
the sun never penetrated the dense fog of air ; but these
were lies to discourage adventurers. False, too, was

their report that the islands were waterless, and that water must be brought here from distant countries, for on Tidore there was a spring of good water gushing out from the mountain. It was hot when it issued, but after an hour it became icy-cold : its heat was due to the fact that it came from a mountain of cloves.

The treaty with Spain was concluded a few days afterwards : the King asked for a Royal Standard to be left with him, and an autograph of the Emperor ; he also desired that some Spaniards would remain and settle here. He hoped to get his nephew crowned King of the neighbouring island of Ternate, with which he had had a long-standing feud, and thus Ternate would also be allied with Spain. He would fight for Spain, he protested, to the death, or if he was compelled to abdicate he intended to come to Spain with his family in the new junk that he was building, and would bring the Royal Standard and autograph with him to establish his identity. Interminable discussions on island politics ensued, and it seems that the effusive friendliness of the King caused some of the Spaniards to wonder whether it could be quite sincere and to suspect treachery. But meantime all went well ; again, as at Sebu, a store was opened on shore for barter, and cloth, linen and knives were exchanged for cloves and cinnamon. Most of the mirrors they had brought were broken, and the King wanted all that were whole. With this suspicion in their minds, the Spaniards were in a hurry to load up with spices and be gone, and the islanders got their goods very cheaply.

The King's affection for Spain grew warmer yet : he even left his island, which no King ever did, to procure cloves for their cargo, and now they were ready. It was his custom to give a feast to the crews of the ships before the cloves were laden, and he invited them all to dinner, to celebrate the arrival of the cloves and also that of the King of Batchian, who was on a visit here. It was no

wonder that Espinosa remembered that treacherous
dinner at Sebu, and the massacre from which he and
Carvalho had escaped.   There was an ominous likeness
between that invitation and this ;   and the Captain-
General, on behalf of himself and his officers and men,
declined to go, and hastened the departure of the ships.

These panic twitterings, so far as we can judge, were
quite unwarranted :   this amiable monarch meant no
treacherous stroke, he was only anxious to pay due
honour to the emissaries of the Emperor, his ally.   His
feelings were hurt at these suspicions, but when Espinosa
asked him to visit the ships again he came, and played
the high-bred monarch indeed, in the grand style, and
said that, for himself, he felt as secure on coming aboard
as he did when he entered his own house.   He depre-
cated this unusual bustle of the Spaniards to quit his
island :   it was not seemly to be in such a hurry, and
November was a bad month for the navigation of these
seas ;   besides, this was the season when Portuguese
ships were in the waters, and the Spaniards might fall
in with them.   Then, when Espinosa still insisted that
his ships must start without waiting for the full cargo of
the cloves to be laden, King Almanzor said that he
himself must return the presents he had received (those
unbroken mirrors) since he had given nothing in return,
and he would have an ugly reputation in Spain, and be
suspected of planning a treachery, if they left in such a
hurry as this.   Finally he had brought to him a Koran,
and made the most solemn oaths in the name of Allah
and the Holy Book that he was a true friend to Spain and
Spaniards.   So cordial and sincere he seemed, that
Espinosa postponed the departure of his ships for another
fortnight.   During these days the King's good faith was
proven, for it came to the knowledge of the Spaniards
" by a sure and certain channel that some of the chiefs
of these islands had indeed counselled him to kill all of

us, by which thing he would have acquired for himself great merit with the Portuguese . . . but he, loyal and constant to the King of Spain, with whom he had sworn a peace, had answered that he would never do such an act on any account whatever."

Kings of the neighbouring islands followed the lead of the King of Tidore and allied themselves with Spain; the King of the great island of Gilolo, and of Batchian and Ternate, all came with presents for their overlord, and it looked as if, by the free will of their choice, the main object of Magellan's voyage, at the goal which he had failed to reach, was to be realized, and the Spice Islands to pass to Spain. Almost every day there were salutes to be fired in honour of some Royal personage who came to visit the ships, presents were exchanged till the Spaniards had no more cloth left, and all the time " they bought cloves like mad." As their stores began to run low, the value of cloves in terms of knives and red caps veered round completely, and, whereas a week ago they were anxious to sell off their goods and be gone, now their purchasing power soared high, for there was a glut of cloves and a shortage of Western wares. Soon the ships grew so heavily laden that it was no longer safe to fire the big guns in honour of Royal visitors, and as the time of departure drew near the price of cloves became derisory; a couple of little brass chains, worth sixpence, would buy a hundred pounds of them, and now that the official merchandise of the ships was disposed of the crew began to sell their shirts and their cloaks and obtained marvellous bargains. There was not room on board for all that the Kings wished to send to the Emperor as presents, and only one-fifth part of the King of Batchian's cloves could be stowed, but there was room for the skins of two birds of Paradise, strange and most precious. They were wing-less, says Pigafetta, but they could hoist long plumelike feathers, which enabled them to fly, or rather to glide, when the wind blew.

But there were dark powers abroad as well on these faery islands, and the King of Tidore warned the Spaniards who lived ashore in the magazine for merchandise not to go out of doors at night, for certain sorcerers on the island took the shape of men without heads, and if they bore ill-will to any they stroked his hand with a magical ointment and he would sicken and die. The King was trying to exterminate these dangerous creatures.

The day of departure was fixed for December 18th, three Kings and a Royal prince came on board to set the ships on their way, but the moment the " Trinidad " weighed anchor it was seen that she was leaking so badly that the water came in " with force as through a pipe." Divers went down to locate the leak ; they wore their hair loose and long, so that as they swam round about the ship it might be sucked into the hole which would thus be located, but even this ingenious device was fruitless, and the " Trinidad " was certainly in no condition to go to sea. The King of Tidore was full of lamentations. " Who will go to take news of me to the King our lord ? " he cried. So it was settled that the " Victoria " should sail at once on the monsoon from the east, while the " Trinidad " remained to be repaired, and the King promised that he would treat her crew as his own children, and employ all his two hundred and twenty-five carpenters on the work so that it might be done with the least delay. But the west monsoon would have set in before the " Trinidad " was ready, and so she was to sail to Panama back across the Pacific. Then the " Victoria " had to be lightened, for she was gorged with cloves, and sixty hundredweight were stored on shore. Some of the crew, fearing the perils of the voyage, remained also, and on December 21st, under

the command of Sebastian del Cano, the " Victoria "
put out to sea with tears and bombards. She had but
sixty souls on board, of whom forty-seven only were
Europeans, the remaining thirteen were native hands
from Tidore.

The route through the Strait of Malacca was of course
avoided, for fear of encountering Portuguese ships, and
the " Victoria," sailing south, passed through Flores
Strait, and then turned eastwards to Ombay. She was
not in condition to make the ocean voyage, and a fortnight was spent here in caulking her seams. Not nice
people, thought Pigafetta, more beasts than men, and
cannibals : he found it also very ridiculous that they
should wrap up their beards in leaves, and put them in
a case, indeed they were the ugliest-looking people he
ever beheld. But though he had not yet seen nearly
enough of the " very great and awful things of the
ocean," this was the last sight he had with his own
eyes of such, for the final records in his inimitable diary
were derived from pilots and the talk of the natives
on board.

Shoal-water prevented the ship from visiting the island
of Aruchete, whose citizens are only eighteen inches
high, and whose ears are as long as themselves, so that
when they go to sleep they cover themselves with one
of them, and lie upon the other as upon a mattress. Nor
did they visit Java, where, so the pilot narrated, there
were very odd practices, nor the gulf to the north of it
where, in the Place of Wind, there grows an enormous
tree in which griffins dwell : these birds can fly about
with a buffalo or even an elephant in their claws. Nor
did Pigafetta see Chiempa, where parties of men hunt
the woods for rhubarb, and sleep in the trees for fear
of the lions ; nor Great China, where the King is never
beheld by common eyes except when he himself wants
to see his people : then he is carried about on a chariot

made to resemble a vast peacock with six ladies all dressed exactly like him, so that none know which is the King. He punishes disobedience by flaying the culprit, whose skin is salted and stuffed, and put up in a public place in the attitude of one doing obeisance.	His palace contains seventy-nine halls and it takes a whole day to go round it.	All these wonders were related to Pigafetta by a Moor, who said he had seen them himself, so down they went in his notebook.

After leaving Ombay the ships coasted along the northern shore of Timor, and then put out on the traverse of the Indian Ocean in the middle of February. Almost at once sickness and shortage of provisions began to cause great suffering among the crew.	The meat putrefied from having been insufficiently salted, and they lived on rice and water.	They were in such evil case that many would have liked to land at Mozambique, where they would certainly have encountered Portuguese and lost their cargo, but the general feeling was to risk everything in the hope of somehow getting back to Spain.	Off the Cape of Good Hope they met with evil weather, gales from the north-west beat against them, and it was not till May 6th, 1522, they could set a course that led straight to Spain.	For two months they crawled north-west up the Atlantic, and during this time twenty-one men died of malnutrition.	The bodies were thrown into the sea, and Pigafetta tells us that the Christians always floated with their faces looking skywards, and the natives with their faces turned towards the water.	So desperate now was their plight that when they came within sight of the Cape Verde Islands Sebastian del Cano decided to put in for provisions. This was a hazardous venture, for the " Victoria " was a Spanish ship laden with cloves from the Portuguese islands, and no hint must leak out that she was one of those five ships whose sailing from Seville in the autumn of 1519 all the devices of Portugal had endeavoured to prevent. So she gave herself out as being a Spanish ship coming crippled from the coasts of America, and on the first journey of her boats ashore to fetch provisions no suspicion was aroused as to her identity. But on the second journey one of the sailors produced a handful of cloves for sale, and it was queer (thought the authorities of the port) that cloves should be coming from America. Then another blurted out that the " Victoria " was the sole remaining ship of Magellan's fleet, and so the boat with its crew of thirteen men was seized. Del Cano from his ship saw that his boat was not returning, but that some Portuguese caravels were putting out from the harbour, and guessing what that meant he set sail and ran for home.

But a sore puzzle had presented itself to our admirable Pigafetta, for the men who had returned from the first trip in safety brought news that on shore the day of the week was Thursday. This was a curious thing, for on board they all thought it was Wednesday, and Pigafetta was more surprised than anyone, for, having enjoyed perfect health ever since he left Seville, he had made an entry in his diary every single day, and his diary said that it was certainly Wednesday. This completely puzzled him, for he was sure he had made no mistake, and it was not till he reached Spain that the conundrum was solved : they had sailed continuously westwards, and so had gained a day. That was already believed to be correct in theory, and Pigafetta's diary was the first document in the annals of the world that proved it to be sound in practice. Extracts from the concluding paragraphs of this vindicated diary are the fittest end to the description of the heroic voyage.

" At last, when it pleased Heaven, on Saturday the 6th of September, we entered the bay of San Lucar : and of sixty men who composed our crew when we left

Maluco we were reduced to only eighteen, and these for the most part sick.

" Monday the 8th of September we cast anchor near the mole of Seville and discharged all our artillery.

" Tuesday we all went in shirts and barefoot with a taper in our hands to visit the shrine of St. Maria of Victory, and of St. Maria of Antigua."

CHAPTER XIV

THE CAPTAIN-GENERAL

HEN the " Victoria," sea-weary and sick, drew up to the quay at Seville, on that day of September, 1522, it was a year and four months since any sure news had come concerning Magellan and his adventures. On May 6th, 1521, the " Santo Antonio," which had deserted during the passage of the strait, had come home, but since then there had been unbroken silence, except for Portuguese rumours from the East that two of Magellan's ships were in the Spice Islands, and that the Captain-General was dead. Captain Mesquita had been put in irons on his own ship, and when she came into Seville she was commanded by Geronimo Guerra, with Estavão Gomez for pilot. These two had fabricated a pretty story on their way home, and they and the crew were word-perfect in it : they had searched (so ran their tale) for the flagship at the rendezvous appointed by Magellan, and having failed to find her could not pursue the voyage alone, and so had returned home. Mesquita had tried to stab Gomez : Gomez had therefore seized him and put him in irons. As for Magellan, Captain and men alike accused him of cruelty and inefficiency, and of the mutiny at Port St. Julian there was, of course, no mention made. India House held an inquiry, the evidence given was not satisfactory ; and, pending further information, Mesquita, Gomez and Guerra were all put

in prison.   Not till the arrival of the " Victoria " was anything more known for certain.

And now came the great news which set Magellan's fame on high, and with it came the true history of the mutiny and of the desertion of the " Santo Antonio." Mesquita was at once released and given such honours as were due to those who had served their King faithfully.   None such could be rendered to the Captain-General himself, for his bones lay somewhere on Mactan among barbarians ; his wife, Donna Beatriz, had died six months ago, in the spring, and his son, Rodrigo, a year before.   But the fame of his exploit, of which he had not lived to see the full accomplishment, but which was now known from those who came home in the " Victoria," flared like a beacon.   Poets and chroniclers of Spain proclaimed him the greatest of all those who had pushed out into the dim immensities which lay beyond the little plot of land and sea which, fifty years before, was all men knew of the world.   Three had there been of this company of adventurous souls whose enterprise was rewarded by vast discoveries : Bartholomew Diaz, who had first rounded the Cape of Good Hope and opened the sea-way to Asia ; Columbus, who had discovered a new world ; and now Magellan, who in all but the actual traverse of seas already known had circumnavigated the whole, thus bracketing in his achievement what the others had won.   All three had started from the Iberian peninsula, and indeed it seemed hardly more than fair that the Holy Father should have apportioned the world between Spain and Portugal, for it was they and they alone who had found it.

But we can best gauge the contemporary estimate of the last of these three greatest of all discoverers not so much from the panegyrics of Spanish poets as from the yells of execration that went up from Portugal.   Now at last was fully manifest the vileness of the man who had left his country where no employment could be found for him, and with the full and contemptuous permission of King Manuel had sought it elsewhere. His crime was that he had won a deathless glory in the service of Spain ; and the splendour of his achievement was the measure of his infamy. He had found, even as he and that lunatic astrologer had said, a route to the Spice Islands by way of Spain, and King Manuel in a frenzy of malice ordered that his coat of arms should be erased from the gateway of his ancestral home at Sabrosa. And how amazingly impotent was that : Magellan needed no coat of arms for his ennoblement and distinction, though King Manuel had no distinction without his. He had not wanted Magellan, but it was monstrous that anybody else should have him. A mean man was King Manuel : a dog in a Royal manger. Magellan's heirs, too, who had remained in Portugal were infected by this national rabies, and a great nephew, grandson of his sister Teresa, to whom by his first Will his property in Portugal descended, endorsed this kingly spite by ordering that this coat of arms should remain for ever erased " as was done by command of my lord the King as a punishment for the crime of Ferdinand Magellan, in that he entered the service of Castile to the injury of this kingdom and went to discover new lands where he died in the disgrace of our King." We should indeed be living in a world of supermen if so glorious a disgrace was other than extremely rare.

It is always difficult to formulate any useful comparison between the great lamps of human enlightenment, and futile to compare the achievements of supreme masters in different spheres : none can hope to decide (or indeed to interest anybody in his attempt to do so) whether Beethoven was greater as a musician than Velasquez was as an artist or Shakespeare as a dramatist. But when three men have gone forth on adventures

similar .in aim and of the same technique there is a
certain common ground on which to build inquiry,
though an obvious limit beyond which it cannot be
pushed.   The aim, in the abstract, of all these three
was to use the sea as a highway to undiscovered lands,
and their technique was navigation.

As far as the ultimate value of their discoveries goes,
there can be no comparison whatever between the results
of what Magellan achieved and of what Diaz and
Columbus achieved.   Diaz by rounding the Cape of
Good Hope, in 1487, opened up a sea-way to India and
the East which remained the only route till, centuries later,
the cutting of the Suez Canal rendered it obsolete ; but,
during these centuries, his enterprise remained of the
very highest commercial value, and, in other hands, of
imperial significance.   But it is impossible to assign
his rank to the pioneer purely on the material result of
his achievement : we have to consider also the circumstances in which it was made, and the difficulty attending its accomplishment.   Since 1431 the Portuguese
had been pushing further and further down the West
African coast ; in that year the Canary Islands, and, in
the half-century that followed, Cape Verde, the mouth
of the Congo, and Cape Negro had all been charted by
explorers who, pursuing known tracks, added a little
to the limits of their predecessors.   Diaz was the last
of this series, and in 1487 he rounded the Cape which
had already been nearly reached, and the route to India
and the East was open.   Enormous was the harvest of
his enterprise, for India and the Spice Islands were set
in the crown of Portugal.

Then came Columbus.   Just as Diaz had said " That
interminable continent of Africa will some time come to
an end, and there will be a sea-way to the East," so
Columbus said " If I sail West, the interminable plain
of the Atlantic will some time be broken by land on its

far horizon," and so it was. He was a very great sea-man ; the love of the unknown and the unattained, which is the chief incentive to noble human endeavour, burned bright in him, but never was an immense dis-covery so easily attained, or so misunderstood by the man who made it. Seven weeks of westward course from the Canaries brought him to his goal, and to the end of his life he held that he had discovered the Eastern coast of Asia. Incalculable indeed in the history of the evolution of the world was his discovery, but it was comparatively simple, and he had no idea what it was.

The third of this trinity was Magellan. He had pro-bably seen in the archives at Lisbon a chart by Christopher Jacques in which was marked far south of Brazil a strait leading from the Atlantic into the great Southern Seas on which Balboa had looked from Darien. It was a postern-gate set at the frozen limit of the known world, and on this hint he founded the logical superstructure which proved to be so sound and surely builded. Nothing could be more certain than that Jacques had not verified the strait as leading into the Pacific, but the possibility was there. That is the supreme gift of those who advance human knowledge, that they can infer from some observation, seen by but insignificant to others, vast causes and deductions : Columbus had it, and exercised it when he saw that piece of tough unknown timber picked up in mid-Atlantic ; Newton exercised it over the falling apple. And, if there proved to be, no strait where he sought for it, Magellan was prepared to go further south yet till he found the open sea at the termination of America. He did not believe that Columbus's new world was but the eastern shore of Asia ; beyond it lay a vast ocean falling within the sphere of Spanish dominions, and he went forth to discover its islands for Spain. He would arrive at the Spice Islands to which his friend Serrano had gone, and which he

himself had approached when he sailed eastwards from
Portugal as far as Malacca, the sea-door into the ocean
where they lay, not by sailing east, but by sailing west.

It is, then, evident how much larger in scope was
Magellan's conception than that of Columbus and Diaz :
it bracketed, so to speak, within its formula the fractions
which they had established and unified the whole. For
the sake of its demonstration he left the country of his
birth, presented himself in Spain with an astrologer of
marvellous knowledge but unbalanced mind, and within
a few months had won the support of the King of Spain
and his Ministers. His scheme had first been turned
down by India House, at every step he encountered the
open and the more dangerous covert hostility of Portugal,
obstacles innumerable were thrown in his path, and yet
he went undeviatingly on to the accomplishment of his
purpose. And, when he was once on the sea, the great
voyage was carried out under circumstances of infinitely
greater danger and difficulty than either Diaz or Columbus
had encountered. Mutiny was brewing before he
started, and it broke out when he was beyond the known
limits of the world. Discontent was corrupting his
men, rations were short, hardships undreamed of were
being faced, the strait was still undiscovered ; yet,
though three ships out of the five openly declared mutiny,
he crushed it within a few hours. Forty men, he knew,
were actively implicated in it, but after executing one
and marooning two others he made no further inquiry,
and the rest, after a period of imprisonment, returned
to their duties. Then he lost one ship, the " Santiago,"
and pushed on with four ; when the passage of the strait
was half-accomplished a second ship, the largest of them
all, deserted, and he pushed on with three. For nearly
four months, with crews decimated with scurvy and
short of water and provisions, he went on across an unknown and islandless ocean, and it was eighteen months

since he started from Seville before he came to the Philippines. Just about twice that number of days had revealed to Columbus the coasts which he had conjectured, and, in comparing the two, neither the actual scope of their adventure, as conceived and planned, nor the perils of its accomplishment must be left out of account. Indeed these form the most substantial items.

But there remains the consideration of the ultimate utilitarian values of the discoveries of these three great explorers, and in that, as has been already briefly stated, it is idle to compare Magellan with the others. Diaz discovered the sea-route to India and beyond, Columbus a new continent, while the practical result of Magellan's voyage and its bearing on the developments of commerce and communication was nil. The finding and the navigation of his strait was not a whit more useful in itself than the discovery of some dangerous and storm-swept route, hitherto unclimbed and deemed unscalable, up a mountain which had already been ascended from the other side. Never did the strait become a water-way for ships owing to its remoteness and the difficulties attending its navigation, and though the Spaniards built on the shore of Broad Reach King Philip's city (aptly rechristened by Cavendish in his first voyage, Port Famine) in order that the ships of " no other nation should have passage through into the South Sea saving only their own," the precaution was a very unnecessary one : it was like putting shards of glass at the top of a wall which no burglar would attempt to scale because there were other ways round it. It was nearly sixty years later that the next navigator attempted it, and Drake's exploit in following Magellan's path was the cause of this starved town being established. But, as soon as Diaz had found his way round the Cape of Good Hope, that route instantly became the populous sea-way for Portuguese ships sailing eastwards to India

and through the Strait of Malacca to the Spice Islands.
Diaz's discovery was immediately rich in practical
results, but for years there was never a sail seen in the
channel of Magellan. Columbus's discovery opened
new trade-routes, and poured the gold of Peru into the
coffers of Spain : ports and cities sprang up on the
Spanish Main, Cartagena and Nombre de Dios and
Panama across the Isthmus. That little voyage of
thirty-six days out from the Canaries was pregnant with
huge issues, and gave birth to a giant.

. But barren was the far greater enterprise, though the
Spaniards guarded it till, finally, in 1616, William
Schouten of Hoorn navigated the Cape which bears his
name, and Magellan's Strait ceased to be anything more
than a geographical term. Never once after the
" Trinidad," the " Victoria " and the " Concepcion "
emerged from it into the Pacific did any Spanish ship
pass through it with gauds for the natives of the islands
which Magellan believed would fall into the Spanish
sphere, and never did one ounce of cloves come back
through it to Spain. The Spanish trade in the Pacific
with the coasts of Chile and Peru, the gold and the jewels
from the western mines, all went up to Panama and thence
by land across the Isthmus to the ports on the Spanish
Main. Indeed it may be said that the sole practical
effect of Magellan's discovery on Spain and Spanish
interests was that it showed Francis Drake (with the
help of Pigafetta's journal) the route into the Pacific,
and the only goods that passed through the strait were
the powder and shot of the guns of the " Golden Hind "
with which she bombarded and sank the treasure-bearing
ships of King Philip, plying from Peru. Magellan's
expedition, in fact, failed in all the objects for which
King Charles had backed it : not only was the route
impracticable for commercial purposes, but the Pacific
was far wider than Magellan or Faleiro had imagined,

and in consequence the Spice Islands actually lay well within the hemisphere assigned to Portugal by Pope Alexander's demarcation. But here was the " Victoria " now unloading by the quay at Seville, with her belly full of cloves ; she had gone westwards to the Spice Islands and the King of Spain still claimed that, as Magellan had set out to prove, they lay in the Spanish sphere. He therefore prepared to send out there another armada of trading ships, but this roused a protest from Portugal, and in 1524 the Badajoz Conference was summoned to settle the question. No conclusion was come to, and after, endless wranglings King Charles finally ceded the Spice Islands to Portugal for 350,000 ducats. The payment of that sum into the Spanish exchequer and the sale of the cloves the " Victoria " had brought home were the only practical benefits that the great voyage brought to Spain.

Yet there probably is not a single man " upon this dull earth dwelling " so blind to the splendour of great adventure, and to the heroism through which it is accomplished, as to dream of measuring Magellan by such results. It is agreed by experts that as a navigator he ranks above all others, and on this score we must place him at the head of the master-mariners. We have no means of judging what his skill as a strategist or tactician in naval warfare would have been ; during his service in the East he was never in command of any squadron or armada, for he went out as a seaman and returned as Captain of one ship, while in the great voyage he never met a hostile ship, and it is therefore idle to compare him with men like Francis Drake or other great fighting admirals. But in the business of discovery and exploration he stands second to none, for we must remember that when Drake made the second circumnavigation of the world he followed Magellan's course into the Pacific, and had Pigafetta's records to consult,

Magellan conceived the biggest project for a voyage that the world contains, he carried through the preparations for it in the teeth of a nation's opposition, and when he died in the Philippines he had accomplished, in the face of overwhelming difficulties, all that made it immortal.

He had no arts of pleasing nor desire for human sympathy : " his men," as Pigafetta tells us, " did not love him," even as King Manuel had always hated him, but the wheels of that steel temperament indifferently ground up the grit of opposition which was pushed in to stay them, and left it behind in powdered dust. Though in all the records of his service we find him devoted to the well-being of those under him, remaining with his seamen on the Padua bank, tending his sick, sharing every privation that must be undergone for the attainment of his goal, doing everything that generally endears a Commander to his men, never once do we find in the pages of Pigafetta, or of others who recorded the great voyage, the slightest hint that anyone felt the smallest personal affection for him. He crushed opposition with the relentless strength of some inhuman machine, his care for his men was dictated by a sense of duty, and he cared as little for himself as he cared for others. He had his work to do and that sufficed him, and, underneath that and directing it, all we can really discover is his belief in the guidance of God. That so dominated him that, at the last, he seems to have lost all sense that he was a man at all, and fired by a fanatical certainty threw into that fierce blaze all human wisdom and prudence, and perished on the threshold of accomplishment.

APPENDIX

IT is a curious coincidence that, both on Magellan's Voyage of Circumnavigation and on Francis Drake's, Port St. Julian was the scene of the execution of mutineers. In Magellan's voyage mutiny broke out here, Quesada was executed, and Juan de Cartagena and the priest, Pero Sanchez de Reina, were marooned: in Drake's voyage Thomas Doughty was here tried for inciting to mutiny and beheaded. This in itself would be noteworthy, but it is only one in a whole chain of coincidences, which together form a remarkable series. In order to compare them it will be necessary to recapitulate quite shortly some of these curiously parallel happenings.

The object of Magellan's voyage was the acquisition by Spain of the Spice Islands then belonging to Portugal, and the preparation for this armada which was to sail " by way of Spain " (i.e. westwards) raised keen opposition from King Manuel, and through numerous agents he sought to stop its starting. One of these agents was Sebastian Alvarez, Portuguese Factor in Seville, who, to discourage Magellan, told him that though he was going as Captain-General " others were sent in opposition, whom he would not know of except at a time when he could not remedy his honour." Alvarez was referring to Juan de Cartagena and Luiz de Mendoza, whose loyalty he had already tampered with. The mutiny, in fact, or in any case such insubordination as would render the voyage impossible, had been planned before the expedition started, and Magellan had been warned. But it set off, and Juan de Cartagena, Captain of the " Santo Antonio," instantly began to act on his instructions, and before the Atlantic had been crossed his repeated insubordination caused Magellan to depose him from his Captaincy and put him in irons. Before Port St. Julian was reached Magellan had given the " Santo Antonio " to his cousin,

Mesquita. Then the mutiny broke out, Quesada was executed and Cartagena marooned. Magellan's conduct in inflicting capital punishment was subsequently questioned, but the power " of rope and knife " (i.e. hanging and beheading) was expressly given him by King Charles. After the punishment of the ringleaders, he took no further reprisals against others whom he knew to have been concerned in it.

Now the coincidences between this episode and the similar one in Drake's voyage are very remarkable. His expedition, the object of which was to sail through the Strait of Magellan into the Pacific, and despoil Spanish treasure-ships plying from Peru to Panama, was supported by Queen Elizabeth, but she insisted that Lord Burleigh, her Lord Treasurer, should know nothing of it, since he was strongly opposed to these maraudings. It was given out therefore that the fleet was to sail to Alexandria. Drake had confided its true destination to his friend, Thomas Doughty, and Burleigh, aware that there was something going on below, got it out of Doughty that the fleet was really going into the Pacific. Burleigh could not stop it, and so eminent an authority as Sir Julian Corbett [1] has suggested that Burleigh instigated Doughty to cause mutiny at sea. Whether this is so or not, Doughty was engaged in treasonable talk before the fleet left England, and Drake was informed of it.[2] He took no notice.

The fleet started : Drake had still unlimited confidence in Doughty, and presently made him Captain of a captured Portuguese ship, which joined his fleet. Accusations of tampering with the cargo were brought against him : Drake deposed him and appointed his own brother in his place. Before the American coast was reached, Doughty made mutinous speeches on the " Pelican " and the " Swan," and was put in irons. He was tried for mutiny at Port St. Julian and executed. Drake's conduct in executing him was questioned, but he produced the Queen's commission which gave him power of life and death. Though he knew that many more were implicated, he took no further steps to investigate or punish.

It will be seen at once that these two stories are so similar as to be practically identical. Both Doughty and Cartagena were

[1] *Drake and the Tudor Navy,* vol. i. pp. 342, 343.
[2] *The World Encompassed* (Hakluyt Society), p. 63.

tampered with before the expedition sailed, and their respective Captains-General knew it; both were deposed from their command and put in irons while crossing the Atlantic. Magellan appointed his cousin to succeed to the Captaincy, and Drake his brother; and, though Doughty was executed and Cartagena marooned, it is stated in one account of Drake's voyage that Doughty had the choice of being marooned and chose to be executed. Both Commanders were called in question for inflicting the death penalty (as was done on Quesada), and in both cases their commissions received from their sovereigns expressly granted them that power. Finally, though both Magellan and Drake knew that many others were privy to mutinous designs, neither of them took any further steps in the matter, and before leaving the ill-omened place and putting out on the great adventure of passing through the strait, they ordered that the whole ships' companies should confess and receive the Sacrament.

The chain of coincidence does not end here. While the exploration of the strait was in progress, the "Santo Antonio" did not keep the rendezvous which Magellan had appointed, but deserted and sailed back to Spain, and similarly the "Elizabeth" of Drake's squadron failed to appear at the rendezvous on the Peruvian coast, deserted and sailed back to England. Guerra, the new Captain of the "Santo Antonio," and Gomez, the pilot, arrived at Seville eighteen months before the "Victoria" returned alone from the circumnavigation of the world, and worked up a case against Magellan, accusing him of cruelty and illegal procedures in his suppression of the mutiny. Winter, captain of the "Elizabeth," and Cooke, the mate, arriving in England some sixteen months before the "Golden Hind" returned alone (Drake having accomplished the second circumnavigation of the world), made precisely similar attacks on their Commander, accusing him of monstrous cruelties and illegal practices in executing Doughty.

Now this chain of coincidences is very surprising, but each link is so well attested that we are bound to accept the whole. But, with regard to other coincidences, it is a different matter. The *locus classicus* for Drake's voyage is a book entitled *The World Encompassed, by Sir Francis Drake*, published in 1628, and compiled by Drake's nephew, of the same name, from notes made by Francis Fletcher, Chaplain to the General. But we have also

Fletcher's notes themselves, as copied by John Conyers, and we notice that the compiler of *The World Encompassed*, though certainly basing his book on these notes (for many sentences are verbally identical), made some considerable omissions, most of which do not concern us. But Francis Drake (circumnavigator) had with him Pigafetta's account of Magellan's voyage, probably the English translation made by Richard Eden, entitled *Magellan's Discovery*, and published in 1555.[1] And it is clear at once that Chaplain Fletcher had read it with some care. He says for instance :

" In the report of Magellan's Voyage, it is said that these people (Brazilian natives) pray to no manner of thing, but live only according to the instinct of nature." [2]

This report is obviously Pigafetta's, for his description of these natives runs thus :

" Its inhabitants are not Christians, and adore nothing, but live according to the usage of nature rather bestially than otherwise." [3]

Again Fletcher in *The World Encompassed* refers to " the line on the course of his (Magellan's) map," and, wrongly, states that Magellan, who experienced much the same treatment as Drake at the Ladrones, had not named them, and that Drake therefore called them the Isles of Thieves. These and many other allusions to Magellan's voyage show that Chaplain Fletcher had studied Pigafetta's journal. A question then arises whether Fletcher did not relate that he had himself seen certain marvellous and unusual things, whereas he had only read about them in Pigafetta's book.

The general matter of giants would seem to offer a fair test on this point. Pigafetta, as we have seen, has much to say about them. He says they were so tall " that the tallest of us only came up to their waists " ; [4] that they covered as much ground at a step as an ordinary man could jump ; [5] that they had ingenious devices to catch guanacos by ambush ; [6] that they made a habit of dancing ; [7] that they had voices like bulls ; [7] and " cried out very

---

[1] *New Light on Drake* (Hakluyt Society), p. 303.
[2] *The World Encompassed* (Hakluyt Society), p. 35.
[3] *The First Voyage Round the World, by Magellan* (Hakluyt Society), p. 44.
[4] *Ibid.*, p. 50.   [5] *Ibid.*, p. 48.
[6] *Ibid.*, p. 51.   [7] *Ibid.*, pp. 51, 52, etc.

loud Setebos, that is the devil whom they name their great God " ; [1] that one at least was a " gentle and gracious person " ; [2] that they were first seen at the River Plate ; [3] and then at Port St. Julian where two young giants came aboard.[4]

Now Fletcher in his original notes describes giants and their ways, precisely as Pigafetta did. He says that the print of a giant's foot was greater in breadth than the length of the biggest English foot ; [5] that " in height and greatness they are so extraordinary that they hold no comparison with any of the sons of men " ; [6] that they catch ostriches (in a wholly incredible manner) by ambush ; [7] that they delight in dancing ; [8] that they call on " Settaboh, that is the Devil, whom they name their great God " ; [9] that they were full of kindness, more so, in fact, than many of Fletcher's clerical brethren ; [10] that they inhabit the country from the River Plate to Port St. Julian ; [11] that they came on board at Port St. Julian.[12]

It would seem therefore at first sight that Pigafetta's account of the giants is corroborated in the most remarkable manner by Fletcher's personal observations, but if we look a little further into the matter we find that it is far more probable that Fletcher does not corroborate at all, but only plagiarizes. For we notice that Francis Drake compiling *The World Encompassed* from Fletcher's notes not only omits all these stories, but denies the existence of such enormous monsters altogether. For we read : " Magellan was not altogether deceived in naming these giants, for they generally differ from the common sort of man both in stature, bigness and strength of body, as also in the hideousness of their voices : but they are nothing so monstrous and giant-like as they were represented, there being some English men as tall as the highest we could see, but peradventure the Spaniards did not think that ever any English man would come hither to reprove them, and therefore might presume the more boldly to lie." [13] Again, when Fletcher records that the giants use certain words

---

[1] *Ibid.*, p. 53.
[2] *Ibid.*, p. 52.
[3] *Ibid.*, p. 48.
[4] *Ibid.*, p. 53.
[5] *The World Encompassed*, p. 40.
[6] *Ibid.*, p. 51.
[7] *Ibid.*, p. 41.
[8] *Ibid.*, p. 51.
[9] *Ibid.*, p. 48.
[10] *Ibid.*, p. 40.
[11] *Ibid.*, p. 40.
[12] *Ibid.*, p. 60.
[13] *Ibid.*, p. 60.

like " Toyt " meaning " cast it down," Francis Drake says that
the *natives* use this precise word with this significance, but does not
call them giants.   Clearly, then, Francis Drake compiling his
narrative from Fletcher's notes does not credit the stories of giants,
and he is supported in this by all other narratives concerning Drake's
voyage.   Cooke, for instance, makes no mention of giants anywhere, either at the River Plate or Port St. Julian or on the
Patagonian coasts, though he tells stories about the natives which
Fletcher tells about giants.   Edward Cliffe similarly denies the
Spanish stories of the existence of giants here,[1] and Nuño da Silva,
Drake's Spanish pilot, only says that the natives of St. Julian were
strong and tall.   In fact, Fletcher alone, among all the narrators
of Drake's voyage, testifies to the existence of giants, and others
specifically deny it.   It would be a strange thing if giants continually and authentically were manifest to Fletcher and to no
other member of the expedition, and stranger still if they habitually
did exactly what Pigafetta describes.

We begin then somewhat to distrust Chaplain Fletcher, even
as Francis Drake did, and our distrust deepens when he tells us
how at Port St. Julian " Magellan had a mutiny against him by
some of his company, for the which he executed divers of them
upon a gibbett, part of which gibbett (being of firwood) we found
here whole and sound." [2]   This cannot have happened, for
Magellan beheaded Quesada, and never hanged anybody ; therefore there can have been no gibbet.[3]   Fletcher clearly needs
corroboration before we accept all he says, but we cannot take
Pigafetta as corroborating him over the giant-business, but only
conclude that he cribbed from Pigafetta.

These coincidences then, between the accounts of Magellan's
voyage and of Drake's, must be divided into two classes : incidents
which are supported, as many of them are, by a consensus of evidence, and those which are plagiarized from Pigafetta.

[1] *The World Encompassed,* p. 278.   [2] *Ibid.,* p. 68.
[3] Mr. Froude (*English Seamen,* p. 88) goes one better than Fletcher and
says that at Port St. Julian Drake found " a skeleton hanging on the gallows
the bones of which were picked clean by vultures."

INDEX

ABREU, Antonio d', 31, 32, 33

Abyssinia, 9

Admiralty Sound, 162, **163**

Adrian, Cardinal, of Utrecht (Pope Adrian VI), 66, 67, 68, 78, 86

Africa, 15
> Sea-route round, Exploration of, 7, 9, 14, 37 ; *see also* Cape of Good Hope
> East coast of, 14, 16
> West coast of, 7, 9, 242

Albuquerque, Alfonso d', 16, 23, 26, 34, 36, 44, 191 ; takes Goa, 28, 29, and Malacca, 30, 31

Alexander VI, Pope, Bull of, and Emendation, territories conferred by, on Portugal and Spain, 11 *sqq.*, 15, 16, 21, 22, 30, 47, 49, 51, 57, 58, 68, 70, 72-3, 76, 83, 119, 149, 196-7, 224, 240, 247

Almanzor, Rajah Sultan, King of Tidore, 230 *sqq.*

Almeida, Francisco d', Viceroy of India, 17, 19, 20 *sqq.*, 36, 38, 44, 56, 105

Alvarez, Sebastian, 90, 91 *sqq.*, conspiracy hatched by, 96, 116, 123, 138, 249

Alvo, log-book of, 150, 173, 176

Amboina, 32, 33

America, the New World of, 51, 58 ; discovery of, 8, 10, 12, 29, 49, 69, 240, 242-3 ; gold from, 6, 76, 97

Andrew of Bristol, master-gunner, 174

Aranda, Juan d', and Magellan's scheme, 60 *sqq.*, 88

Argensola, —, 31

Aruchete, Island, 235

Asia, eastward route to (*see also* Cape of Good Hope), 8, 10, 240

Atlantic Ocean, the, 7, 73, 115, 236 ; meeting of, with the Pacific, 16, 168 ; Papal line of demarcation through (*see also* Alexander VI), 72-3 ; Strait from, to the Pacific (*see also* Strait of Magellan), 243

Azamor, 38, 39, 40

Azores, Islands, 12

BADAJOZ Conference, the, 247

Balboa, Vasco Nuñez de, first sight by, of the Pacific, 11, 15, 47, 154, 243

Bambino, the, at Sebu, 203, 204

Banda, and the Banda Sea, 32

Baptista, the Genoese pilot, 113, 145, 146, 150, 175, 176, 179

Barbosa, Beatriz, wife of Magellan, 61, 64, 81, 82-3, 105, 108 ; death of, 107, 240

Barbosa, Diego, 57 *sqq.*, 81 *sqq.*, 107, 115, 116, 119

Barbosa, Duarte, 57, 103, 113, 132, 133, 149, 163, 165, 166, 209, 217, 219

Barcelona, 10, 111

Barros, —, 166

Batchian, King of, 231, 233

Belem, 18, 20

Birds of Paradise, 233-4

Bohol, Island, 225

Borneo and its King, 227-8

Braganza, Duke of, 38

256 FERDINAND MAGELLAN

Brazil, 13, 15, 16, 36, 47, 48, 49, 51, 71, 73, 117, 119, 243 ; natives of, 143 ; Strait, south of, see Strait of Magellan
Broad Reach, Magellan's Strait, 154, 155, 158, 163, 165, 245
Brunei, River, 227
Burleigh, Lord, 250

CABRIAL, —, 15, 16
Cagayan, 226
Calicut, 9, 14, 16, 56, 191
California, 173
Cananor, Battle of, 20, 21
Canary Islands, 10, 94, 113, 114-15, 157, 246
Cannibals, 120, 121
Cano, Sebastian de, "the Captain," 127, 128-9, 229, 235, 236, 237
Cape of Desire, 162, 168, 170, 186, 229
Cape Froward, 159, 161
Cape of Good Hope, the, 9, 11, 14, 16, 21, 23, 30, 37, 55, 56, 81, 236, 240, 242, 245
Cape Horn, 141, 168, 246
Cape Negro, 242
Cape Sagres, 6-7
Cape St. Augustine, 15, 119
Cape St. Vincent, 6, 10, 154
Cape Valentyn, 155, 159, 163
Cape Verde, 242
Cape Verde Islands, 12, 117, 236
Cape Virgines, 152
Caragua Island, and its King, 186, 189
Cartagena, Juan, 113 ; treachery of, 95-6, 104, 116, 117 ; arrest and release of, 118, 123-4 ; in the mutiny, 126, 127, 129, 134, 136, 143, 156, 163 ; marooned, 138-9, 149, 165, 166, 249, 250, 251
Carvalho, Juan, pilot, 120, 220 ; treachery of, 221-2, 226, 228, 232 ; deposition and death of, 229
Castelbranco, —, 25, 26

Cathay (China), 7, 15, 22, 29, 30, 176, 192
Catherine, Princess, of Sebu, 203
Cavendish, Thomas, circumnavigator, 8, 245
Celebes, the, 30
Central America, 15, 36
Ceylon in Seilani (Leyte), 189
Charles, King of Sebu, 202
Charles V, and Magellan, 45, 49, 53, 55, 62 sqq., 69, 72, 73, 74 sqq., 85, 97 sqq., 106, 113, 115, 116, 123, 129, 136, 137, 139, 141, 149, 156, 164, 166, 176, 182, 183, 191, 193, 199, 200, 202, 203, 204, 208, 213, 216, 219, 222, 223, 224, 230, 231, 232, 233, 246, 247
Capitulation of, with Magellan, 78 sqq., 83, 87, 88, 137, 139, 200 ; further powers accorded by, to Magellan, 83, 137, 139
Cession by, of the Spice Islands, 13, 247
Elected Emperor, 111, 112
Standard of, 105, 202, 231
Cheregato, Mgr. Francis, 111
Chiempa, 235
Chile, Spanish tradé-route to, 246
China, see Cathay, and Great China
Chinese junks, attack by, 25-6, carrying trade of, 29
Christopher, converted Siamese Moor, 191, 193, 194, 202, 210, 212
Circumnavigators of the World, see Cavendish, Drake, and Magellan
City of Jesus, the, 203
Cliffe, Edward, 254
Coca, Antonio de, traitor, 124, 126, 128, 163
Cochim, 20, 25, 26, 28, 114
Coco-nuts, Pigafetta on, 180-1
Coelho, Gonzalo, explorations of, 15, 48
Columbus, Christopher, discoveries of, 8, 9, 11, 12, 13, 15, 29, 36, 46, 49, 56, 61, 68, 240, 242

" Concepcion," ship, 88, 113, 120, 124, 127 *sqq.*, 134, 136, 148, 149, 150, 152, 155, 157, 158, 159, 161, 162, 163, 164, 165, 170, 217, 220, 246 ; fate of, 225

Congo River, mouth of, charted, 242,

Cooke, —, of the " Elizabeth," 251, 254

Correa, Gaspar, *cited*, 136

Cortez, Hernando, 47

Costa, Alvaro da, Portuguese ambassador, 83 *sqq.*, 93, 101, 102

Covilhão, Pedro de, 9, 14

Croy, Guillaume de, 65, 68

Crusade, the Holy, 107

DARIEN, Balboa's sight from, of the Pacific, 11, 47, 154, 243

Deduction, gift of, 243

Diaz, Bartholomew, voyage of, round the Cape of Good Hope, 9, 11, 30, 37, 55, 81 ; comparative value of his discoveries and those of Columbus and Magellan, 240, 242 *sqq.*

Diu, Battle of, 20, 21

Doughty, Thomas, mutineer, execution of, 138, 149, 249, 250, 251

Drake, Francis, compiler of *The World Encompassed*, sources of, 112, 251 *sqq.*

Drake, Sir Francis, 247 ; circumnavigator, 8, 16, 77, 112, 138, 141, 154, 168, 170, 172, 173, 175, 245, 246, 247, 251 ; dealings of, with natives, 193 ; and the mutiny of Doughty, 138, 149, 249 *sqq.* ; piracies of, 6, 8, 12, 19, 76, 250

EASTER DAY 1520 and 1521, 127, 186, 187

Eden, Richard, 112, 252

Elizabeth, Queen, and her piratical captains, 6, 12, 14, 76-7, 250

" Elizabeth," Drake's ship, desertion by, 251

Elizabeth Island, 154, 155

Elizabethadæ Islands, 154

Enrique, the slave, 56, 59, 67, 69, 109, 183 *sqq.*, 192, 199, 202 ; treachery of, 109, 218 *sqq.*

Espinosa, Gomez de, 132, 133, 220, 229, 232

FALEIRO, Francisco, 103

Faleiro, Ruy, astronomer, 49 *sqq.*, 56-7, 61 *sqq.*, 83, 85, 95, 103, 113, 120, 163, 178, 224, 241, 244 ; globe made by, 50 *sqq.*, 56-7, 61 ; knighted, 83, 84 ; trouble with, 100 *sqq.*

Ferdinand, Don, 202, 206

Fez, the King of, 39

First Voyage Round the World, by Magellan, 112, 136

Fletcher, Francis, Drake's Chaplain on the Voyage of Circumnavigation, 112, 175, 251 *sqq.*

Flint knives, 120

Flores Strait, 235

Florida, 15

Fonseca, Mgr., Bishop of Burgos, 66 *sqq.*, 78, 80, 86-7, 90

Froude, Antony, 254

GAMA, Vasco da, 14, 16, 19, 44, 176

Gilolo, King of, 233

Globes, Faleiro's, 50, 56-7, 61 ; Schöner's, 48, 71

Goa, 28, 29, 56

Golconda, 22

" Golden Hind," the, 77, 172, 246, 251

Gomez, Estevão, pilot, 156, 164, 165, 167, 171, 239

Great China, King of, 235-6

Great South Sea, the, *see* Pacific Ocean

Guadalquivir, River, 105

Guam, 173

Guanacos, 145

Guerra, Geronimo, 165, 239, 251

Guillemard, F. H. H., *cited*, 176
Guinea Coast, the, 117

HAKLUYT SOCIETY, the, 112, 136
Hammocks, derivation of the word, 120
Haro, Christopher de, 71, 74, 97, 98
Hawkins, Sir John, 6, 12, 115
Henry the Navigator, Prince of Portugal, K.G., 6 *sqq.*, 13, 22, 48, 53
Henry VI of England, 7
Herrera, —, *cited*, 150, 155, 158
Humabon, King of Sebu, 190 *sqq.*; baptism of, 202
Humunu, Island, 177

INDIA, 3, 7, 10, 14, 16, 21, 30, 31, 34, 38, 51, 58, 69; Magellan in, 3, 18 *sqq.*
Indian Ocean, the, 14, 23, 55, 84, 236, 240
Infante's Town, the, *see* Sagres Castle, *and* Cape Sagres
Isabella, Queen of Massava, 203

JACQUES, Christopher, and his chart, 15, 36, 48, 68, 71, 84-5, 98, 119, 243
Java, 30, 32, 235
Jehane, Queen of Sebu, 203, 204
John, Christianized Patagonian, 145, 146
John I, of Portugal, 6
John II, of Portugal, 3, 43; sea explorations under, 8 *sqq.*, 13; and Columbus, 9, 10, 49, 56, 68; and the Papal Line of Demarcation, 15, 72, 76

KING PHILIP'S CITY, or Port Famine, 245
King of Portugal and India, Manuel's title, 19

LABOUR, Bay of, 122
Laccadive Islands, *see* Padua Bank
" La Diane " ship's watch, 114

Ladrone Islands and natives, 172, 173 *sqq.*, 177, 178-9, 181, 252
Lamego, Bishop of, 87, 90
Lateen Sails, Isles of the, 174
Legaspe, Miguel Lopez de, 203
Lendes da India (Correa), *cited*, 136
Leo X, Pope, 111
Leonardo da Vinci, map by, 15-16
Leonora, Queen, wife of John II, 3, 5, 10
Leonora, Queen, wife of Manuel of Portugal, 85, 89
Leyte (Seilani), 189
Lisbon, 16, 22, 23, 27, 28, 30, 31, 32, 34, 35, 37, 49, 51, 61, 128
Court of, Magellan's connection with, 3, 4, 5, 10, 21, 30, 34 *sqq.*, 193; salaries at, 43 *sqq.*
Royal Library at, 8, 48, 51, 68, 84, 150, 243,
Lorriaga, Juan de, 128, 136
Luzon, King of, son of, 228

MACTAN, Island, Magellan's attack on, and death, 208 *sqq.*, 214-15, 229, consequences, 216 *sqq.*, 222, 223, 225
Magellan, Diego de Sousa, 4, 106, 107
Magellan, Ginebra, 4
Magellan, Ferdinand, birthplace, birth and family of, 1 *sqq.*; Court life of, 3, 21, 35 *sqq.*; Indian and Malacca voyages of, 3, 17 *sqq.*, 23 *sqq.*; in the Moroccan affair, accusation against, and wound resulting from, 38-9 *sqq.*; rebuffed by Manuel, 41 *sqq.*; service sought by, with Charles V, 55 *sqq.*; scheme of, to secure the Spice Islands for Spain, 55 *sqq.* (*see also* Strait of Magellan), approved of, by the King, his Capitulations and power conferred by, on Magellan, 75 *sqq.*, 80, 137, 250; marriage of, 61-2; knighted, 81; voyage of, in

Magellan, Ferdinand (*continued*)—
search of the Strait (*q.v.*), 97
sqq.; flagship of, *see* "Trinidad"; the mutiny, 115-16,
118, 123, 125 *sqq.*; success, 140,
177-8, compared with that of
Diaz and of Columbus, 242
sqq.; passage into the Pacific,
152 *sqq.*, the Philippines annexed, 177 *sqq.*; the attack on
Mactan, and death of Magellan,
208 *sqq.*; accusations against,
by deserting captains, 239
Accounts of the Great Voyage,
111 *sqq.*, 175, 251
Achievement of, 247-8
Characteristics of, 18-19, 25, 27, 28,
Christianizing zeal, 201 *sqq.*,
and miracle ascribed to, 205
sqq., 210, unpopularity of, 116,
123, 126, 248
Children of, *see* Magellan, Rodrigo
Circumnavigation of the world by,
8, 20-1, 32, 240, parallels between this voyage and Drake's,
250 *sqq.*
Dealings of, with natives, 193
Death of, 32, 105, 109, 110, 113,
218, 219, 222, 225, 228, 229,
230, 240, 248
Fame of, established, 240-1
Naval services of, 56
Wife of, *see* Barbosa, Beatriz
Wills of, 3 *sqq.*, 18, 27, 56, 105,
106 *sqq.*, 218
Magellan, Isabella, 4, 106, 107
Magellan, Pedro, father, 3, 4, 5, 18
Magellan, Rodrigo, 4, 105, 106, 107,
179, 240
Magellan, Teresa, 3, 4, 18, 19, 105, 241
Magellan, Strait of, *see* Strait
Magellan's Discovery (translation by
Eden), 112, 252 *sqq.*
Malacca, 23 *sqq.*, 29, 30, 31, 34, 35,
36, 46, 56, 59, 69, 71, 84, 109,
179, 183, 191, 244
Malacca, Strait of, 22, 23, 29, 235,
246

Malacca, Sultan of, 23 *sqq.*, 30
Malay Archipelago, the, 30
Manuel, King of Portugal, Empire-builder, 13-14, 17, 19, 20, 21,
24, 27, 33, 84; and Magellan,
3, 30, 33, 34, 35 *sqq.*, 39 *sqq.*,
60, 62, 69, 79, 81, 82, 83-4,
85 *sqq.*, 101, 103, 106, 123,
128, 142, 154, 191, 192, 241,
248, 249; meanness of, 14, 69,
70-1, 77, 81, 98; Moorish
expedition of, 38-9
Massava Island, and its King, 183 *sqq.*,
208
Matienzo, Don Sancho, 91
Medina Sidonia, Duke of, 105
Melinda, 14
Melchizedek, 9
Mendoza, Luis de, traitor, 96, 104,
113, 115, 126, 127, 149,
mutiny of, 129, 132; death
of, 133, 136; disgrace of,
137, 138
Meneses, General de, 38, 39
Mesquita, Alvaro de, 103, 124, 127,
128, 136, 149, 152, 153 162,
163, 164, 165, 186, 239, 240,
250
Mesquita, Martin de, 103
Mesquita Pimenta, Alda de, 3, 124
Mindanao, Island of, 225, 226, 229
Molino, Luiz de, 127, 138, 139
Molucca Islands, 8, 30, 32, 83, 175,
176, 197, 224, 238; friendly
kings of, 230 *sqq.*
Mombasa, 14
Moors, the, Christian captives of, 107;
expeditions against, 6, 38-9,
110; oriental trade of, 7-8, 9,
16-17, 21, 22, 23, 191, 193,
202, 236
Morocco, expedition against, Magellan
in, 38, 110
Mozambique, 236
Mutiny, conspiracy of, 96, 104, 115,
118, outbreak and quelling of,
125 *sqq.*, 244
Mysore, 22

NATAL, 14
Nombre de Dios, 8, 66, 246
North America, Early maps of, 15

OMBAY, 235, 236
Oriental trade of the Moors (q.v.), 7-8
Osorius, Bishop, cited, 43-4, 45
Our Lady of Barrameda, Church of, 105

PACIFIC OCEAN, the, 10-11, 15, 16, 29, 30, 36 ; first European voyage in, 31, 33-4, 36 ; gates to, see Malacca, and Strait of Magellan ; Magellan's scheme for entering, 46 sqq., Spanish support for, 57 sqq., the voyage, 96 sqq., the passage into, found, 150 sqq., 168-9 ; islands discovered in, 172 sqq. ; return of the ships, 237 sqq. ; storms of, 123, 147, 154, 170
Padua Bank, Magellan's ship ashore on, 26, 27, 28, 35, 56, 114, 248
Palowan, Island of, 226
Panama City, 246
Panama, Isthmus of, 8, 47, 76, 234, 246 ; expedition to, proposed, 98 ; Spanish Canal scheme for, 68
Papal Demarcation, Line of, see Alexander VI, and Tortesillas Capitulations
Patagonia, 15, 36 ; derivation of the name, 147
Patagonian natives, giants, 143 sqq., 171, 252-3
Paul, the Patagonian, 147, 160-1, death of, 171
Payva, Alfonso de, 9
" Pelican," ship, 250
Penguins, 122
Pereira, Nuño Vaz, 20
Perestello, Felipa (Señora Columbus), 9
Pernambuco, 15
Persian Gulf, the, 16

Peru, gold of, 246
Peter Martyr, 113
Philip II of Spain, 8, 77
Philippine Islands, the, 30, 32, 229 ; discovery of, 177, 179, 181, 245 ; kings of, allied to Spain, 192 sqq., 196, 198, 204
Pigafetta, Antonio, and Magellan's voyage to the Strait, 111 sqq., 237-8, passim ; in the fight at Mactan, 213 sqq., wounded, 216, 220 ; omissions by, 143, 179, 194
Pinzon, —, 15
Place of Wind, near Java, 235
Plate, River, 121, 253 ; giant-cannibals near, 121
Pliny, 115
Port St. Julian, 148, 161, 253 ; winter at, 143 ; short rations, 156-7 ; mutiny at, of Magellan's captains, 104, 115, 126 sqq., 147, 163, 179, 194, 229, 239, 244, 254, aftermath of, 164, 165 ; Drake's trial and execution at, of Doughty, 138, 149 ; the mutinies at, compared, 249 sqq.
Portugal, 12 ; maritime power of, and explorations, 5 sqq. ; purchase by, of the Spice Islands, 13, 247 ; sphere of, under the Bull of Alexander VI, 11 sqq. passim, 247 ; wrath of, at Magellan's success, 19, 240-1
Portuguese seamen in Spanish employ, 57, 71, 85, 89
Portuguese, the, at Tidore, 230-1
Presbyter John, 9

QUESADA, Gaspar, 113 ; mutiny by, 126, 163, 229, trial and execution of, 137 sqq., 149, 249, 250, 251

RAINING TREE, the, of the Canaries, 115
Red Sea, the, 16

Reina, Pero Sanchez de, priest, traitor, 143 ; marooned, 149, 150, 151, 165, 166, 249, 251

Rhodes, the Grand Master of, 111, 112, 116

Rhodes, the Knights of, 111

Ribeiro, Nuño, 93

Rio, Bay of, 119 ; natives near, 119, 120

Roberto, Christopher, 109

Rome, sack of, 113

Rota Island, 173

SABROSA, home of the Magellans, 4, 5, 10, 14, 18, 19, 105, 107, 241

Sagres Castle, 8, 55

St. Anselm's fire, 117, 122

St. Clare's fire, 122

St. James, Order of, 81, 84, 167-8, 196

St. Lazarus, Archipelago of, see Philippine Islands

St. Matthias, Gulf of, 121-2

St. Nicholas, fire of, 122

St. Philippo, Bay of, 154

Salzburg, the Cardinal Archbishop of, 113

Samar, Island of, 177

San Lucar, Bay of, 105, 110, 237

San Martin, Andres de, 120, 149, 164, 165, 167, 220

San Salvador, Church of, Sabrosa, 18, 107

Santa Cruz, Rio de, 147, 148, 149

Santa Maria de la Vittoria, Church of, Seville, 105, 108, 129, 238

" Santiago," ship, 88, 114, 121, 127, 129, 130, 132, 134, loss of, 147 sqq., 244

" Santo Antonio," ship, 88, 101, 103, 104, 113, 116, 118, 123, 124, 126 sqq., 146, 149, 152, 155, 157, 158 sqq., 186, 229, 249 ; desertion by, 166 sqq., 179, 240, 251 ; arrival of, at Seville, 239 ; first ship to go round the World, 127-8

Sebu, Island of, King and people of, 189, 190 sqq., 199 sqq., 208, 212, 213, 228 ; Christianizing of, 195-6, 199 sqq., 223 ; Magellan's miracle at, 206-7, 213-14 ; massacre at, 221 sqq., 229

Seilani (Leyte) Island, 183, 189 .

Sequiera, Diego Lopes de, and the Malacca Expedition, 23 sqq., 29, 35

Serrano, Francisco, friend of Magellan, 23 sqq., 28, 31, 35, 37, 51 ; remains in Ternate, and corresponds with Magellan, 32 sqq., 36, 46 sqq., 51, 52, 56, 59, 69, 110, 114, 170, 176, 179, 183, 243 ; death of, 187, 225, 230

Serrano, Juan, 114, 127, 134, 147 sqq., 162, 165, 167, 168, 209, 210, 217, fate of, 219 sqq.

Setebos, Patagonian devil, 161, 253

Seville, 53, 83, 84, 107, 123, 126, 237 ; Magellan at, 56 sqq., 88, 90, the riot over the flag, 91 sqq., 133 ; the departure to seek the Strait, 105, 108, 110, 111, 129, 170, 236, 245 ; the mutiny hatched at, 95-6, 115 ; the return to, 113, 127, 165, 229, 238, 239 sqq., 251

Archives at, 100

India House at, Board of, 58, 61, 63, 65 sqq., 70, 74, 76, 80, 83, 87-8, 98, 113, 244 ; inquiry by, on the return of the " Santo Antonio," 239

Lepers near, 107

Merchants of, support of, for Magellan, 97

Sharks, 117, 172

Siam, trader from, at Sebu (see also Christopher), 191

Silapulapu, Rajah, in Mactan, 208, 209 sqq.

Silva, Nuño da, 254

Skuas, gull-harrying by, 117

Solis, Juan de, and Brazil, 119, 120
South America (*see also* Brazil, *and*
    Patagonia), 138 ; discoveries
    concerning, 14 *sqq.*, 48, 71,
    141, 168
South Pole, the, 141, 168
Southern Cross, constellation, 171
Spain, sea-power of, and the discovery
    of America, 6, 10-11
  Share of, under Pope Alexander's
    Bull and Magellan's views on,
    11 *sqq.*, 21, 30, 183, 243 *et*
    passim
Spain and Portugal, meeting of,
    among the Spice Islands, 191
Spanish Main, the, 19, 246
Spanish Treasure Fleets, 6, 8, 97, 246
Spice Islands, the (*see also* Moluccas,
    and Strait of Magellan), ques-
    tion of sphere including, 13,
    52, 56 *sqq.*, 75, 76, 108, 196-7,
    242 ; Serrano in (*see also*
    Serrano), 51 ; search for way
    to, by d'Abreu, 31 *sqq.*, and
    by Magellan, 7, 10, 29, 32, 33,
    37, 83 *sqq.*, 110 *sqq.*, 132, 141
    sqq., 166, 170, 176 *sqq.*, 179,
    243, reached at last, 191, 205,
    229 *sqq.*, 246, 247 ; purchase
    of, by Portugal, 13, 247
Stanley of Alderley, Lord, 112
Strait of Magellan, indications of, 15,
    16, 36, 47, 48, 51, 57, 59, 69,
    71, 84-5, 243 ; search for, 95,
    97 *sqq.*, 111 *sqq.*, 126, 250 ;
    finding of, 150, 224, 243, 245 ;
    traverse of, by Magellan, 152
    sqq., and by Drake, 250
Suez Canal, the, 242
Suluan Island, 177, 181 ; gold on,
    186
Sumatra, 32
Susa, Garcia de, 23, 24, 25
"Swan," ship, 250

Tagus, the, 8, 17, 18, 19, 20
Telles, John da Silva, and his wife,
    3 *sqq.*, 18, 105

Telles, Luiz da Silva, 3
Tenerife, 115, 116
Ternate, King of, 233, and Francisco
    Serrano, 33, 46, 51, 56
Terra Australis Incognita, the, 16,
    37, 141, 168
Tidore, 229 ; arrival at, of Espinosa,
    230 *sqq.* ;
  King of, 33, 233
Timor, 236
Tortesillas Capitulations, the, 12
Trade-winds, the, 15
Transylvanus, Maximilian, 113, 146,
    149, 207
Traz-os-Montes, province, 1, 2
"Trinidad," the, Magellan's flag-
    ship, 88, 90, 91, 110, 114, 127,
    129 *sqq.*, 138, 152. 153, 162,
    167, 170, 173, 174, 181, 183,
    186, 190, 199, 210, 220, 221,
    225, 230, 234, 246

Unfortunate Islands, the, 172, 178
Useless Bay, 155

Valladolid, 63, 64, 65, 69, 70, 83
Vartema, Luigi, 23
Venice, 112
Vicenza, 111
"Victoria," ship, 88, 104, 113, 129
    sqq., 148, 149, 152, 158, 159,
    161 *sqq.*, 170, 217, 225, 229,
    234 *sqq.*, 246 ; arrival at
    Seville, 238, 239, 240, 247
Vincente, Martin, 9

Where East is West, 11 *sqq.*, 21, 192
Winter, Captain of the "Elizabeth,"
    accusations by, of Drake, 251
World, The, Encompassed by Francis
    Drake (Fletcher), 112, 175,
    251

Zamal, Island, 177
Zanzibar, 9
Zenith, the, 120.
Zula, of Mactan, 209

CPSIA information can be obtained
at www.ICGtesting.com
Printed in the USA
BVHW040834010219
539250BV00003B/89/P